A Risk-Benefit Perspective
on Early Customer Integration

Contributions to Management Science
www.springer.com/series/1505

Christoph Kausch

A Risk-Benefit Perspective on Early Customer Integration

With 49 Figures and 29 Tables

Physica-Verlag

A Springer Company

Dr. Christoph Kausch
Rehalpstrasse 7
8008 Zurich
Switzerland
christoph@kausch.eu

Library of Congress Control Number: 2007931486

ISBN 978-3-7908-1961-8   Physica-Verlag Heidelberg New York

Physica-Verlag is a part of Springer Science+Business Media

springer.com

© Physica-Verlag Heidelberg 2007

Production: LE-TEX Jelonek, Schmidt & Vöckler GbR, Leipzig
Cover-design: WMX Design GmbH, Heidelberg

SPIN 12074051   88/3180YL - 5 4 3 2 1 0   Printed on acid-free paper

Foreword by Prof. Dr. Oliver Gassmann

Customers - a source of irritation and disturbing factor for R&D or a source for innovation? The involvement of customers into the innovation process has a long tradition; following the early work on lead users in the eighties, the importance of users as a source of innovation has been widely recognized today. Today the degree of user integration has increased from specification delivery to virtual users that develop products they desire by themselves. The recent success of open source development has increased the speed and acceptance of user innovation. Opening up the innovation process seems to be the imperative of todays R&D management. The expected benefits are better market orientation, reduced time-to-market, lower costs, better evaluation of required functions, access to new application and technology knowledge and relationship oriented advantages.

But is 'democratizing of innovation' (von Hippel 2005) always more profitable for a company? Practice in B2B industries shows that many customer integrations in the fuzzy front of innovation do not keep the promises. Risks of customer integration consists of a strong bias towards the individual customer and his interests and experiences. Additional time and costs because of the highly iterative process, and unintended knowledge diffusion are risks which have to be addressed. Christoph Kausch is challenging this widely spread attitude that more customer integration is always better. Instead he provides a balanced approach of risk-benefit analysis.

On the base of a case analysis of four Swiss companies Christoph Kausch develops a theoretical framework and a formal decision model on customer integration. He provides a framework for the question: Is customer integration advisable in a specific situation? What are the positive and negative effects of customer integration into the early innovation process? This is a convincing book for business practitioners and academics in the field of user innovation. I wish for this work a wide distribution and for the companies employing these concepts the best of success.

St. Gallen
March 2007

Prof. Dr. Oliver Gassmann
Institute of Technology Management
University of St. Gallen

Foreword by Prof. Dr. Tom Sommerlatte

As innovativeness is gaining decisive importance for profitable growth and competitive advantage, the search for new product and service ideas is being intensified and, in many cases, more systematically organized.

One oft the sources of innovative ideas that an increasing number of companies go after is the customer. Integrating customers in the search of new problem solutions, of product and service improvements and of differentiation opportunities – customer integration in the early innovation phase – has been praised as a particularly effective way of strengthening the innovation power of companies.

Substantial research has been directed at the so-called lead user approach, i.e. the exploration and testing of ideas and concepts together with selected customers known to be open to and interested in innovation leadership in their own business area. However, recent on-hand experience gained by a number of companies shows that the virtues of early customer integration are sometimes questionable, negative side-effects even outweighing in certain cases the expected advantages.

This book shows that there are indeed risks in customer integration the balance of which with the benefits depends on which access a company can gain to its customers' needs and knowledge, what role these insights can play in the innovation process and how customer integration is being managed,.

Based on in-depth empirical research with 4 Swiss companies, all of them active in international markets, the author applies a comprehensive model of the innovation process, especially of the basic tasks in the early stage of the process, to examine the potential contributions of lead users and the benefits and risks emanating from their involvement. He then proposes measures that can be taken to enhance the benefits and to minimize the risks.

This work is an eye-opener: Involving lead users in the early innovation process can no longer be considered a reliable recipe as such but can be expected to produce valuable returns only if (a) the dependency on customer knowledge justifies the effort, (b) the benefits and success factors of integrating customers are skilfully managed, and (c) the risks involved are explicitly addressed and carefully contained.

What then are the success factors of customer integration?

The author arrives at 4 leading factors the application of which must be improved through a continuous learning process:

- Senior management must show strong commitment to innovation and customer integration,
- both technology and marketing departments must be involved in the process,
- responsibilities for cooperation must be clearly defined on the company's and the customers' part, and
- people involved must be selected based on their open-minded personality and their positive attitude to customer integration.

He also assesses the risks and the measures that can be taken to reduce their effect, e.g.

- the risk of biased results due to customers' functional fixedness, for example, can be reduced or avoided by careful customer selection, involving a sufficient number of lead users and using appropriate simulation methods (such as mock-ups, conjoint analyses etc.).

If the dependency on customer knowledge is considered low and the cost of risk reduction measures estimated to be high, then the author suggests that customer integration is simply not advisable.

For the decision whether or not to deploy customer integration as a channel of ideation and concept testing, the author puts forward a formal decision model showing the prospective outcome, i.e. the risk-benefit-ratio, as the quotient of the sum of the identified risks as modified by risk reducing measures over the sum of the expected benefits and success factors.

To objectively use this decision model in real-life situations, the author recommends that a team of company representatives involved in the innovation process individually and then jointly assesses the various risk and benefit factors, applying a rating scale, thus minimizing subjective bias.

The reader will take away a new understanding of when and how early customer integration can be made a meaningful, fruitful and reliable source of innovative product and service ideas – and when not. The academic controversy on the subject and the resulting hesitations of practitioners can thus be overcome. The way is open to successfully working with lead users whenever a lucid assessment of the benefits and risks justifies it.

It was a great pleasure to follow, together with Prof. Dr. Oliver Gassmann, the thorough, perspicacious and dedicated work of Dr. Kausch leading to obtaining his PhD at the University of St. Gallen and to this book.

Prof. Dr. Tom Sommerlatte
Engenhahn-Wildpark, April 16, 2007

Acknowledgements

This thesis is the result of my doctoral studies at the Institute of Technology Management at the University of St. Gallen/Switzerland and the Harvard Business School at Boston/USA. It was written between December 2003 and December 2006, considering external scientific and empirical research up to June 2006.

It is my pleasure and desire to thank all those who have contributed directly or indirectly, in a major or minor way, to the completion of my work.

First of all, I want to thank Professor Oliver Gassmann, my thesis supervisor, for asking me to join his team as a research associate after obtaining my diploma in mechanical engineering and for supporting me throughout my research. I gladly extend these thanks to Professor Tom Sommerlatte, my co-supervisor, who was always ready to sacrifice his time on short notice in order to advance the progress of the thesis and to speed up the doctorate procedure.

A major debt of gratitude is owed to Professor Stefan Thomke, my faculty sponsor at the Harvard Business School. I will never forget the kind reception and the many fruitful discussions he had with me despite his overload of doctoral students of his own.

With regard to my stay at the Harvard Business School, I gratefully acknowledge the financial support by the Swiss National Science Foundation.

Special thanks go to my parents Veronika and Professor Peter Kausch for their endless emotional and financial support during the whole time of my academic education. Without their encouragement, it would have been more difficult to reach my goals in occasionally controversial circumstances.

Last but not least, I would like to express my thanks to all colleagues at the Institute of Technology Management, especially to my officemates Lorenz Keller and Gerrit Reepmeyer for the friendly working atmosphere.

Zurich   Christoph Kausch
May 2007

Contents

1 Introduction

Quidquid agis, prudenter agas et respice finem!

(Aesop, approx. 600 BC)

Whatever you do, act prudently, and think of the outcome – especially when considering customer integration!

1.1 Relevance of the topic

1.1.1 Relevance of customer integration

Innovations are essential for securing and expanding a company's position in the market (Larson 2001).

The time of strictly segregated innovative activities either within or outside companies has been replaced by the era of Open Innovation (Chesbrough 2003c; Gassmann 2006). It started when more and more companies wished to commercialize both their own ideas and external innovations and tried to deploy other firms' processes for their internal research activities. This required a considerable change in a company's innovation policy: the solid boundaries between the company and the outside world had to be transformed into a semi-permeable membrane enabling at least a limited flow of information (Chesbrough 2003b). "True innovation never occurs in isolation" also is the dogma of the newly developed "Next Generation Innovation" approach (Jonash and Sommerlatte 2000: 2).

The more recent integration of customers into the innovation process complements the longer-standing cooperation with suppliers and scientific partners in this field. Among the most important triggers for customer integration is the high failure rate of innovative products (Atuahene-Gima 1995) that applies to industrial as well as consumer goods (Lüthje 2003). Customer integration can reduce this rate: customers know what they want and need and thus guarantee that new products developed accordingly will satisfy the market. At the same time, integrated customers constitute a reliable buyer potential.

The second important reason for integrating customers is the growing speed of technological development, which makes quick innovations imperative in order to avoid product obsolescence (Cordero 1991; Mabert et al. 1992). Combining forces with customers in the search for and the development of new products often shortens the innovation process considerably.

Another cause of innovative activities with customers is the need for securing access to new skills or technologies (Littler et al. 1995) that the company does not possess. External customer knowledge is not only welcome but also sometimes essential for gaining a competitive advantage.

The following diagram shows the importance companies of all branches attach to customers:

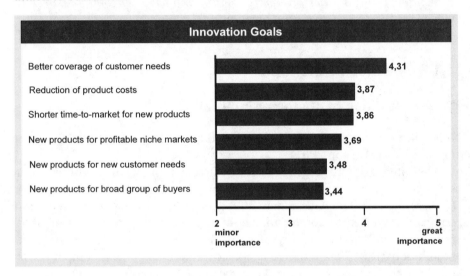

Source: Arthur D. Little (2004)

Fig. 1.1. Reasons for innovation with customers

1.1.2 Relevance of the early innovation phase

Customers have been integrated to different degrees in every phase of the entire innovation process. The first part, best known as the early innovation phase, sets the course for all following activities. With its maximum impact on R&D, it is the best starting-point for customer integration (Biemans 1991; Kohn and Niethammer 2002; Reichart 2002). At this early stage, the integrated customers' knowledge and experience can speed up the process of finding and selecting innovative fields and ideas most effectively. This advantage is augmented by the fact that the early consideration of customers' wishes minimizes the risk of a later change of construction in the product development phase, caused by dissatisfied customers having tested a model that did not meet their needs or expectations. The unwelcome consequence of a delayed market introduction with a sometimes considerable reduction of profits (Atuahene-Gima 1995; Bacon and Beckman 1994; Biemans 1991; Herstatt 2002; Kohli and Jaworski 1990; Murphy and Kumar 1996, 1997; Thomke and Fujimoto 2000: 132) can be avoided by integrating customers from the beginning.

These recognized facts and developments have led to the almost general consensus that customer integration is an indispensable prerequisite for a successful early innovation phase.

1.1.3 Relevance of a risk-benefit perspective

Of late, the positive connection between customer integration and a successful new product has been questioned (Brockhoff 2005a). Growing experience with customer integration has shown that the involvement of customers, advantageous as it is, can lead to disadvantages as well, such as biased results or loss of know-how, among other unwelcome aspects (Hamel et al. 1989; Jonash and Sommerlatte 2000: 16; Littler et al. 1995). In some cases, the disadvantages of customer integration may even outweigh its advantages, thus suggesting abstention from the concept altogether.

The prevailing strategy of generally including customers in the innovation process, which has been the result of the concept being considered best practice, has mostly prevented the question of whether customers should be integrated in a specific project, leaving only the questions of when and how this should be done. This thesis aims at replacing the current paradigm of customer integration as a natural asset to innovation activities without questioning its usefulness altogether. The objective is to find a way of assessing the prospective value of customer integration for every specific integration project, thus leading from the general recommendation to a consideration of the particular case.

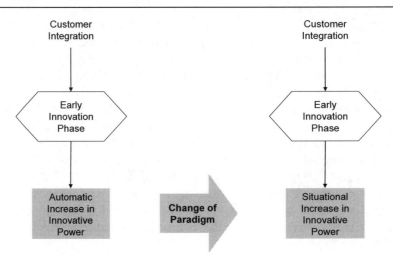

Fig. 1.2. Change of paradigm

In the day-to-day business of innovation management, such a situational investigation of the concept's advisability is not likely to meet with approval unless it can be achieved in a comparatively easy way. The thesis therefore focuses on establishing practical managerial guidelines that facilitate the prediction of whether customer integration will be a profitable course of action in any given innovation project. This prediction departs from the axiom that any activity is economically advisable when its resulting advantages are greater than its resulting disadvantages. The problem with customer integration is that its results only become effective when the integration project is over; beforehand, the element of uncertainty is attached to them, turning benefits into mere chances and disadvantages into risks. A model risk-benefit analysis, considering the effects and influencing factors of customer integration, will help with the individual assessment.

Such a model has to be based on points of reference that apply to any company. While every company will arrange its early innovation activities in a way best suited to its specific goals and means, which implies that few arrangements are similar, certain tasks are the same no matter in which way the early innovation phase may be subdivided. These tasks, e.g. finding opportunities for innovative products or selecting concrete ideas, all have specific characteristics that decide whether customer integration is fundamentally helpful in the first place or not. Certain tasks may exclude customer integration because customers cannot supply the respective required knowledge. The question of what can or cannot be learned from customers therefore has to be answered prior to any concrete thoughts on customer integration. This answer also decides which type of customer should be integrated, for a special kind of knowledge or skill requires a specific category of customers. Based on the characteristics of each task, various typical positive or negative effects of customer integration are likely to occur. Accordingly, the question of when customer integration is recommended in a risk-benefit perspective can only be answered with respect to each particular task such as finding, selecting, testing, etc.

The central point of a comprehensive risk-benefit analysis is the fact that all integration measures will have one or more effects that may be positive or negative. For instance, the integration of customers into workshops on roadmapping and scenario analysis for identifying opportunities may lead to the desired better market orientation but also to an unwelcome and unforeseen leakage of knowledge. To get an idea of the likely overall outcome of an envisaged integration measure, its prospective negative effects (risks) have to be balanced against its prospective positive effects (benefits). If risks and benefits are equal, neutralizing each other, the ultimate outcome is the same as without customer integration, which, accordingly, does not make sense. In case the risks even outweigh the benefits, customer integration would be downright uneconomic.

In the context of this study, "risk-benefit perspective" does not mean a money-based balance resulting in concrete figures but an overall weighing of advantages and disadvantages that answers the question of whether customer integration is advisable in a concrete innovation task.

1.2 Shortcomings of existing research

1.2.1 Conceptual research gap

The research for this thesis has been conducted in the context of strategic R&D management of investment and consumer goods. It focuses on the research fields of early innovation phase and customer integration with its positive and negative effects.

The integration of customers/users into the innovation process, especially into its early stages, has met with intensive research centering on the type of customers to be integrated (Brockhoff 1998, 2003; Nambisan 2002), on integration methods (Herstatt and von Hippel 1992; Leonard and Rayport 1997; Thomke and von Hippel 2002; Ulwick 2002; Urban and von Hippel 1988; von Hippel 1986), and on integration stages within the early innovation phase (Herstatt and Verworn 2003; Lüthje and Herstatt 2004; Murphy and Kumar 1997; van Kleef et al. 2005). Whereas various benefits of customer integration have already been given ample scientific attention (Bacon and Beckman 1994; Gruner and Homburg 1999; Kristensson et al. 2002; Lettl 2004: 66-69), its disadvantages and risks have not been investigated as closely. So far, the negative aspects of customer integration have mainly been discussed in the context of collaborative product development between two or more independent organizations (Littler et al. 1995) or with regard to discontinuous innovations (Veryzer 1998b). Very few other references to "disbenefits" (Littler et al. 1995) can be gathered (Bower and Christensen 1995: 44; Farr and Fischer 1992; Hamel et al. 1989; Kujala 2003; Reichart 2002; Wilson et al. 1995). The question of how negative side effects of customer integration detract from the value customers may add to the innovative success has not been the focus of research yet, although first answers have been given (Campbell and Cooper 1999; Enkel et al. 2005). Uncharted regions remain in respect of the economic sense of customer integration; the problem has as yet been mentioned in passing only (Brockhoff 2003: 471; Littler et al. 1995; Nambisan 2002). The question of what can or cannot be learned from customers – which decides whether customer integration is a priori a futile, i.e. economically absurd, or a possibly worthwhile effort – has been broached (Lettl 2004: 48ff), but only in the context of disruptive innovations. The success or failure of in-house development as compared to customer partnering has been discussed (Campbell and Cooper 1999), however only en bloc and not with respect to specific innovation tasks. In summary, literature, varying in intensity, is available on all relevant literature streams but not on their respective interfaces. The overlap will constitute the basis for a comprehensive economic assessment of an intended customer integration project. In order to answer the questions pertaining to this research gap, further conceptual research on the general and particular suitability of customer integration to solve certain problems and on its positive and negative side effects is necessary.

1.2.2 Empirical research gap

Various positive results of customer integration have been established by empirical research (Biemans 1992; Johne and Snelson 1988; Kohn and Niethammer 2002; Lynch and O' Toole 2003; Rothwell et al. 1974). Negative consequences are less well investigated but have entered the limelight of empirical researchers (Brockhoff 1997; Herstatt et al. 2003; Kohn and Niethammer 2002; Littler et al. 1995; Lynn et al. 1996: 13ff; Reichart

2002). The potential knowledge contribution of customers has been investigated in various case studies (Lynn et al. 1996: 13ff; Veryzer 1998b: 143ff), however only with regard to radical innovations and limited to customers' aptitude for evaluating innovative ideas. An explicit weighing of advantages and disadvantages of customer integration, resulting in a risk-benefit analysis, has not been carried out yet, although first general empirical investigations were undertaken (Ganesan 1994; Li and Calantone 1998). These omissions leave an empirical research gap for investigation.

A risk-benefit analysis of customer integration, based on a holistic perspective of the positive and negative side effects of customer integration, can close both the conceptual and empirical research gap.

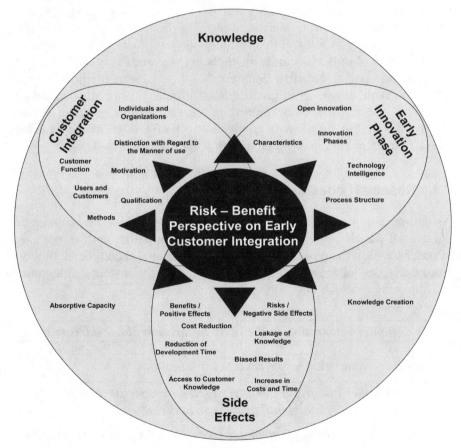

Fig. 1.3. Research gap

1.3 Research concept

This research project, inspired by the phenomenon of open innovation and the increasing relevance of customer integration into the early innovation process, has the objective of finding out if this concept can still be considered advisable on a general level or, if this is not the case, if and when it can be recommended in particular projects.

In order not to imply any preference for or aversion to the concept, the main research question is put in the form of an open question that retains the possibility of customer integration as a generally advisable practice. On a strictly logical basis, this issue has to be cleared first. If customer integration is recommendable a priori, its benefits are taken for granted, at least in the way that they generally outweigh possible disadvantages. The resulting company strategy of integrating customers on a routine basis will lead to a consideration of only risks and risk-reducing measures if at all, not paying attention to special benefits. Sub-questions pertaining to those will be pointless. With an answer in favor of a situational decision, theoretical and empirical research has to be more comprehensive. For practical reasons and purposes, the thesis will combine the partly overlapping research, which is reflected in the research question and the research design.

1.3.1 Research question

As demonstrated with the research gap, a comprehensive investigation of the overall positive outcome of early customer integration does not exist. In order to reach the research goal of either a general recommendation or a risk-benefit model for economically advisable early customer integration, the following research question is posed:

> *Is customer integration in the early innovation phase advisable?*

This research question raises several sub-questions:

> *Can customer integration be investigated irrespective of different individual process structures?*
>
> *Which possible effects of customer integration have to be taken into account?*
>
> *Can the potential success of customer integration be predicted?*

1.3.2 Research approach

The research is conducted from the perspective of companies considering customer integration, not from the customer's point of view or interests.

With the partly overlapping, partly conflicting research goal of assessing the general or particular value of customer integration, a special recognized research approach (Lettl 2004) has seemed to be appropriate.

General literature research is compiled in Chapter 2, which gives a comprehensive overview of all aspects of customer integration in the early innovation phase. In addition, supplementary theoretical research entered the development of a reference model for a risk-benefit analysis in Chapter 3, containing detailed theoretical characteristics of aspects already mentioned in Chapter 2, e.g. of risks and benefits in the context of special innovation tasks. This supplementary, targeted research has led to the deduction of several propositions, preparing the envisaged concrete risk-benefit model, the necessity of which still depends on the outcome of subsequent empirical research. This empirical research in the form of case studies and mini-cases therefore has to test propositions as well as provide characteristics for the overall success of customer integration. The dual use of empirical data influences the structure of the thesis to a considerable degree.

The trigger for this thesis was a practical problem of managers and companies and not a phenomenon originating in scientific discussions, which would be the typical object of basic research. The dissertation project therefore follows the University of St. Gallen's research tradition, which understands the theory of business management as an application-orientated social science (Bleicher 1991; Ulrich 1981). Management theory must stay in close contact with practice and contribute to the solutions of practical problems.

Due to the novelty of the empirical phenomenon of side effects of customer integration and to the existence of diverse case material, this study uses an exploratory approach. With such an approach, the emphasis is predominantly on the exploration of interesting situations, correlations, and contexts in companies and on the conceptualization of the investigated material (Ulrich 1981). These concepts can be refined in subsequent empirical research. This reiterating learning process aims at both generating questions and presenting propositions relevant to explaining typical phenomena (Kromrey 1995).

Following Kubicek (1977), Tomczak (1992), and Gassmann (1999), the research process is highly iterative (see Fig. 1.4.). In addition to validating propositions created solely upon theory, the targeted new knowledge covers questions to reality which are based upon both theory and practice (Kubicek 1977). The image of reality that is created upon the initial framework and data collection is critically reflected in order to achieve differentiation, abstraction, and changes in perspective. The new theoretical understanding leads to new questions about reality. Consequently, at the time of writing the publication the research process must be frozen in a pragmatic way. All open questions at that stage in the research process have to be made explicit as part of the research results.

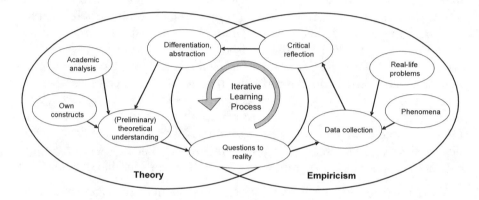

Source: following Kubicek (1977), Tomczak (1992), and (1990)

Fig. 1.4. Exploratory research as an iterative learning process

1.3.3 Research methodology

As the side effects of customer integration constitute a very young empirical phenomenon, an exploratory research method has been chosen, focusing on qualitative research in accordance with Eisenhardt (1989), Yin (1994), and Gassmann (1999).

From the four basic types of design for case studies, this research follows a multiple-case design with customer integration - the joint project - as the single unit of analysis (see Yin 1994). In addition to four case studies, mini-cases will be used to illustrate theoretical concepts and approaches for coping with different challenges in customer integration. These mini-cases deepen the understanding of the topic in its particular context and are favored by the practice, having a close link to its activities and being easy to remember (Tsoukas 1994). Throughout the study, these mini-cases or narratives will be used to deepen the understanding of a subject under study (see von Zedtwitz 1999).

Organizational research relies on case studies for two reasons that normally are mutually exclusive: either to test propositions, thus inducing hypotheses, or to build new hypotheses or theories (Eisenhardt 1989). The case studies and mini-cases serve both purposes, because the development of the finally aspired model for predicting the value of customer integration can be equaled to building a new theory or formulating a new hypothesis. The cases will be used to prove or disprove the propositions derived in Chapter 3 and will provide the empirical basis for the final model, which will be developed from theoretical reflections and from empirical findings. As both approaches resort to partly overlapping methods (Eisenhardt 1989), there is no fundamental obstacle against using the case studies and mini-cases both ways. On the contrary, the research question suggests the combined use, serving as it does to open up a new research field that does not have extensive analyzable data. In cases like this, case studies are ideal to record human behavior and its reasons and to help recognize superordinate relations of cause and effect (dos Santos et al. 2003).

The main criteria in qualitative empirical research are validity of results and reliability. Usually, three types of validity can be distinguished: (i) construct validity, (ii) internal validity, and (iii) external validity. According to Yin (1994), construct validity can be increased by using multiple sources of evidence, establishing a chain of evidence between question, data, and conclusion, and having key informants review the draft case study report and agree upon it. Internal validity of causal relationships requires a reliable process of analyzing data and comparing emerging concepts and theories with previous literature for generalization and validation of theories from cases. In addition, the concept of triangulation is central with respect to internal validity (Lamnek 1993; Yin 1994). External validity confirms that the findings can be generalized. Finally, reliability is required to enable other researchers to conduct the same research with the same procedure at later times (Eisenhardt 1989).

In this research, validity and reliability are ensured by combining the semi-structured data with the results of thoroughly conducted desk research, internal R&D documentation, and presentations by R&D personnel. The interpretations are confirmed in follow-up interviews.

The methodic backbone of this qualitative, exploratory research is the contingency approach, claiming that there is no single right way of acting (Child, 1972; Kubkicek and Welter, 1985). Everything depends on the respective situation. Abandoning the paradigm of universal, absolutely and unconditionally valid answers to organizational questions (cf. McKenna 2000: 14; Wolf 2003: 153), which was the predominant concept of theoretical science up to the 1960s, the contingency approach holds the view that "there is no one best way to manage an organization" (Drazin and Van de Ven 1985: 514). Scientists as well as managers have to find out "which technique will, in a particular situation, under particular circumstances, and at a particular time, best contribute to the attainment of managerial goals" (Stoner 1982: 54). All answers are contingent on the specific circumstances in each organization or company; a company must adapt its organizational structures to the respective prevailing conditions (Kieser 2001: 169).

The research project is guided by the theory of the contingency approach with regard to the main research question in general and in the context of the sub-questions two and three in particular.

1.3.4 Research design

Even though there is an increasing awareness of the relevance of early customer integration, only few pertinent studies have focused on a management perspective. Therefore, the Institute of Technology Management of the University of St. Gallen, Switzerland, conducted various research projects from March 2003 until spring 2006 which are part of the basis for this thesis, providing empirical examples for mini-cases:

- Bilateral research project with *Bayer Material Science* with the scope of optimizing and visualizing their early innovation process.
- Bilateral research project with *BASF* with the aim to improve and implement ways of integrating customers in the very early phase of *BASF's* innovation process.
- Bilateral research project with *ZF Friedrichshafen AG* about the optimization of their technology strategy and early innovation processes.
- Research project, partly sponsored by the Commission for Technology and Innovation (CTI - Swiss research fund), with six Swiss-based companies (Bircher Reglomat AG, Gallus Ferd. Rüesch AG, Schindler Elevators Ltd., Schurter AG, Sefar AG, Zimmer GmbH) with the aim of improving the companies' market orientation by way of an early customer integration. Special emphasis is put on the adaptation and modification of customer integration tools, such as the lead user method, to the companies' individual needs.

- From February 2004 to October 2004, a series of workshops on early customer integration was held for a group of nine multinational core participant companies (BASF AG, Getzner Werkstoffe GmbH, Helbling Technik AG, Henkel KGaA, Infoterra GmbH, Kaba AG, Merck KGaA, Schindler Elevators Ltd. and SIG allCap AG) and five guest speaker companies (Bayer Material Science AG, IBM - ISL, Siemens AG, Sulzer Hexis AG, Zumtobel AG). The objective was to assess how competitive advantages can be reached, kept, and increased with the help of strategies for early customer integration.
- Various personal interviews were also conducted during the projects mentioned above and in conferences as guest speaker and/or participant. More than 206 interviews with managers and experts from R&D and Innovation, providing insights into companies from various industries, constitute additional empirical material (see Table 1.1.)

Table 1.1. Overview of empirical data set

Industry	# of Interviews	# of Companies
Engineering & Manufacturing	126	21
Chemicals	13	7
Consumer Packaged Goods	18	8
Pharmaceuticals & Medical Products	37	6
Software/Electronics/Telecommunication	12	6
Total number of interviews and companies	206	48

The main focus of empirical research was on the case studies. Several German-speaking companies strongly involved in early customer integration (Gallus, Schindler, Schurter, and Zimmer) have supplied material for the thesis. The detailed criteria for their selection and the structure of the case study research will be introduced in the context of the cases in Chapter 4.

The empirical investigations pertaining to the case studies started in 2004 and were finished in the fall of 2005.

1.3.5 Thesis outline

The thesis is structured as follows (see also Fig. 1.5.):

Chapter 2 demonstrates that the integration of customers in the innovation process has been a focus of scientific research for about three decades. This chapter highlights the state of the art in literature with regard to the key issues of customer integration in order to develop conclusive reference points for a risk-benefit perspective.

The next chapter (Chapter 3) describes and characterizes in detail the core components for successful customer integration in the early innovation phase, establishing categories of components and deriving propositions relating to them. Existing theoretical and empirical findings are combined with own new perspectives and considerations in the course of developing this analytical reference frame. A summary of the propositions concludes the chapter.

Chapter 4 shows how companies have dealt with the issues raised in the previous chapters. Different companies serve as an example of good or bad practices regarding customer integration and its related benefits or risks. Four detailed case studies give first-hand information on the practical answers to most theoretical questions raised in Chapter 3.

Chapter 5 deals with the characteristics of advisable customer integration that emerge from a cross-case comparison of the four case studies and additional mini-cases. Based on typical patterns resembling the findings of the Research Dependence Theory, the chapter points out ways of successful integration practices, proving the propositions of Chapter 3 all along.

The following Chapter 6 develops a managerial model for predicting the prospective success of customer integration.

The final Chapter 7 sums up the concrete answers to the research questions and lists the validated propositions/hypotheses. It also discusses the immediate implications for management theory and practice and points out where future research is necessary.

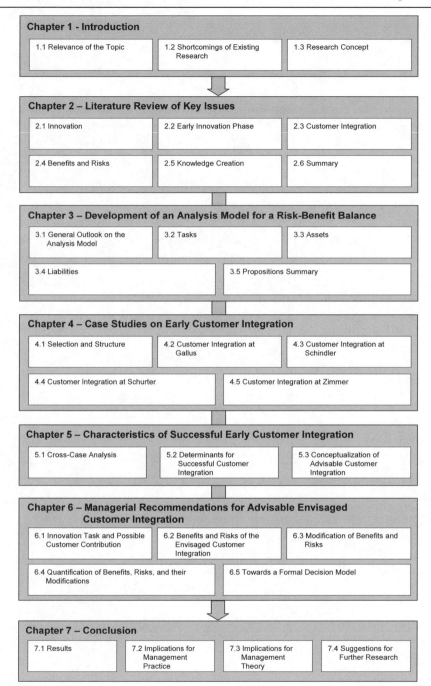

Fig. 1.5. Structure of thesis

2 Literature review of key issues

2.1 Innovation

For most companies, innovations are an indispensable prerequisite of survival in increasingly competitive markets and the main trigger for customer integration.

The definition of this term varies from one scientific discipline to another, e.g. economics, social sciences, or technical sciences, and even within each discipline it largely depends on the author's scientific background and point of view (Reichart 2002). In the context of this study, the term innovation is mainly used in the technical sense, referring to developments that result in a new product or a new service (Kobe 2001). The novelty lies in the perception of the relevant unit of adoption - the market - and the designation to benefit individuals, groups, or wider society (Zaltman et al. 1973).

With the focus on customers' contribution to innovations, a further breakdown of the term is necessary regarding the degree of novelty. Innovations improving existing products are called incremental, whereas those finding completely new solutions, e.g. developing new functionalities or leading to a drastic cost reduction or an improvement in performance by at least 500%, are called radical. Innovations that can be used without extra investments, additional acquisition of knowledge, and new process structures are termed sustaining. If a change in one of the three mentioned fields is necessary, the innovation is disruptive (Bower and Christensen 1995).

Most incremental innovations are sustaining, and radical innovations tend to be disruptive, but this correlation is not cogent.

2.2 Early innovation phase

2.2.1 Temporal delimitation and character

The innovation process as a whole comprises all activities from the finding and shaping of a concept for an innovative product to its production and final commercialization. This entire process is often termed product innovation process, product development process, or just product development (Schlaak 1999: 1; Specht and Beckmann 1996: 17). The English-speaking countries refer to the whole process as "New Product Development" or NPD (Verworn 2005: 12), whereas elsewhere this term is often also used for the second part of the innovation process following the concept development (Linner 1995: 8; Pleschak and Sabisch 1996: 160; Schmelzer 1999: 208; Zuberbühler 1979: 73f.).

Since the 1960s, efforts have been made to structure this whole process (Cooper 1994: 4ff; Verworn 2005: 13). The results vary regarding their content and level of abstraction (Vahs and Burmester 1999: 83f). The only correspondence that can be found is the rough subdivision into early and late phases (Verworn 2005: 14). The early phases have been comprised into "the early innovation phase" which has many names: fuzzy front end (Cooper 1997: 21; Kim and Wilemon 2002b; Massey et al. 2002: 39f; Moenart et al. 1995: 144f; Montoya-Weiss and O'Driscoll 2000; Smith and Reinertsen 1991: 43), phase zero (Khurana and Rosenthal 1998; Zien and Buckler 1997: 283), cloudy phase (Gassmann and Zedtwitz 2003), initiation stage (Souder and Moenart 1992: 492), early stages (Nobelius and Trygg 2002: 331), early phases (Herstatt 1999: 72f; Kobe 2001: 49; Verganti 1999: 363), pre-project phases (Cooper 1983), up-front homework (Cooper 1996), predevelopment or up-front activities (Cooper 1988: 237).

The early innovation phase starts - in this respect all models more or less agree - with an impulse or a suddenly emerging opportunity (Verworn 2005: 15); an impulse consists of new or changed customer needs, a new product launched by a competitor, new regulations or technological progress (Buchholz 1998: 23f; Saynisch 1979: 90; Smith and Reinertsen 1992: 4), an opportunity is a new innovation field or a new trend (Gassmann et al. 2006a). The end of the early innovation phase differs according to the various process models.

Some authors include the technical process of product development into the early innovation phase (Cooper 1988: 238; Nihtilä 1999: 56f; Nottrodt 1999: 3), others (Jonash and Sommerlatte 2000: 50; Schwankl 2002: 8) consider prototype development as part of the fuzzy front end.

The usual definition in literature is the one used by Verworn (2005: 15): The early innovation phase covers all activities from the first impulse or the first emerging opportunity for a new product to the final go/no go decision prior to the actual product development.

The next phase comprises the technical development including development and testing of prototypes, first tests in the market, a final design, and a preparation of serial production. The last phase consists of serial production and market introduction (Herstatt and Verworn 2003: 9).

Whatever the structure of the different fuzzy front end models, they all have to consider the specific aims of the early innovation phase: reducing uncertainties by collecting information about ideas, assessing them, and developing a concept or project plan (Herstatt 1999: 76; Kim and Wilemon 2002a: 70; Madauss 1994: 1; Moenart et al. 1995: 244; Rosenau 1997: 103).

Its character, as the name "fuzzy" indicates, is rather vague and escapes the term "structure" in the strict sense of the word. The seeming semi-chaos is necessary and intended to bring about an atmosphere conducive to creative ideas.

2.2.2 Various structure models

With these characteristics in mind, two main categories of structuring approaches have been developed: descriptive and normative process models (Cooper 1983: 6; Verworn 2005: 21). The first category describes innovation processes as found in practice. The second one deduces a picture of an ideal process from successful actions. This distinction, however, is not very convincing because it does not further scientific conclusions: a process found in practice is hardly worth describing unless it is considered exemplary for others, and by being described it is transformed into an "ideal" process model. The following models are introduced in detail:

- Stage Gate Process (Cooper 1988: 242)
- Development Funnel by Wheelwright and Clark (1992)
- Front End Model by Khurana and Rosenthal (1998)
- New Concept Development Model (Koen et al. 2001)
- Customer-oriented Concept Development Model by Gassmann, Kausch and Enkel (2006a)

The Stage Gate Process

The Stage Gate Process, developed by Cooper and further refined by Cooper and Kleinschmidt (Cooper 1988; Cooper and Kleinschmidt 1990, 1993), centers on a break-down of the innovation process into distinct, consecutive, multifunctional "stages", separated from each other by "gates". At these gates, the innovation activities within the previous stage are evaluated and judged according to certain fixed criteria. This assessment results in a go/no decision: the process is irretrievably stopped if the evaluation is negative. This way it is guaranteed that only suitable projects are pursued. The model has been criticized for its sequential design that excludes considerations turning up at later stages (Herstatt 1999: 77; Verworn 2005: 30).

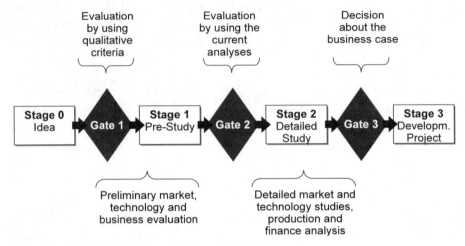

Fig. 2.1. Stage-Gate-Process (Cooper 1997:22)

The Development Funnel

Wheelwright and Clark (1992) developed a model based on an approach that is basically similar to the Stage Gate Process: the Development Funnel. This "funnel" structures the innovation process into three "phases" separated by two "screens". The main idea – and the reason why the picture of a funnel was chosen – is that at the outset of the innovation process a wide opening for all kinds of challenges and opportunities has to be provided, whereas the necessary concentration on just a few concepts asks for an elimination process by which only the most promising ideas pass through the narrow final opening prior to serial production. In the first phase, which comprises idea generation and concept development, all persons involved are encouraged to come up with more and better ideas (Kobe 2001: 59). These are screened, and the best ones are analyzed in detail in phase 2, which also serves to establish and procure the knowledge their realization will require. In a second screening, the final projects are selected. The following phase 3 endows the remaining projects with the necessary resources, turning them into focused developments quickly.

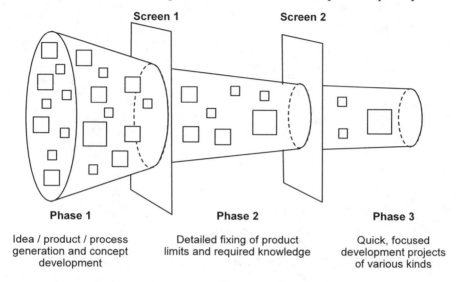

Fig. 2.2. Development Funnel by Wheelwright and Clark (1992)

The Front End Model by Khurana and Rosenthal

Khurana and Rosenthal, having established in empirical studies that the success of development projects depends on the fit of idea generation and project definition with the company's strategy (Khurana and Rosenthal 1997), emphasized the importance of the "Front End" of innovative processes. They recommend a procedure that starts with two input streams: a pre-phase consisting of opportunity identification, idea generation, and market/technology analysis on the one hand and a company-driven strategy, comprising a strategic vision and the assigning of responsibility, on the other hand (Khurana and Rosenthal 1998: 64ff). The streams join up in Phase Zero that analyzes customer needs, competitors, and market segmentation. By means of feasibility studies and project planning, a go/no go decision is made, opening or closing the way to the project's technical execution.

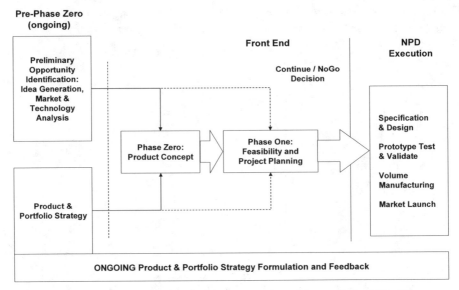

Fig. 2.3. Model of the front end of NPD (Khurana and Rosenthal 1998: 59)

The New Concept Development Model by Koen

Whereas the previously described models all follow a linear structure with various consecutive steps in which decisions on selection and elimination are made in a chronological order, Koen advocates a completely different approach (Koen et al. 2001; Koen et al. 2002). He developed a model of the fuzzy front end, the New Concept Development Model, in which the diverse segments or sub-phases of the early innovation phase are not strictly separated but interact with the others, influencing them and being influenced in turn. To illustrate this interaction, which allows iterative assessments and reconsideration, he chose the picture of a circle with five revolving elements, symbolizing the free circulation and up to a point flexible sequence of the different sub-phases. The "driver" or "engine" of the whole innovation process is the company's strategy, management, and innovation culture; the influencing factors consist of the company's organization and structure, its customers' and competitors' influence, and its ability to develop new technologies.

Fig. 2.4. New Concept Development Model by Koen, Ajamian et al. (2001: 47)

The Customer-oriented Concept Development Model by Gassmann, Kausch and Enkel (2006a)

With the main focus on customer integration rather than on technical or organizational processes, the authors, combining Koen's New Concept Development model (Koen et al. 2001) with the imperative necessity of knowledge creation (Jonash and Sommerlatte 2000: 22), have developed a circular model with five sub-phases (Gassmann et al. 2006a).

The first phase, Opportunity Identification and Analysis, centers on finding and selecting opportunities. The second phase, Idea and Knowledge Creation, is a novelty, asserting that idea generation presupposes knowledge that, in its turn, is broadened and enriched by these very ideas to be used immediately or stored for future use. The following sub-phase is termed Idea and Functionality Selection, an idea referring to a new product, a functionality being a new or better way of using an existing product for its intended purpose or a way of opening up new purposes. The fourth sub-phase is called Concept Definition and resembles the respective sub-phases of other models, especially Koen's. Prototype Testing, constituting the last sub-phase, has been included in this model for the sake of its vast possibilities of customer integration.

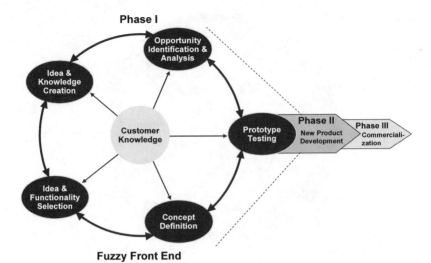

Fig. 2.5. Customer-oriented Concept Development Model by Gassmann, Kausch and Enkel (2006a)

Table 2.1. Literature streams of the early innovation phase

Author(s)	Literature Stream	Conceptualization	Empirical Validation	Outcome	Related Research
Reid and de Brentani (2004)	Early Innovation Phase	Three perspectives of innovation and their relation to the fuzzy front end (FFE): 1. environment, 2. individual, 3. organization	Theoretical paper	Model of the early innovation phase, defining the NPD process for discontinuous innovations as a combination of individual and corporate decisions at different interfaces: boundary, gate keeping, and project interface	Buckler (1997), Buggie (2002), Boutellier, Gassmann et al. (2000), Cooper (1997), Dahan and Hauser (2001), Gassmann and von Zedtwitz (2003), Kim and Wilemon (2002a; 2002b), Koen et al. (2001; 2002), Khurana and Rosenthal (1997; 1998), Montoya-Weiss and O'Driscoll (2000), Nobelius and Trygg (2002), Reinertsen (1999), Rice, Kelley et al. (2001), Smith, Herbein and Morris (1999), Thomke and Fujimoto (2000), Tidd and Bodley (2002), Walls (2002), Zhang and Doll (2001)
Cooper (1988)	Phase Structure of Early Innovation Phase	n/a.	Theoretical paper	Management model for structuring early innovation activities in a so-called Stage Gate Process	Albach (1994), Cooper (1990; 1996; 1997; 1997), Cooper and Kleinschmidt (1990; 1993), Ebert, Pleschak et al. (1992), Gassmann, Kausch and Enkel (2005b; 2006a), Geschka (1993), Herstatt (1999), Hughes and Chafin (1996), Hwang (2004), Khurana and Rosenthal (1997; 1998), Koen, Ajamian, Boyce et al. (2002), Muller (Muller 2005), Nobelius and Trygg (2002), Pleschak and Sabisch (1996), Rochford (1991), Schumpeter (1939), Smith and Herbein (1999), Stalk (2006), Thom (1980), Ulrich (1995), Vahs and Burmester (1999), Wheelwright and Clark (1992), Witt (1996)
Koen, Ajamian, Burkart et al., (2001)	Phase Structure of Early Innovation Phase	Establishment of best practices for the Innovation FFE	Mixed-methods approach, comparison of results obtained via case research in eight companies and multiple-respondent questionnaire surveys in 23 companies	Development of a theoretical construct (NCD) for the FFE, consisting of three elements: 5 interacting sub-phases, an "engine" that powers them, and external influencing factors.	

2.3 Customer integration

To achieve a comprehensive view of customer integration, this term has to be broken down into its components because different customers require different integration measures and vice versa.

2.3.1 Customers

In the normal sense of the word a customer is a person who takes up a service or buys goods, no matter if he actually uses them (Lettl 2004). Users, on the other hand, are always considered customers as the last link in the value chain, whether they bought a product or received it in another way. For the purpose of simplification, the terms customer and user will be employed in the same sense and more or less at random, apart from the fixed combinations "customer integration" and "lead user".

The term customer may refer to the individual level (Gemuenden 1981: 4ff; Karle-Komes 1997: 41; Kirchmann 1994: 15) or to the organizational level (Herstatt 1991: 7; Herstatt et al. 2002: 65ff; Shaw 1985: 287; von Hippel et al. 2000: 23). With customer integration, it is obvious that only persons and not companies are considered, but these persons may act on their own as individual customers or as representatives/employees of organizations/other companies.

In the course of this research, various types or categories of customers will play an important role.

Distinction with regard to the manner of use

Users often differ considerably regarding the frequency and intensity of product use. A "normal" customer uses a product for a special private purpose and with changing, rather low intensity (Kohn and Niethammer 2002). A professional customer makes use of a product in a constant, highly intensive manner as an "extreme user" (Kohn and Niethammer 2002). If a customer uses a product in another than the originally intended field, e.g. a diamond drill in the exploration of oil fields, he is called "analogous user" (Herstatt 2002).

Such users will be professional customers for the most part, but sometimes "normal customers" also find ways of using a product in a different way or for different purposes compared to the producer's envisaged use.

The manner of use can differ in another way as well: Most customers will use the acquired product themselves as so-called "direct" users. "Indirect" users are people who recommend an approved product to others on a professional or private basis without actually using it themselves, e.g. an architect recommending elevators or lighting systems to his clients or a soccer coach recommending sportswear to his players (Gassmann et al. 2006a).

Qualification and motivation

Customers differ with regard to their knowledge of processes or products (Lüthje 2000: 34-40). It goes without saying that "normal" customers usually know less about a product than professional users.

A customer's motivation for wanting a new product and his readiness to be integrated into the process of developing it may have various reasons that are classified by scientific research as extrinsic or intrinsic (Lüthje 2000: 41-44). Extrinsic motives are money – financial remuneration in various forms is a very potent incentive (Brockhoff 2005a; Gebert and von Rosenstiehl 1981: 38-43; Lüthje 2000: 42; von Rosenstiehl 1980: 272) – or the expected profit a customer will have using the future product (Eliashberg et al. 1997; Haman 1996; Lilien et al. 2002). Intrinsic motivation is a reward for customer activities by the customer himself: he feels important being able to help, he gains reputation among his peers, he increases his own knowledge and expertise or he just enjoys the process (Achtenhagen et al. 2003; Gassmann 2001; von Krogh 2003; von Krogh and von Hippel 2003). Of late, a new category of motivation has been discovered: the social motivation (Reichwald and Piller 2005). Users interact with each other on user Internet platforms, thus establishing contacts with people of similar interests; their contribution to the interests of the company providing the platform is a mere by-product. Another "social" motive is the wish to influence the environment (Kollock and Smith 1999).

Based on the customers' qualification and motivation, von Hippel described a type of customer whom he termed „Lead User" (von Hippel 1986).

Being highly qualified and progressive, these customers

- "face needs that will be general in a marketplace – but face them months or years before the bulk of that marketplace encounters them, and
- are positioned to benefit significantly by obtaining a solution to those needs" (von Hippel 1986: 796).

Both qualification and motivation restrict the circle of lead users to extreme and professional analogous users, excluding the remaining customer group of "normal" users.

Customer function

Brockhoff (1998: 8f; 2003: 466ff), concentrating on forms and ways of customer input, discerns five types of customers: 1. the "demanding" customer, i.e. the representative of the demand side of the market, who expresses his needs either directly or by his behavior and thus supplies new ideas, 2. the "launching" customer, who actively takes part in the innovation process, 3. the "innovative" customer, whose own almost completed innovative solutions to his problems form the basis for a new product - this term coincides more or less with the term lead user -, 4. the "reference" customer, who passes on his experience of using a certain product to the producer and/or to other users/customers 5. the "first buyer", who helps reduce uncertainties about market expectations within the company (see Fig. 2.6.).

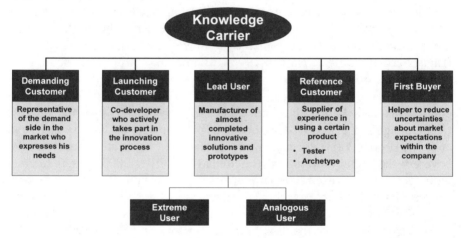

Source: modified from Brockhoff (1998)

Fig. 2.6. Customer functions

2.3.2 Integration

Definition

The interaction between company and customers may have many forms, each varying in type and intensity, e.g. a short buyer-seller contact, a questioning via conventional market research, or a long-term cooperation in product development. Integration (for a detailed description cf. Engelhardt et al. 1993) implies a certain time element, excluding the brief moment of handing over products or rendering a service. In addition, the interaction must be intentional on both parts and aimed at cooperation, even if it is a short one as in conventional market research. Its main characteristic is the consequent orientation towards a customer's proactive role in innovative activities (Reichwald and Piller 2005). The strongest form of integration is customer partnering, defined as a "formalized working relationship between a customer and a manufacturer which involves performing coordinated development activities to develop a new product" (Campbell and Cooper 1999: 508).

Table 2.2. Forms of interaction between company and customers (based on Reichwald and Piller 2005)

Manufacturer-Customer Interaction in the New Product Development Process	
Indirect Contacts	
Listening in: Using customer data from search portals, web-based advisors, or product catalogs to explore unmet customer needs ("design for customers")	**Indirect collection of market / customer information** - Evaluation of literature and trade journals of customers' industries - Evaluation of patents - Evaluation of feedback based on analysis of CRM systems etc. **Customers as passive targets of observation** - Customer observations (during use of product) - Empathic Design - Click-stream analysis, web-based content analysis etc. - Exploring search mechanisms, searches in product catalogs
Integration	
Asking about: Asking customers explicitly about new product features or product concepts, using surveys, web-based conjoint analysis, and other means to get access to customer preferences and needs ("design with customers")	**Manufacturer-initiated dialogue with customers** - Customer / user panels; user surveys on (future) requirements - Consumer-idealized design - (Web-based) conjoint analysis - Quality function deployment and Kansei engineering - Securities trading of concepts (virtual stock markets) - Creativity workshops with customers - (Virtual) concept testing and prototyping - Piloting and field tests, (web-based) critical incident technique - Product clinics (also in form of online discussions) **Customer initiated dialogue with manufacturers** - Evaluation of complaints - Evaluation of customer requests / customer recommendations - Systematic complaint management - Screening of user groups and user communities
Taking part: Allowing and enabling customers to design their own solution (at least partly) by the use of user innovation platforms ("design by customers")	**Customers are equal partners of the organization** - Manufacturer-initiated and operated toolkits for innovation - Intermediary-initiated and operated toolkits for innovation - User design: Using visual drag-and-drop, respondents trade off features against price or performance - Joint product development with customers (lead users) - Temporary employment of supplier's staff at customer's site - Temporary employment of customer's staff at supplier's site - Lead user workshops initiated by the manufacturer **Customers as independent innovators** - Lead user activities without manufacturer's initial motivation - Community innovation (e.g. open source) - Customer-initiated and operated platforms/ toolkits for innovation

Historical development of customer integration

Innovations are expensive and risky. The two triggering reasons for customer integration have been to upgrade company resources by customer input, thus lessening own costs (Krapfel et al. 1991; Lengnick-Hall 1996) and to overcome information deficits which pose risks (Helten 1994; Li and Calantone 1998). Both motives for customer integration are described in detail by Hayes and Wheelwright (1988).

Since the 1970s, active cooperation with customers has been an object of scientific research, starting with Achilladelis et al. (1971) and Rothwell et al. (1974) who stressed the importance of understanding customers' needs for a successful product development.

An active role for customers as idea generators was first suggested in the 1960s (Enos 1962; Freeman 1968). Concrete recommendations for customer integration in the idea generation stage were advocated by von Hippel who developed the Customer-Active-Paradigm (CAP) (von Hippel 1978: 40, 1979: 84) as opposed to the Manufacturer-Active-Paradigm (MAP) (von Hippel 1978: 40, 1979: 84). Within MAP, the customer, being considered incapable of own innovative activities, is only active when expressly asked by the manufacturer -"speaking only when spoken to"- (von Hippel 1978: 243), whereas within CAP most innovative activities of the idea generation phase are instigated and carried out by customers (von Hippel 1979: 87). The CAP model was modified by Foxall and Tierney (1984) and Voss (1985) into a CAP 2 model, increasing the possible places of customer integration within the innovation process.

A partly similar perspective, considering not only customers but also other external participants of the innovation process, has led to another comparatively young paradigm. It departs from the fact that all companies used to share one characteristic: they restricted the innovative efforts to company resources, closing off the outside. This attitude, in retrospect, has been termed "closed innovation paradigm" (Chesbrough 2003c). In the 1990s, however, the high costs and risks of developing and launching innovative products led to an increased number of alliances between companies in their common goal to discover customer requirements in a more cost-effective way (Miotti and Sachwald 2003). By and by, this cooperation was extended to suppliers and to external experts such as research institutes or universities. In 1995, the external knowledge input into the companies' innovation activities amounted to 34-65% (Conway 1995). Customers were the last to be actively included. This opening of the innovation process, first described by Chesbrough (2003c), has led to the era of the so-called "Open Innovation Paradigm" (Chesbrough 2003b, c, 2004; Rigby and Zook 2002).

Without this paradigm shift, customer integration into the early innovation phase would not have reached the widespread extension it has nowadays.

Table 2.3. Literature streams of customer integration

Author(s)	Literature Stream	Conceptualization	Empirical Validation	Outcome	Related Research
Bonner and Walker (2004)	Customers and Users	Focus on new product advantages: Their degree is influenced by the customers' "embeddedness" into the company and by the heterogeneity of knowledge among the set of influential customers	Quantitative research, n=137	Importance of relational embeddedness and knowledge heterogeneity of influential customers taking part in NPD projects	Achtenhagen, Müller-Lietzkow et al. (2003), Alba and Hutchinson (2000), Athaide and Stump (1999), Bossink (2002), Brockhoff (1998; 2003; 2005a), Bruce, Leverick et al. (1995), Callahan (2004), Eliashberg, Lilien et al. (1997), Gary (2003), Gruner and Homburg (1999), Harhoff, Henkel and von Hippel (2003), Herstatt, Lüthje et al. (2002), Hillebrand and Biemans (2003), Ishii (2004), Jeppesen and Molin (2003), Kahn (2001), Karle-Komes (1997), Kok, Hillebrand and Biemans (2003), Kristensson, Gustafsson and Archer (2004), Lengnick-Hall (1996), Lettl (2004), Lilien, Morrison et al. (2002), Lüthje (2000; 2004), Markham and Griffin (1998), Miotti and Sachwald (2003), Morrison, Roberts and Midgley (2004), Nambisan (2002), Pitta, Franzak et al. (1996), Reichwald and Piller (2005), Salomo, Steinhoff and Trommsdorff (2003), von Hippel, Thomke et al. (2000), von Krogh and von Hippel (2003)
Von Hippel (1986)	Customers and Users	Examination of users' general aptitude to create or assess novel product possibilities	Theoretical paper	Identification and integration of "Lead Users" in the R&D process	
Brockhoff (2003)	Customers and Users	NPD described from the customers' point of view	Theoretical paper	Establishment of different customer types and recommendations on their integration in specific stages of the innovation phase	

Table 2.3. (cont.)

Author	Topic	Definition	Method	Contribution	References
Van Kleef, van Trijp and Luning (2005)	Customer Integration	n.a.	Theoretical paper	Classification of customer integration methods according to three performance dimensions: need elicitation, task format, and need satisfaction	Battarbee, Mattelmäki et al. (2000), Christiano, Liker and White (2000), Dahan and Hauser (2002), Franke and Piller (2004), Franke and von Hippel (2002), Gassmann, Kausch and Wolff (2006b), Lakhani and von Hippel (2003), Leonard and Rayport (1997), Lilien, Morrison et al. (2002), Lüthje and Herstatt (2004), Olson and Bakke (2001), Ozer (2003), Park et al. (2000), Paustian (2001), Thomke and von Hippel (2002), Urban and von Hippel (1988), von Hippel and Katz (2002), von Hippel, Thomke et al. (1999), von Hippel (1986; 1988; 2001a; 2001b)
Chesbrough (2003a)	Open Innovation	Open innovation is conceptualized as a knowledge spillover of human resources across company boundaries	Theoretical paper based on numerous mini-cases	New paradigm: Open Innovation replaces company-intern innovation; recommendations for managing/protecting intellectual property	Chesbrough (2003b; 2003c; 2003d; 2004), Gassmann (2006), Gassmann, Sandmeier and Wecht (2004), Hagedorn and Duysters (2002), Hattori and Lapidus (2004), Jones, Conway and Steward (2000), Kirschbaum (2005), Klee (2004), Linda, Jarvenpaa and Davenport (2003), Muller and Välikangas (2002), Powell, Koput and Smith-Doerr (1996), Reichwald and Piller (2005), Rigby and Zook (2002), Stupay (2004), Tapon and Thong (1999), Tidd (1997), Whittaker and Bower (1994), Wolpert (2002)

Methods

Various methods of customer integration are being practiced, often in combination.

The Lead User approach (Herstatt and von Hippel 1992; Lilien et al. 2002; Olson and Bakke 2001; Urban and von Hippel 1988; von Hippel 1986, 1988; von Hippel et al. 1999) counts among the most famous and best established integration methods. It is based on the selection and integration of visionary opinion leaders described above. Von Hippel's original four steps –identification of important market or technical trends; identification of lead users; analysis of data referring to lead users' needs; projection of these data onto the general market of interest (von Hippel 1986) – have been detailed and modified. The latest process model of the lead user method was developed by Lüthje and Herstatt (2004: 53ff):

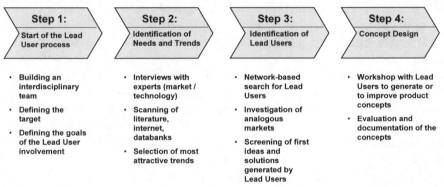

Fig. 2.7. The process of the Lead User method (Lüthje and Herstatt 2004: 561)

The User Toolkit method, also decisively shaped by von Hippel (Franke and von Hippel 2002; Thomke and von Hippel 2002; von Hippel 2001a, b; von Hippel and Katz 2002), was made possible by modern communication and interaction technology. This technology has created toolkits (computer-supported programs allowing a completely mathematical description of technological frameworks and ways of functioning) enabling customers to design parts or functions of a product or a whole new one. The User Toolkit method is recommended when the following conditions prevail: (a) a company's shrinking shares in a market with customers increasingly demanding individual products; (b) a product solution requiring several feedback loops; (c) a company or a competitor using very modern, IT-based tools for developing new products (Thomke and von Hippel 2002). Under these circumstances, the User Toolkit method demands the following steps (Thomke and von Hippel 2002):

1. Develop a user-friendly toolkit for customers
2. Increase the flexibility of your production process
3. Carefully select the first customer to use the toolkit
4. Evolve your toolkit continually and rapidly to satisfy your leading-edge customer
5. Adapt your business practices accordingly.

The User Toolkit method presupposes a certain degree of computer-related knowledge on the customer's side (von Hippel and Katz 2002) and functions best with lead users (Thomke and von Hippel 2002); however, normal customers with IT-related knowledge also may make useful contributions in certain markets (Dahan and Hauser 2002).

The *Empathic Design method*, going back to Leonard and Barton (1995), was further developed by Leonard and Rayport (1997) and taken up by Batterbee, Mattelmäki et al., (2000), and Nichani (2002). It departs from the empirical discovery that customers often are unable to articulate their needs, either because they lack the necessary descriptive abilities or, more frequently, because they are not aware of their wishes relating to a product. The conclusion drawn from this discovery is that rather than asking customers about their needs, these ought to be established by experts watching and analyzing customers' behavior on using a product. Customers using products in unfamiliar surroundings – e.g. in special consumer labs – tend to behave in a different way compared to their using it at home, feeling compelled to employ it "intelligently" in strict accordance with the producer's instructions and with their idea of the research goal. Even at home, they may alter their usual mode of use when they know they are being observed. The Empathic Design method therefore prefers – as far as this is legally and technically possible – an observation process that is unnoticed by the objects (Leonard and Rayport 1997: 110).

The Empathic Design method relies on five steps:

1. Organizing the observation process (Who shall be watched? Who shall watch? Which behavior shall be watched?)
2. Collecting data (via video cameras, cameras or questionnaires)
3. Analyzing and interpreting data (in order to discover the customers' problems)
4. Finding solutions for these problems (by means of creativity techniques)
5. Developing and testing prototypes (the latter being done by customers as well).

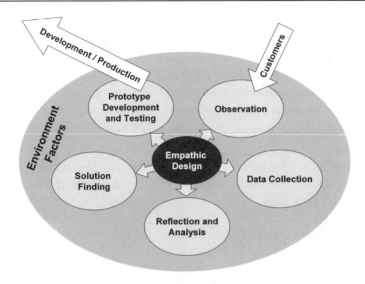

Source: according to Leonard and Rayport (1997) and Koen, Ajamian et al. (2002)

Fig. 2.8. Elements of the Empathic Design method

The *Ulwick method* first came into use in 2002. On observing the innovation process in various companies, Ulwick (2002) discovered that many innovative products failed in the market although customers had been involved in the concept development. In contrast to the previously described integration methods, he put the failure down on too much and too early reliance on customers' wishes. According to him, it is not the customers who should decide on the form of a new product but the company experts. The customers can and should give information only on the reasons for wanting a new product, not on the product itself or its specifications (cf. Dehne 2003: 13). Ulwick terms this desired information "outcome". His method centers on identifying outcomes by interviewing customers. The outcomes are then screened, categorized, and rated, and the best ones are used for innovative activities without customers.

The Ulwick method comprises five steps:

1. "Plan outcome-based customer interviews" with a group of customers as heterogeneous as possible
2. "Capture desired outcomes" by interviewers/presenters who are able to identify even badly expressed or hidden outcomes and can distinguish mere anecdotes or comments from crucial contributions
3. "Organize the outcomes" by listing the results, leaving aside redundant outcomes and categorizing the remaining ones

4. "Rate outcomes for importance and satisfaction" by interviewing a different group of customers and making them grade the product ideas according to their impression of importance and satisfaction – this step is very important to avoid biased results –
5. "Use the outcome to jump-start innovation" in all stages of the early innovation phase (Ulwick 2002).

Conjoint analysis is an advanced analytical technique that originated in mathematical psychology. In applied sciences, especially in marketing and New Product Development, it is used to determine ideal product configurations by asking consumers to express their preferences towards varied product profiles or features (Baker and Burnham 2002; Green and Srinivasan 1978; van Kleef et al. 2005). The underlying theory is that buyers view products as composed of various attributes/characteristics (e.g. color) each of which is made up of various levels/degrees (e.g. green, red, blue). The objective of conjoint analysis is to find out which combination of a limited number of attributes is most preferred by customers. By observing how they evaluate products in response to changes in the underlying attribute level, innovation managers can estimate the impact each attribute level has on overall product preference. Typical conjoint studies are based on up to six attributes, each described on about two to five levels. Participants rank or choose between combinations – the latter alternative is called "choice based conjoint" or "discrete choice analysis" – (cf. Dahan and Hauser 2002; van Kleef et al. 2005). The collected data is fed into a statistical software program producing utility functions for each feature.

The *Focus Group* concept was developed by Calder (1977) and has been readily accepted and modified by others (Bruseberg and McDonagh-Philp 2002; McQuarrie and McIntyre 1986). This widespread and comparatively cheap (McQuarrie and McIntyre 1986) method, belonging to the qualitative tools of market research, consists of bringing together 6-12 customers to discuss relevant problems that, by their complexity, defy normal market research procedures. A company expert leads the usually two hours' discussions. Of late, "virtual" focus groups join on the Internet in certain markets, which is made possible by IT-based tools. Focus groups are normally used for identifying search fields, but they can also contribute valuable insights in the concept definition phase (McQuarrie and McIntyre 1986).

Problem analysis, in contrast to the Focus Group concept, is not about finding solutions for recognized problems but about finding problems in the first place. Customers are asked about problems they may have had when using a certain product. The identified problems give a clue about customer needs, thus instigating innovative solutions.

Three types of Problem analysis have been established: the Problem Detection System (Fornell and Menko 1981), the Opus Analysis (Winiger 1986), and the Problem Inventory Analysis (Tauber 1975).

The *Problem Detection System* comprises four steps. In the first one, users – either individually or in a group – are asked about problems with a certain product or a product area. In a second step, company employees assess these problems, eliminating problems that appear technically insoluble or specifying them. In a third step, users rate the remaining problems according to their intensity, frequency, and uniqueness in comparison to competing products. The last step consists of evaluating the data in order to establish the most urgent problems and to get an idea about possible product improvements.

The *Opus Analysis*, which derives its name from the business consultant group Opus Development, uses a similar approach. In a first step, a company team establishes a list of products to be modified and a customer target group. Only few customers with experience in the established product area are invited to discuss and identify problems with the listed products. The problems are written down on small cards. In a following step, a bigger group of users is asked to put these cards into the so-called Opus Box containing five compartments that indicate different levels of problem intensity. According to this grading, users, developers, and other experts generate ideas for product improvement that are graded in the same way.

The *Problem Inventory Analysis* also stresses the importance of problem discovery to unearth consumer needs. This method is based on two assumptions: "The general ways in which products and services can improve the quality of life are rather limited" and "It is much easier for consumers to relate known products to suggested problems than to generate problems for a given product" (Tauber 1975: 68). In consequence, a problem inventory for a particular industry should be developed, containing statements that mention a problem but not a product. Respondents are asked to fill in the blanks, completing the sentences by spontaneously naming a product with just this specific problem. A following analysis gives clues for further investigation.

A complete list of customer integration methods is shown in Table 2.4.

Table 2.4. Customer integration methods (modified and expanded from van Kleef et al. 2005)

Method	Theoretical Basis	Operating Procedure	Key References
Lead user technique	Diffusion of innovations	Start of the Lead User Process: building an interdisciplinary team; defining the target; defining the goals of the Lead user involvement and von Hippel (1992), Li- Identification of needs and trends: interviews with experts (market / lien, Morrison et al. (2002), technology); scanning of literature, internet, databanks; selection of Lüthje and Herstatt (2004), most attractive trends Identification of lead users: networking-based search for lead users; Nagel (1993), Urban and investigation of analogous markets; screening of first ideas and so- von Hippel (1988), von lutions generated by lead users Concept design: workshop with lead users to generate or improve Hippel and Katz (2002), product concepts; evaluation and documentation of the concepts	Herstatt (1991), Herstatt and von Hippel (1992), Li- Morrison et al. (2002), Lüthje and Herstatt (2004), Olson and Bakke (2001), Nagel (1993), Urban and von Hippel (1988), von Hippel (1986; 1988), von Hippel and Katz (2002), von Hippel, Thomke and Sonnack (1999)
User Toolkit method	Experimental Design	Develop a user-friendly toolkit for customers Increase the flexibility of your production process Carefully select the first customer to use the toolkit Evolve your toolkit continually and rapidly to satisfy your leading-edge customer Adapt your business practices accordingly.	Dahan and Hauser (2002), Franke and Piller (2004), Franke and von Hippel (2002), Gassmann, Kausch and Wolff (2006b), Lakhani and von Hippel (2003), Ozer (2003), Park et al. (2000), Paustian (2001), Reichwald and Piller (2003), Thomke and von Hippel (2002), von Hippel and Katz (2002), von Hip- pel (2001a; 2001b)

Table 2.4. (cont.)

Empathic Design	Theories of anthropological investigation and tacit knowledge	Organizing the observation process (Who shall be watched? Who shall watch? Which behavior shall be watched?) Collecting data (via video cameras, cameras or questionnaires) Analyzing and interpreting data (in order to discover the customers' problems) Finding solutions for these problems (by means of creativity techniques) Developing and testing prototypes (the latter being done by customers as well)	Battarbee, Mattelmäki et al. (2000), Leonard-Barton (1994; 1995), Leonard and Rayport (1997), Leonard and Sensiper (1998), Polanyi (1966)
Ulwick method	Theories of anthropological investigation and tacit knowledge	"Plan outcome-based customer interviews" with a group of customers as heterogeneous as possible "Capture desired outcomes" by interviewers/presenters who are able to identify even badly expressed or hidden outcomes and can distinguish mere anecdotes or comments from crucial contributions "Organize the outcomes" by listing the results, leaving aside redundant outcomes and categorizing the remaining ones "Rate outcomes for importance and satisfaction" by interviewing a different group of customers and making them grade the product ideas according to their impression of importance and satisfaction "Use the outcome to jump-start innovation" in all stages of the early innovation phase (Ulwick 2002)	Dehne (2003), Ulwick (2002)
Conjoint Analysis	Experimental design	The researcher selects attributes relevant to the product category (e.g. by means of a focus group with target consumers) The researcher selects the levels of each attribute to be used in study. Typically, studies use between two and five levels for each	Baker and Burnham (2002), Dahan and Hauser (2002), Frewer, Howard, Hedderley et al. (1997), Green,

Table 2.4. (cont.)

		attribute. Hypothetical products are defined as combinations of attribute levels	Krieger and Wind (2001), Green and Srinivasan (1978), Lilien and Rangaswamy (1998), Krieger, Cappuccio, Katz et al. (2003)
		The respondent is given a set of these hypothetical profiles (constructed along factorial design principles in the full profile case)	
		The respondent ranks or rates the stimuli according to some overall criterion, such as preference, acceptability, or likelihood of purchase	
		In the analysis of the data, "part-worths" (van Kleef et al. 2005) are identified for the attribute levels such that each specific combination of part-worths equals the total utility of any given profile. A set of part-worths are derived for each respondent	
Focus Group	None specific	A group of participants, usually 8–10, sits together for a more or less open-ended discussion about a product or a specific topic	Bruseberg and McDonagh-Philp (2002), Calder (1977), Dürrenberger and Behringer (1999), Greenbaum (1993), Krueger & Casey (2000), Langford & McDonagh (2003), McNeill, Sanders and Civille (2000), McQuarrie and McIntyre (1986), Morgan (1988)
		The discussion moderator makes participants introduce themselves and feel comfortable and makes sure that the topics of significance are brought up. To help participants verbalize their needs, interaction between group members is encouraged	
		The report summarizes what was said, and perhaps draws inferences from what was said and left unsaid in the discussion	

Table 2.4. (cont.)

			Fornell and Menko (1981), Tauber (1975), Winiger (1986)
Problem Analysis:	None specific	Problem Detection System	
		Users are asked about problems with a certain product or a product area; Company employees assess these problems, eliminating problems that appear technically insoluble or specifying them	
Problem Detection System		Users rate the remaining problems according to their intensity, frequency, and uniqueness in comparison to competing products	
Opus Analysis		Evaluating the data in order to establish the most urgent problems and to get an idea about possible product improvements	
Problem Inventory Analysis		Opus Analysis	
		A company team establishes a list of products to be modified and a customer target group. Only experienced customers are invited to discuss and identify problems with the listed products. The problems are written down on small cards	
		A bigger group of users is asked to put these cards into the so-called Opus Box containing five compartments indicating different levels of problem intensity. According to this grading, users, developers, and other experts generate ideas for product improvement that are graded in the same way.	
		Problem Inventory Analysis	
		A problem inventory for a particular industry is developed, containing statements that mention a problem but not a product	
		Respondents are asked to fill in the blanks, completing the sentences by spontaneously naming a product with just this specific problem	
		A following analysis gives clues for further investigation	

Table 2.4. (cont.)

Category appraisal	None specific	The researcher selects a set of competing products of interest (possibly including a product concept)	Carroll (1972), Coombs (1964), Green and Carmone (1969), Greenhoff and MacFie (1994), Guniar, Uotani and Schlich (2001), Moskowitz (1985; 1994), Richardson-Harman, Stevens, Walker et al. (2000), Tucker (1960)
		The products are presented to the respondent	
		The respondent directly ranks, rates or sorts the products on sensory, preference or perceptual attributes or on their perceived (dis)similarity	
		One of the widely available statistical procedures (e.g. factor analysis, multidimensional scaling) is used to graphically portray stimuli, respondent's individual preferences and/or attributes in a geometrical space	
		The resulting map captures many significant factors defining the competitive structure of the product category. Depending on the applied technique, the map	
		shows intensity of competition between products—the closer two products are together, the more similar they are perceived or preferred	
		summarizes how consumers perceive products on each attribute	
		shows relationships between attributes and how well these attributes differentiate between products	
		indicates areas of the map that are desirable to certain segments of consumers	
Free elicitation	Theories of spreading activation	The researcher presents stimulus probes or cues (usually words) to the participant	Anderson (1983), Collins and Loftus (1975)
		The participant is asked to rapidly verbalize the concepts that come to mind and that he/she considers relevant in the perception of the	

Table 2.4. (cont.)

		stimulus. For example, when the stimulus is a product name, the objective is to activate all nodes associated with this product name in the respondent's memory. It is assumed that statements mentioned first are most important The interview is generally recorded and transcribed before analysis Results can be analyzed in a variety of ways, depending on the goal of the research, for example by displaying associative knowledge networks or classifying statements in meaningful categories	
Information acceleration	Diffusion of innovations and decision-flow models	The researcher constructs a virtual buying environment simulating the information that is available to consumers at the time they make a purchase decision Respondents are 'accelerated' into the future by the provision of alternative future environments that are favorable, neutral, or unfavorable towards the new product. In this virtual buying environment, they are allowed to search for information or shop Measures are taken of respondents' likelihood of purchase, perceptions, and preferences Based on these measures, a model is developed to forecast sales and simulate strategy alternatives	Urban and Hauser (2004), Urban, Hauser, Qualls et al. (1997), Urban, Hauser and Roberts (1990), Urban, Weinberg and Hauser (1996)
Kelly repertory grid	Personal construct theory	The participant is provided with a set of products presented in groups of three For each triple combination, the participant is asked to think carefully about the products and decide in what way two of them are similar, and at the same time, different from the third one Having identified the reasons to discriminate between the products,	Bech-Larsen and Nielsen (1999), Kelly (1955), Sampson (1972), Thomson and McEwan (1988)

Table 2.4. (cont.)

	the participant is asked what he thinks is the opposite. This procedure is repeated until all products are evaluated in combinations of three	
	The attributes (called constructs) are all written down on a grid sheet. A repertory grid is a matrix representation of products and constructs. In addition, all products can be scored against each construct to establish its importance	
	Grids can be clustered by content analysis, frequency counts, or principal component analysis to analyze what is relevant, similar and different in the eyes of the consumer	
Laddering Means-end chain theory	The participant is provided with a set of products	Claeys, Swinnen and Vandeen Abeele (1995), Gutman (1982), Nielsen , Reynolds and Gutman (1998), Walker and Olson (1991)
	The participant is asked to make distinctions between the products (by means of triadic sorting on perceived meaningful differences or by means of preference differences or by means of perceived differences by occasion)	
	Each mentioned distinction is the starting-point for a series of 'why'-probes by the researcher, to determine sets of linkages between attributes, consequences, and values	
	Once all interviews are completed, key elements of the interview are summarized by standard content-analysis, taking into account the different levels of abstraction	
	A summary table is constructed representing the number of connections between elements	
	From the summary table dominant connections are graphically represented in a tree diagram, called a hierarchical value map (HVM).	

Table 2.4. (cont.)

		Hierarchical value maps consist of a number of ladders (or association networks), and represent the combinations of attributes, benefits, and values that consumers use as a basis for distinguishing between products in a given product class	
Zaltman metaphor elicitation technique (ZMET)	Theories of non-verbal communication, metaphors as representations of thoughts, mental models	Participants are given instructions about the research topic (e.g. a brand name, a corporate identity, a product design) and the task to take photographs and/or collect pictures (e.g. from magazines/books) that indicate what the topic means for them. 7 to 10 days later a personal interview is planned	Christensen and Olson (2002), Coulter, Zaltman and Coulter (2001), Zaltman (1997), Zaltman and Coulter (1995)
		Participants bring their pictures and photographs and tell their stories about the topic (storytelling)	
		Participants are asked to make distinctions between products (e.g. by means of triadic sorting). Each mentioned distinction is the starting-point for a series of 'why'-probes by the researcher to determine sets of linkages between attributes, consequences, and values (laddering technique)	
		Participants are asked to indicate a picture that (1) most represents their feelings, and (2) might describe the opposite of the task that they were given. In addition, they are asked to use other senses to convey what does and does not represent the topic being explored	
		The interviewer reviews all the constructs, and participants create a map to illustrate connections among important constructs (mental map)	
		Next, a summary image or montage is constructed by the participant or a graphic technician to express important issues (e.g. by	

Table 2.4. (cont.)

digital imaging techniques)

A consensus map is created with the help of analyzing the number of constructs and the frequency of related ones. The consensus map is a diagram showing linkages among constructs. Connector constructs serve as linkages between them. In addition, an interactive CD can be composed including the visual, sensory and digital images and vocal descriptions along with vignettes

2.4 Benefits and risks

Customers are integrated with the purpose of increasing the effectiveness and the overall success of innovative activities. The intended effect of their integration therefore is to gain as much additional value as possible.

Integration measures, e.g. installing workshops with customers or siphoning off their knowledge via toolkits, are carried out in the hope of positive effects, for example a spillover of knowledge from customer to company. These aspired positive effects are sometimes accompanied or even totally replaced by undesirable and often unforeseen negative effects which, not being intended in the first place, are called side effects. "Effects" is the generic term of benefits and risks; whereas the term "negative side effects" (Gassmann et al. 2006a) has become a synonym of risks.

2.4.1 Benefits

In the context of economics, the term benefit is a synonym of profit (Link 2001). It describes the added value that calculated actions or coincidence bring about as compared to the status quo. Chance, in comparison, is defined as the possibility to make profit or obtain benefits; put in a mathematical formula, it is the result of benefit multiplied by probability of occurrence (Link and Marxt 2004). In literature and practice the terms benefit, chance, advantage, and positive effect are often used at random for the same phenomenon without attention to different meanings (this thesis will use the predominant term benefit in a general way, referring to "chance" only when the element of uncertainty is of special importance).

Various benefits of customer integration have been described in literature and verified by experiments. Those with widespread practical relevance are:

Better market orientation

Marketing considerations play an increasingly important role in the innovation process. A profit-orientated company has to consider the prospective sales possibilities for future products, the sooner the better. Integrated customers can provide the necessary information on market needs and wishes; products developed accordingly will sell well. The benefit of better market orientation as a consequence of early customer involvement can even be considered as the most cogent argument in favor of this concept (Kujala 2003; Littler et al. 1995; Wilson et al. 1996).

Reduction of development time

One of the most frequently mentioned benefits of customer integration is the resulting speeding up of the development process (Cordero 1991; Littler et al. 1995: 18; Mabert et al. 1992; Millson et al. 1992; Qualls et al. 1981; Reichart 2002: 92). According to Hagedoorn (1993), time reduction is one of the most important motives and outcomes of alliances with customers. Empiric studies by Zahn, Komes et al. (1995: 60ff) have shown that 57% of the investigated companies could reduce the time for product development by integrating customers.

Customer involvement in the early innovation phase may either have an immediate time-reducing effect, e.g. a customer's idea may make further research unnecessary, or it may abbreviate the later production process or preparations for market launch. However, recent empirical research has questioned this benefit; the high hopes placed in time-reducing effects of customer integration have not been fulfilled to the expected extent (Brockhoff 2005a).

Cost reduction

A number of authors (Cordero 1991; Littler et al. 1995; Mabert et al. 1992; Millson et al. 1992; Qualls et al. 1981) have advocated sharing and thus reducing the costs of product development by collaboration. It is true that this aspect has been discussed almost exclusively in the context of collaboration between independent organizations (Freeman 1991; Gugler 1992; Lorange 1991), but it also applies to the integration of customers (Reichart 2002: 92).

Access to new knowledge

Gaining additional know-how, skills, expertise, and experience from customers also ranks among the strongest reasons for customer integration (Campbell and Cooper 1999; Littler et al. 1995) and has become one of the most desired effects of this concept (Holmes 1999; Schilling and Hill 1998). This information spillover (Harhoff et al. 2003: 1753) from customer to company brings with it a broadening of scope and vision for innovations and a higher chance of developing break-through products.

Strategic advantages

Customer integration can also lead to long-range strategic advantages. It may pay off in the future to cultivate relationships with customers, even if an immediate advantage in the context of an envisaged imminent project is uncertain. By integrating an important customer, a company may ensure that this customer remains a faithful, reliable buyer of the company's products. Also, access to new customers may be a longer-term strategic perspective when integrating already well-known ones (Campbell and Cooper 1999). Collaboration with another company or with an important lead user, leading to a long-term learning effect, may improve the company's competitive position in the market, in the expectation that the customer's knowledge will go to the company only and will not boost competitors (Hagedoorn 1993; Wilson et al. 1995).

While the list of recognized benefits in the wake of customer integration is impressive, first warnings are uttered that "there are no automatic short-term commercial benefits associated with customer partnering when compared to in-house development" (Campbell and Cooper 1999: 516), implying that benefits depend on the special circumstances of each particular integration project.

The research stream for overall benefits comprises studies by Bacon and Beckman (1994), Gruner and Homburg (1999), Kristensson, Magnusson et al. (2002), and Lettl (2004: 66-69).

2.4.2 Risks

By linguistic standards, the counterpart of benefit is disadvantage or damage. In the context of economics, the terminology varies. Besides disadvantage, the terms negative side effect (Gassmann et al. 2006a), "disbenefit" (Littler et al. 1995), and risk are employed synonymously. As for risk, the use as counterpart of benefit is not quite correct: risk is the other side of chance. It is "an uncertain event which, should it occur, has a negative impact on achieving the objects" (Simon 1999). Risk consists of two components, the impact or consequence of an event and the probability or frequency of its occurrence; the mathematical formula is risk = impact level multiplied by probability of occurrence (Muessig 1997).

The negative side effects of customer integration are about to gain more scientific interest: Bower and Christensen (1995: 44), Littler, Leverick and Bruce (1995: 18-19), Veryzer (1998b: 143ff), Kujala (2003), Wilson, Littler et al. (1995), Gassmann, Kausch and Enkel (2006a).

With the focus on practical customer integration, rare and untypical or sociological and psychological effects, e.g. Rosenthal and Hawthorne effects, will not be considered.

Biased results

A customer who is integrated in the early innovation phase consciously or subconsciously puts his stamp on the outcome. In whichever way he is integrated, his personal and professional interests and qualifications are a decisive shaping factor of the final innovative product. Exactly this enrichment with external market views and ideas is the gist of the benefit "better market orientation", but it may also have the contrary effect of limiting or impairing the outcome in several ways. This risk may turn up in various forms:

Biased results due to customers' views

A customer's point of view influences the direction of his innovative activities, e.g. his search for innovative ideas (Gruner and Homburg 2000; Wynstra and Pierick 2000). This is normally a welcome contribution, but eccentric tastes or "idiosyncratic preferences" (Lengnick-Hall 1996: 799) may ruin its original value and bias the search in an unfavorable way. If an integrated customer convinces the company of his unusual point of view, which is not shared by the market, the final product may not sell well even though it meets the highest aesthetic standards.

Biased results due to customers' interests

Customers' specific interests may also pose risks. Having to invest considerable time on an integration project, customers often agree to the integration only because they expect a personal benefit (von Hippel 1986). If they, correctly or not, perceive a clash of interest between the company and themselves, they tend to act for their own benefit, blocking off the development of innovative products that might interfere with their own line of production. This is, for example, the case when collaborative activities lead to the identification of ideas that might well become blockbusters for the integrating company but would mean the end or at least a restriction of the customer's product line.

Customers' interests may cause problems in another way as well. Their willingness to be integrated is often based on the desire for a "customized" product, i.e. one adapted to their particular needs. The advantage of this customization is that customers constitute a reliable buyer potential for products that were designed according to their needs (Prahalad and Ramaswamy 2000), but the advantage may turn into a disadvantage when these customers, representing only a small group, are the only ones interested in the new product. The result is an admittedly unrivaled niche product, which may be desirable with certain product types (Garvin 1988;

Lengnick-Hall 1996), but normally a mere niche market will hardly meet the company's expectations regarding sales and profit.

Biased results due to customers' experience

To get hold of customers' experience is one of the most powerful reasons for integrating them (Urban and von Hippel 1988; von Hippel 1988). Sometimes, however, this experience is grossly overrated: customers may lack the necessary first-hand experience of product use, encountering the "barrier of inability" (Lynn et al. 1996), and their integration turns out to be useless. The more critical and frequent problems with customers' experience lie in the opposite direction: normally customers do have first-hand knowledge of existing products and can tell in which respect these do not fulfill their needs and expectations. This experience, however, often makes them direct their innovative efforts in one direction only: to improve the familiar product rather than create a radically new solution. The underlying state of mind is called "functional fixedness" (Adamson and Taylor 1954; Birch and Rabinowitz 1951; Leonard 2002; von Hippel 1986). The resulting limitation to incremental innovations is not necessarily a disadvantage; there may be companies that are content with such innovations and are not fixed exclusively on breakthrough ones. Normally, though, a company will attempt to discover possibilities for radical innovations, because they usually are more profitable.

Additional time

This risk refers to the increase in time to be spent on innovation activities due to customer integration; the short form *additional time* has become an established term (Campbell and Cooper 1999).

The modern methods of market research, requiring stronger customer participation such as the Empathic Design method or Focus Group discussions, presuppose a careful selection of the participating customers in order to reach meaningful results, and this selection process takes time. Extra time is also needed for preparing the method itself, e.g. setting up the agenda or installing the necessary programs with IT-based tools. With customers as participants of workshops, e.g. for the identification of opportunities, the search for suitable lead users takes up a considerable amount of time. Harmonizing different management styles in the case of integrated representatives of other companies or playing a mediating role among incompatible workshop participants may also add time to the innovation process (for additional "time costs" cf. Farr and Fischer 1992; Littler et al. 1995).

In some cases, keeping up integration activities becomes more important than the prime object of finding and developing new products (Littler et al. 1995: 19). Empiric studies have shown that customer integration, instead of reducing the time of innovation activities, increases it in a number of cases (22% according to Zahn et al. 1995: 60ff).

Additional costs

All the factors that add time also bring about an increase in costs for innovation projects with customers: it takes money to track down lead users or to develop special toolkits for customers etc. (Farr and Fischer 1992). Secondly, customers often expect a monetary remuneration for their willingness to participate in innovative activities (cf. 2.3.1). In addition to these obvious extra costs, opportunity costs (Campbell and Cooper 1999) and transaction costs (Williamson 1979; Wilson et al. 1995) have to be considered. "Undue effort and resources [may be] directed toward the collaborative product development project, such that the maintenance of the collaboration itself becomes the prime objective, at the expense of the specific product development" (Littler et al. 1995: 19).

Leakage of knowledge

This risk goes by several names: loss of know-how (Enkel et al. 2005), leakage of expertise (Wilson et al. 1995), leakage of skills (Littler et al. 1995), or negative spillover (Gassmann et al. 2006a). As this study has chosen knowledge as the generic term (cf. 2.5.1), the risk will be referred to as leakage of knowledge.

A customer who takes part in the innovation process unavoidably acquires company or other integrated customers' knowledge while contributing his own (Li and Calantone 1998; Lukas and Ferrell 2000). This knowledge gain may not even be limited to the knowledge received in the project in question but can pertain to skills and know-how the company uses in other business areas (Littler et al. 1995) or to information and insights on market possibilities that so far have been the company's exclusive domain (Farr and Fischer 1992). The inherent risk of almost every customer integration project is that the customer may use the newly gained knowledge either for purposes of his own or trade it to an existing competitor. Developing new competitors or boosting marginal competitors through leakage of skills has been observed (Wilson et al. 1995 with further references). The worst case scenario is that the customer takes over the producing company's role, making it redundant at least for the production of the jointly investigated/developed product (Brockhoff 2005a). Even if customers do not use the acquired knowledge in a clandestine and illegal way, they may openly require its exclusive or combined use, claiming that the knowledge had already existed in their sphere or that it has arisen through the combination of company and customer know-how (Hagedoorn 2003). This quarrel over intellectual property rights may not only be costly and time-consuming but also lead to the eventual loss of the new knowledge in the course of legal proceedings.

Strategic risks

Permanently damaged relationships with key customers as a consequence of failed integration projects are cited as not uncommon disbenefits of customer integration (Campbell and Cooper 1999). Another strategic purpose on integrating customers, namely to boost a company's standing among its competitors, may also go wrong. Instead of increasing a company's competitive power, strong integrated companies as customers may misuse their power (Brockhoff 2005a; Campbell and Cooper 1999) and interfere with the company's strategic decisions, which leads to reduced managerial control (Littler et al. 1995; Wilson et al. 1995: 174 with further references). In the worst case, e.g. if a strong customer as the company's currently biggest or only buyer demands exclusive rights to the outcome of combined innovative activities, the company may end up as nothing more than the customer's subcontractor (Campbell and Cooper 1999; Johne 1994). Another strategic risk is that customers, intentionally or not, induce a company to embark on looking for products that cannot be realized for technological or economic reasons. Competitors in the guise of customers may do so in order to cause expenditures not in tune with market conditions, whereas other customers without bad intentions, but with unrealistic expectations may repeatedly make unfeasible suggestions that still need considering (Brockhoff 2005a).

2.4.3 Risk-benefit balance

The common juxtaposition or comparison of risks and benefits (Baird and Thomas 1985; Rowe 1977; Wilson and Crouch 2001) demonstrates the rather imprecise use of the word risk: strictly speaking, risks can only be measured against chances and disadvantages against benefits. However, this thesis will employ the specialist combination.

On integrating customers it is difficult, if not impossible, to attribute definite sums to positive or negative effects of integration measures within the innovation process, which would be the objective of a strict cost-benefit analysis. A risk-benefit analysis without a subsequent balance would be of little use: the analyzed effects can lead to proactive decisions on customer integration only if and when the established and graded effects are weighed against each other, showing which kind predominates. However, assessing risks and chances within innovation projects is a highly subjective affair (Link 2001), largely depending on the company's special situation and on the people involved. That is why an overall risk-benefit balance should lean primarily on qualitative analysis methods, which use words to describe the magnitude of potential good or bad consequences and the likelihood of their occurrence (Covello and Merkhofer 1993; Link 2001; Muessig 1997).

Even with qualitative methods, risks and chances, due to specific quantifying processes, can be described in figures indicating impact and frequency. The outcome of this figure-based risk-benefit balance is called the risk-benefit ratio. A ratio of >1 means that the prospective risks outweigh the prospective chances.

Table 2.5. Literature streams of benefits and risks

Author(s)	Literature Stream	Conceptualization	Empirical Validation	Outcome	Related Research
Gruner and Homburg (2000)	Customer Integration: Benefits / Positive Effects	Customer integration in the NPD process as a means to increase new product success	Mixed-methods approach, 12 field interviews in the German machinery industry, survey and statistical analyses of a sample (n= 317) in the machinery industry	Customer involvement has a positive impact on new product success in some, but not all stages of the NPD process. Customers' characteristics have a significant effect on new product success	Callahan and Lasry (2004), Gassmann, Kausch and Enkel (2006a), Franke and Shah (2003), Gruner and Homburg (1999), Harhoff, Henkel and von Hippel (2003), Holmes (1999), Kristensson, Gustafsson and Archer (2004), Kristensson, Magnusson et al. (2002), Lengnick-Hall (1996), Lettl (2004), Littler, Leverick et al. (1995), Millson and Raj (1996), Ornetzeder and Rohracher (2006), Reichart (2002), Schilling and Hill (1998)
Brockhoff (2005a)	Customer Integration: Risks / Negative Side Effects	Manufacturer-customer cooperation and its information flows	Theoretical paper	Only specific customers should be integrated in the early product development process; a game theory model describes fruitful forms of cooperation	Brockhoff (1997), Dabholkar and Bagozzi (2002), Enkel, Kausch and Gassmann (2005), Gassmann, Kausch and Enkel (2006a), Helm and Kloyer (2004), Hutt and Stafford (2000), Kujala (2003), Ofek and Srinivasan (2002), Tollin (2002), Veryzer (1998b), Wheeler, Mansfield et al. (1980), Wilson, Littler, Leverick et al. (1995)

Table 2.5. (cont.)

Campbell (1999)	Customer Integration: Risk – Benefit Analysis	Comparison of success of NPD with or without customer partnering	Quantitative research, survey sample size n=88	Partnership projects are normally as successful as in-house projects. Not all New Product Development is improved by close cooperation with customers	Alam (2002), Campbell (1999), Das and Teng (1999), Ernst (2004), Farr and Fischer (1992), Gassmann, Kausch and Enkel (2006a), Kujala (2003), Kujala and Mäntylä (2000), Knolmayer (2002), Link (2001), Link and Marxt (2004), Littler, Leverick et al. (1995), Lüthje, Lettl and Herstatt (2003), Muessig (1997), O'Connor and Veryzer (2001), Veryzer and Borja de Mozota (2005), Zahn, Komes and Walfort (1995)
Kujala (2003)	Customer Integration: Risk – Benefit Analysis	n/a	Theoretical paper	User involvement generally has positive effects, especially as a primary information source for product requirements. The role of users must be considered carefully; more cost-efficient practices are needed for gathering users' implicit needs and wishes	

2.5 Knowledge creation

2.5.1 Definition of knowledge

In the sense of this thesis, particularly in the context of customer integration, knowledge is used as a generic term for all kinds of customer contribution: know-how, skills, experience, information on special needs, or points of view. Unless expressly employed in a specific meaning, knowledge, in the following text, comprises whatever can be learned from customers and whatever knowledge resources a company has on its own.

The definition of knowledge is not an easy task; philosophy has tried from its very beginnings to answer the questions about the dimensions, importance, meaning, and different kinds of knowledge (Nonaka 1994). Depending on the respective author's point of view, special aspects of knowledge may dominate the definition as a whole. Davenport and Prusak, from a strategic perspective, define knowledge as a "fluid mix of framed experience, values, contextual information, and expert insight that provides a framework for evaluating and incorporating new experience and information" (Davenport and Prusak 1998: 5).

For practical purposes, the easiest way to define the term knowledge is to measure it against the similar, but not identical terms data and information. These, together with knowledge, form a "hierarchy of terms" (Enkel 2005: 45). Data are represented by signs or functions (Probst et al. 1997: 34; Rehäuser and Krcmar 1996: 4) and do not contain hints for further use (Davis and Botkin 1994: 166). When interpreted in a special context, data turn into information (Vicari and Trioilo 1997). Information is transferred into knowledge if and when the recipient can learn from it (Enkel 2005: 45), which also depends on this person (Probst et al. 1997: 35). In other words: information is a flow of messages, while knowledge is created by this flow and is shaped by the personality of its recipient (Nonaka and Takeuchi 1995: 58).

The theory of knowledge discerns two dimensions of knowledge with various pairs of names. The most frequently used ones are implicit - explicit and tacit - articulated (Enkel 2005: 46; Hedlund and Nonaka 1993). Articulated/explicit knowledge is codified, e.g. in the form of mathematical formulae, construction plans, or written texts that enable its transfer via formal communication systems. Tacit/implicit knowledge is "embedded" (Berger and Luckmann 1966) in a person and is difficult to transfer (Hedberg et al. 1997). It consists of technical and cognitive elements. The technical components are best described by the term "know-how" (Nonaka et al. 1997: 19), the cognitive elements comprise "working models" of reality - schemata, mental models, beliefs - which are taken for granted (Nonaka et al. 1997: 8), e.g. the assumption that a wheel will turn.

In summary, knowledge can be defined as "information combined with experience, context, interpretation, and reflection" (Davenport et al. 1998: 43).

2.5.2 Knowledge creation

Based on the Resource-Based View, developed in the 1980s (Barney 1991, 2001; Grant 1991; Prahalad and Hamel 1990) and focusing on a company's relevant resources rather than on the until then valid Structure-Conduct-Performance-Paradigm (Porter 1980, 1985), the Knowledge-Based-View stresses the importance of knowledge for a company's success (Grant 1996; Nonaka 1991; Spender 1996). "In an economy where the only certainty is uncertainty, the one sure source of lasting competitive advantage is knowledge" (Nonaka 1991: 96). Creating new knowledge therefore has become an imperative aim of management activities.

The starting-point for knowledge creation is the individual, gathering tacit knowledge via his/her actions and experiences. This individual knowledge, when communicated to other individuals, turns into collective tacit knowledge, meaning it is at more than one person's disposal (Enkel 2005: 49). The process of converting individual knowledge into collective knowledge, mostly by interaction among individuals in a group (Leonard and Sensiper 1998: 121), is called socialization (Nonaka 1991, 1994). The transformation from tacit knowledge into articulated knowledge, e.g. writing a report about experiences, is termed externalization, whereas the opposite process of learning/acquiring articulated knowledge goes by the term internalization (Nonaka 1994). New and more complex articulated knowledge is created by rearranging existing articulated knowledge or combining separate articulated pieces of knowledge - this process used to be termed combination (Nonaka 1994) and is now called systematization (Nonaka 2000). For a company wishing to improve its knowledge creation management as part of its entire knowledge management the processes of externalization and socialization are the most important ones (Enkel 2005).

With regard to customer integration, which is in fact customer knowledge integration, the main task is to get hold of the customers' mostly tacit knowledge in order to transfer it into articulated knowledge, to combine it with the existing company's knowledge, and to make it accessible to employees for further analysis. Creating knowledge networks has become the key to sustainable and customer-oriented innovations (Johannessen et al. 1999). Permanent technology and competency networks, supplying knowledge for innovation projects whenever the need arises, are a prerequisite of a successful "Next Generation Innovation Organization" (Jonash and Sommerlatte 2000: 9).

2.5.3 Absorptive capacity

Knowledge creation as described in 2.5.2 is connected with another aspect of knowledge: the absorptive capacity. This concept, which was developed by Cohen and Levinthal, concerns both knowledge generation and application, being defined as a firm's ability to evaluate, assimilate, and apply external knowledge (Cohen and Levinthal 1990). According to the authors, the ability to assess external knowledge depends on a company's past experience and prior investments. The capacity to assimilate this knowledge is contingent on the characteristics of the knowledge in question, on the organizational characteristics such as alliance or joint venture, and on the technological overlap. The ability to apply/exploit the gathered and assimilated knowledge is based on the company's technological opportunity and its means to protect its innovation.

Mowery and Oxley (1995) define absorptive capacity in a different way as a broad set of skills needed to deal with the tacit component of transferred knowledge and the need to modify this imported knowledge.

The concept of absorptive capacity has been adopted in the fields of strategic management (Lane and Lubatkin 1998; Nahapiet and Ghoshal 1998) and technology management (Schilling 1998). In recent years, it has been re-conceptualized by Zahra and George who define absorptive capacity "as a set of organizational routines and processes by which firms acquire, assimilate, transform, and exploit knowledge to produce a dynamic organizational capability" (Zahra and George 2002: 186). The novelty lies in the division of absorptive capacity into the two sub-sets of potential capacity (knowledge acquisition and assimilation) and realized capacity (transformation and exploitation) as well as in viewing absorptive capacity as a dynamic capability, thus making it amenable to change through management actions (Zahra and George 2002: 186).

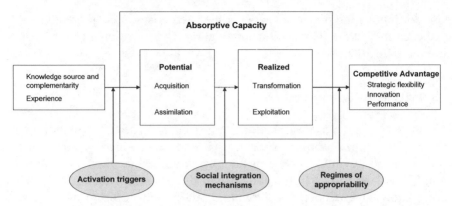

Fig. 2.9. A model of absorptive capacity (Zahra and George 2002: 192)

Table 2.6. Literature streams of knowledge creation

Author(s)	Literature Stream	Conceptualization	Empirical Validation	Outcome	Related Research
Von Krogh. Nonaka and Aben (2001)	Knowledge Management	Knowledge management practices at Unilever	Single case study. Time span for data collection: 3 years	Strategies for managing knowledge: Leveraging, Expanding, Appropriating, and Probing. The core processes of knowledge creation and transfer are central to applying these strategies	Cai (2006), Danskin, Englis, Solomon et al. (2005), Davenport, De Long et al. (1998), Davenport and Prusak (1998), Gebert, Geib, Kolbe et al. (2003), Gibbert, Leibold and Probst (2002), Grossmann (2006), Malhotra (2005), Neef (2005), Nonaka (1994), Nonaka and Takeuchi (1995), Probst, Romhardt et al. (1997), Rehäuser and Krcmar (1996), Vicari and Trioilo (1997), Zhang (2006)
Grant (1996)	Knowledge-based view	Concept of companies as absorbers of external knowledge	Theoretical paper	Techniques of integrating external experts' knowledge; consequences for organizational design and for company boundaries	Conner (1991), Conner and Prahalad (1996), Kogut and Zander (1992; 1996), Grant and Baden-Fuller (1995), Spender (1996), Grant (1997; 2002), von Krogh, Ichijo and Nonaka (2000)
Nonaka (1994)	Knowledge Creation	Focus on knowledge as a continuous flow between tacit and implicit knowledge	Theoretical paper	Various kinds of knowledge transformation and actors: individuals mostly create tacit knowledge, whereas organizations articulate and amplify it.	Johannessen, Leonard and Sensiper (1998), Johannessen, Olaisen and Olsen (1999), Jonash and Sommerlatte (2000), Kusunoki, Nonaka and Nagata (1998), Leonard-Barton (1995), March (1991), Mascitelli (2000), Nonaka (1991; 2000), Nonaka and Takeuchi (1995), Olson et al. (1999), Pitt and Clarke (1999), Shapiro and Varian (1999)

Table 2.6. (cont.)

| Cohen and Levinthal (1990) | Absorptive Capacity | Definition of Absorptive Capacity as a company's ability to integrate external knowledge | Research of 1,719 business units representing 318 firms in 151 lines of business | Absorptive capacity depends on a company's prior experience and existing knowledge | Boynton, Zmud and Jacobs (1994), Cockburn and Henderson (1998), Garud and Nayar (1994), George (2002), Huber (1991), Keller (1996), Kim (1998), Lane, Koka et al. (2002), Lane and Lubatkin (1998), Lim (2000), Mowery and Oxley (1995), Mowery, Oxley et al. (1996), Stock, Greis et al. (2001), Szulanski (1996), Veugelers (1997), Zahra and George (2002), Zahra and Veugelers (1997) |

2.6 Summary

The aggregated literature streams lead to the conclusion that customer integration, on the whole, is a research field where most aspects appear to be covered.

The early innovation process, which is the temporal and local point of reference for customer integration, has been investigated with regard to its process structure (see 2.2.2 with further references), to the predominant integration methods (see 2.3.2 with further references), to customers with special attention to the different types (see 2.3.1 with further references), to their main input into the innovation process, namely knowledge, and its pertaining issues (see 2.5 with further references), and, with special emphasis, to the benefits and risks of customer integration (see 2.4 with further references). The overview has revealed that within the well-established concept of customer integration, the focus has shifted from organizational or structural aspects to new challenges:

- Increase in the perception of risks
- Uncertainty of the value of customer integration.

Whereas the recognized benefits of customer integration have so far supported the concept with only minor modifications as to recommended integration methods, the growing awareness of risks has led to a tentative reassessment, which is summarized in the statement that the ROI on customer partnering is unknown (Campbell and Cooper 1999: 508). Accordingly, the literature overview suggests a reappraisal of the paradigm that customer integration is a necessary and promising part of successful innovation activities. In view of the evolving questions of if and how this paradigm ought to be changed or replaced, the compiled literature confirms the research gap outlined in Chapter 1.2.

A perspective of individual evaluation, weighing risks and benefits in a particular case, challenges the assumption of overall and always predominant benefits.

The degree of involved benefits as well as the degree of involved risks will define the outcome of customer integration projects.

A positive balance on the benefit side therefore is a key issue of successful customer integration. The core components for such a balance, combining further research and own theoretical deductions, will be discussed within the framework of an analysis model to be developed in the following chapter.

3 Development of an analysis model for a risk-benefit balance

As explained in the previous chapters, this thesis aims at establishing the general or particular value of customer integration with the aid of case study research. In order to guarantee meaningful statements and comparable results, this type of empirical research requires an analysis model or reference framework on which the practical investigations are based (Miles and Huberman 1994; Voss et al. 2002). For a close link with theory and a fit with the novel perspective on customer integration, the analysis model has to combine findings of existing research and own theoretical deductions, thus showing why and how the case study research has to be conducted. This combination will lead to several propositions that are to be validated or refuted by the ensuing empirical research in the case studies or with additional support of mini-cases.

The first proposition, however, is based on the theoretical and empirical findings described in the preceding chapters:

> **P1:**
> Customer integration does not automatically add value to the innovation process but needs a project-oriented risk-benefit analysis.

3.1 General outlook on the analysis model

The analysis model to be developed has to be applicable to companies of all sizes, branches, and with different process structures.

As was expounded in detail in Chapter 2.2.2, theory and practice offer a plethora of structure models for the early innovation phase. A risk-benefit model of customer integration, following whichever structure model, would have a limited scope of application from the very beginning, because only few companies would happen to use the chosen structure for their own individual innovation process. Especially small and medium-sized companies, while eagerly pursuing innovation activities, seldom implement an acknowledged structure for their early innovation process at all.

However, there are a number of problems every innovation manager has to solve no matter what his company's innovation process actually looks like, such as finding ideas for innovative products. A risk-benefit outlook on customer integration, based on tasks or themes rather than on sub-phases of the early innovation phase, may be of more extensive use, leaving it to a manager's discretion to choose the innovative task he considers performing with the help of customers without having to restructure the entire early innovation process.

This leads to the following proposition:

> **P2:**
> Certain tasks occur in the course of every innovation process irrespective of the concrete process structure.

Companies integrate customers in the hope of improving the innovative result. This result depends on the solution of various tasks/problems that turn up in the innovation process. The question of customer integration cannot be answered with regard to the early innovation phase as a whole but only in the context of a special task to be performed; with some problems/tasks customer integration may be advisable, with others rather not.

These considerations back up the next proposition:

> **P3:**
> Risks and benefits of customer integration pertain to the particular task customers are involved in.

The concrete tasks will differ depending on product complexity, branch, competitors, and so on. Still, several universally valid questions have to be answered, either in a strictly chronological order, iteratively, or if and when the need arises.

The most obvious task is the identification of possibilities for innovative actions. This task comprises the discovery of both opportunities and concrete ideas for innovative products. In both cases, the element of search is predominant, requiring a flair for desirable and feasible new products. Both opportunity identification and idea generation rely more or less on the same techniques, e.g. creativity techniques or patent analysis. It is true that they are not identical, but the basic task of coming up with suggestions for innovation is the same.

Once opportunities and ideas are established - usually there are more than just one -, the logical next step is selecting those that seem worth pursuing. This task is often harder than the previous search (Koen et al. 2002).

A wrong choice may ruin a company or at least damage either its financial resources or its reputation. A thorough analysis or screening of opportunities and ideas, eliminating less promising ones, is a vital task to be performed in almost any innovation process.

Defining a technology and business concept for the further pursuit of the selected product idea is another task of innovation managers. Drawing up a technology proposition and a business plan requires numerous considerations; the evaluation criteria for the "gate document" are well established (cf. Cooper and Kleinschmidt 1994a; Linton et al. 2002; Meade and Presley 2002).

A further task to be performed at least in technical innovation processes is the testing of prototypes or dummies. This testing may occur at very early stages in the case of rapid prototyping when a working model of various parts of a product or system is developed after a relatively short investigation (Sandmeier 2006) or at a rather late stage in the case of evolutionary prototyping when a complete model is finally tested (Sandmeier 2006). In both cases, the task lies in confirming the functionality and suitability of the new product in order to avoid later changes in hardware or software.

A comparatively new task, which has become more and more significant, is the development of an effective knowledge creation management, also called knowledge creation (Sandmeier 2006). This task, centering on gathering and managing knowledge (cf. chapter 2.4.2) that turns up as a by-product of innovation activities, enables a company to be ahead of others in the innovation race by "keeping the idea basket constantly to overflowing" (Jonash and Sommerlatte 2000: 43).

These tasks, not necessarily all of them, have to be performed in the course of most companies' early innovation process.

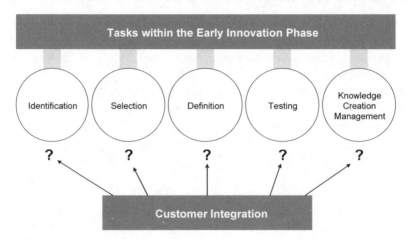

Fig. 3.1. Tasks and customer integration

Within each task, the characteristics of the particular innovative activities form the basis for possible customer integration and its economic value. Depending on the aims and the respective methods with which the tasks are to be accomplished, the question of a fundamentally useful customer contribution has to be answered, preventing an almost automatic integration because customer integration seems to be best practice. Based on the integration measures that appear sensible in answer to the previous question, certain benefits and negative side effects are likely to occur, improving or impairing the innovative success. A risk-benefit balance intended to support the decision on customer integration will list the expected potential benefits as assets and the unwanted potential disbenefits as liabilities. Although in the fixed term "risk-benefit" analysis or balance risks come before benefits, ergonomic and logical reasons suggest the prior investigation of benefits: if there should be no benefits in customer integration, the possible risks are of no importance because customer integration would be no sensible option in the first place. If, on starting with risks, no risks were to be discovered, it would still be necessary to investigate benefits in order to compare the results of innovative activities with or without customers. Before balancing the thus examined benefits with the risks, it is necessary to establish if and how they can be influenced. In some cases, factors that are not directly related to integration measures may increase the value of the combined benefits, constituting an additional asset. Risks, on the other hand, may be avoided or minimized. The respective measures will eliminate the pertinent liabilities or at least reduce their weight in a risk-benefit balance. These considerations lead to the following analysis model:

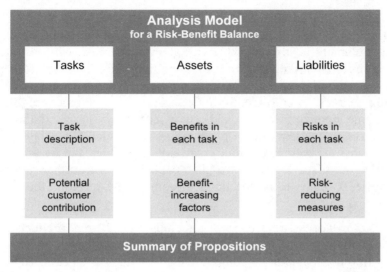

Fig. 3.2. Outlook on analysis model

3.2 Tasks

As outlined in 3.1, certain specific tasks have to be carried out in the course of every innovation process, whether with or without customers' additional support. Companies used to perform the respective duties on their own or with external experts only (cf. 2.3.2 "Historical development of customer integration"), and some still do so, which shows that customer integration is not an absolute necessity but a question of convenience and economic good sense.

The details of each task will define which particular type of innovation tools are to be used (3.2.1). Depending on the characteristics of each task, the potential customer contribution (3.2.2) will answer the question of what can or cannot be learned from customers, which is the foundation of why they should be included in the first place.

3.2.1 Task description

Identification

In the context of innovation management, identification means the discovery of new products the market actually or possibly needs or wants. This applies to finding opportunities as the general field for innovative activities and to generating ideas for a particular product within this field. It is true that these activities, apart from the different object, are not identical: the creative element is stronger where ideas are concerned, whereas with opportunities the main focus is on the recognition of existing, but not obvious business fields. However, creative and detective demands are made, if to varying degrees, in both identifying opportunities and generating ideas. It takes some creative efforts to add a new technology to an existing procedure, thus discovering a new opportunity, and an idea has to be identified in a rough way before different creativity techniques can be applied and expanded on it (see 2.4.1 and Rosenau et al. 1996 with further references). Therefore, it seems to be the thing to combinedly examine the basically similar tasks.

An *opportunity* is a business or a technical need - e.g. products for old people whose sight or hearing is impaired - that a company may wish to satisfy in order to capture a competitive advantage (Koen et al. 2002), or it can consist in a new trend as opposed to need that appears worth following, such as "wellness". An opportunity can also be a scientific discovery; for example the observation that crab fishers usually have excellent teeth due to often biting on the crabs' chitinous exoskeleton has led to the development of a whole range of chitosan-containing products such as toothpaste, cosmetics, surgical filling material, wound dressing, and so on (Handelsblatt 2006). Other opportunities consist in a way of simplifying or speeding up operations, a cost-reducing approach, or a new manufacturing process or marketing procedure (Koen et al. 2002), in short in the possibilities offered by applying new technologies or procedures.

Within the vast, almost unlimited area of possible innovations, a search-field narrows down the search for innovative activities to a thematically restricted space (Gassmann and Kausch 2005). Finding or rather recognizing such opportunities is vital for every company because at a time of fast technological progress and quickly changing trends existing products outside these opportunities are unlikely to support a company's success over a long period. In accordance with opportunities related to its product line a company is able to start looking for innovative products that are based on ideas within the opportunity frame. An opportunity therefore is the basis of the entire innovation process, preceding, as a rule – but not necessarily so – the idea generation process.

Opportunities are not being advertised. Their identification may occur spontaneously now and then when a single person happens to recognize an unmet customer need, e.g. a key account manager hearing complaints or wishes from his customers, but normally it takes special methods, tools, or techniques to find them.

In the context of an opportunity defined as a need, the normal way of discovery is market research. In addition to its more traditional methods, the Empathic Design method, the Ulwick method, the User Toolkit method, the Focus Group concept, and the Problem Analysis method (cf. Chapter 2.2.2 Methods) are useful to establish new need-based opportunities.

Apart from market research, a need can be discovered by company staff with close contact to customers, for instance salespeople, key accountants, or call center employees. This contact can also be brought about by sending staff to trade fairs or by organizing sales conferences and seminars with customers. A promising way of identifying needs is to arrange meetings or trips with users, e.g. inviting owners of Harley Davidson motorbikes, or to provide testing and training opportunities for interested potential or actual customers, e.g. farmers trying out combine harvesters (examples from Förster and Kreuz 2005). Evaluating customers' complaints or suggestions (Brockhoff 2005a) and organizing discussions via e.g. a forum or a focus group with customers complete the list of methods for identifying needs (for a detailed description of need assessment practices cf. Herstatt 1991; Koen et al. 2002).

With opportunities defined as trends, it is necessary to distinguish between customer and technology trends.

The identification of customer trends is the process of mining collected data for hidden common patterns or traits. Various means of identification are at hand:

The easiest, if rather expensive way is to take up the services of external professional trend scouts or market research organizations, e.g. The Everest Group, or of research portals like Mind Branch or providers like Mintel (Houghton 2006). For a company's own activities, a plethora of pertinent software has been developed, e.g. DecisionMaker, IBM Intelligent Miner, or Vantage Print (for more examples cf. www.businessintelligence. ittoolbox.com/topics). The Internet also offers online services and trend watching sites, such as InfoCentricity or TrendWatching.com, which supplies open source trend identification. Some search engines provide a quantitative measure of customers' likes and dislikes online, e.g. Google (www.google.com/press/zeitgeist.html), thus enabling companies to draw conclusions about certain trends. Digital libraries and user communities, too, allow the identification of customer trends (Bollen et al. 2003).

Apart from these special ways, the identification of customer and technology trends follows the same lines.

The more traditional methods of trend identification are patent analysis, literature research, and bibliometrics (Lichtenthaler 2000), especially with technology-driven opportunities.

Other methods such as roadmapping, scenario analysis, trend extrapolation, and creativity techniques have become the preferred methods in the context of opportunity identification (Koen et al. 2002).

In addition, competitive intelligence methods – collecting, analyzing, and communicating in a structured way information on competitive trends outside the company (Belliveau et al. 2002; for further reference see Fuld 1994; and Kahaner 1998) are at hand.

Idea generation usually is the second aspect of the identification task, normally based on previously established and selected opportunities. However, a company may not feel compelled to look for new opportunities if it is well established in a market for an existing long-lasting need or if it follows an acknowledged new trend. In this case, it can restrict its identification activities to seeking concrete innovative ideas within the already given opportunity.

In the context of the early innovation phase, an idea is the most embryonic form of a new product, service, or environment solution (Koen et al. 2002). Idea generation comprehends a continuous process of tossing up, turning around, modifying, discussing, combining, rejecting, and finally shaping ideas (Koen et al. 2002).

Its foremost techniques include the above-mentioned market research methods, the evaluation of customer suggestions and complaints, the organization of competitions for creative ideas (Brockhoff 2005a), and creativity techniques, i.e. brainstorming, brainwriting, method 635, mindmapping, and the Russian TRIZ system - Theory of inventive problem solving - (Altshuller 1984; Altshuller 1999). The methods suggested by Tanner (Tanner 1992), i.e. lateral thinking, metaphorical thinking, association trigger, and capturing and interpreting dreams, may be helpful as well. With idea generation, the methods of roadmapping, scenario analysis, trend extrapolation (Geschka 1995; Kern and Schröder 1977), and the Delphi method are also to be recommended (for a comprehensive review cf. van Kleef et al. 2005). Idea banks and the newly developed IT-based tools complete the list.

Selection

Having identified opportunities or ideas, a company has to decide which ones are worth pursuing. Even in the rather unlikely case of only a single discovered opportunity or idea, it is necessary to assess its potential and determine its future use. Selection, therefore, consists of two parts: in the first step, opportunities/ideas are analyzed and graded according to specific

criteria, and in the second step, the less promising ones – or all – are eliminated, leaving only potential hits.

In the context of opportunities, this process is usually termed "analysis",
whereas with ideas the term "selection" has become established (Koen et
al. 2002). Still, the respective activities are basically identical; their different scientific name is based on which part of the task happened to be
stressed. This suggests the joint examination of both innovation tasks.

On selecting *opportunities*, the first thing to do is to set up a list of criteria a company deems important for future innovative activities. These criteria will differ from one company to another and comprise many company-intern considerations, e.g. resources, the company's position among
competitors, and the opportunities' correspondence with the company's
strategy and culture, as well as technological and market considerations,
such as development potential and market needs and wishes.

In a second step, the opportunities are carefully examined with regard to
each given criterion. According to how well the opportunities match up to
these criteria, they are graded. The overall grade allows a comparison between several opportunities or the decision to pursue or abandon a single
one, depending on a previously fixed minimum grade to be reached.

The final selection also has to consider the decision makers' risk tolerance because many uncertainties still remain (Koen et al. 2002). This selection in the strict sense of the word among opportunities with similar
grades boils down to a weighing of chances.

The methods and tools required for this task are more or less the same as
with opportunity identification (see 3.1.1), but they now serve another end:
instead of helping identify opportunities, they are now directed at extracting the most promising ones. An additional measure, which is highly recommended by practitioners, is the assignment of a multifunctional team,
working full-time on the analysis and consisting of three to five members
with at least one marketing and one R&D expert.

With *idea selection*, the task starts with compiling the ideas generated in
the identification task, including those that do not pertain to new products
in the strict sense of the word but to new functionalities of existing products. "Functionality" is a new way of using a known product for its intended purpose or a way of opening up new purposes, or, to put it in a scientific way, "any property other than nutritional that affects utilization"
(University of British Columbia 2004).

Ideas and functionalities are evaluated in various ways that will also differ among companies; there is no "best" way to do so. Formalized portfolio management methods or a multistage business process may be as effective as measuring ideas against criteria set up by the company. In

whichever way ideas are assessed, feedback loops to opportunity selection are recommended (Koen et al. 2002).

Koen also found out that a decision process allocating business resources to the new ideas, giving their originators feedback, and installing an innovation culture facilitates the selection process (Koen et al. 2002).

The usual financial measurements, such as cash flow calculations, sales and profit forecasts, and net value considerations, as well as certain portfolio methodologies are also methods of choice.

Normally it takes at least two preliminary decisions before the final selection is made because the intention, in most cases, is to save the ideas from rejection. Generally, the people involved in the selection process should pay more attention to helping the ideas move forward by modifying them, if necessary, than to stifling them (Koen et al. 2002).

Definition

An idea selected for future realization still is not ready for the production process. Before spending more resources on the physical creation of a product, a company will examine in detail if and how a product based on the selected idea will survive in the market. The resulting proposition has to be submitted to senior management that will open or close the gate to the necessary investments. That is why this business or technology proposition is aptly referred to as "gate document" (Koen et al. 2002).

The task of drawing up this gate document comprises several steps. In the first one, which leads to a project definition - also termed project development (Gruner and Homburg 2000) or technology development (Koen et al. 2002) -, the idea is evaluated once again but with special attention to technical feasibility and concrete production procedures. Empirical studies have shown that companies tend to combine idea selection and project definition in the case of ideas pertaining to incremental and therefore rather concrete innovations; with radically innovative ideas, it is necessary to separate these processes (Savioz et al. 2001).

The subsequent drawing up of a business plan, the concept definition, requires numerous considerations before the actual financial needs are specified. Diverse evaluation criteria have been established, regarding the product itself - e.g. innovativeness; feasibility; environmental, health, or safety risks; product uniqueness -, the market - e.g. market potential; time to market; market/customer needs -, or the company itself - e.g. fit with the company's strategy; demand of resources; synergies within the company - (Cooper and Kleinschmidt 1994b; Linton et al. 2002; Meade and Presley 2002).

These considerations are much more detailed and specific than those concerning idea selection (Savioz et al. 2001).

Every company will have a different list of criteria for a business plan, because, as with idea selection, they largely depend on the nature and type of the company's product line and on the decision makers' attitudes towards risk (Koen et al. 2002). In accordance with the fixed criteria, the formality of the business plan varies, paying attention to the company's level of resources, the organizational requirements, and the business culture.

In case a concept does not get the necessary clearance to pass through the gate, it will be rejected for the time being or for good. If the "knock out" reasons are reversible, it will be subjected to another round of reshaping. In any case, the knowledge pertaining to a rejected idea should be stored away for possible future use together with other dormant ideas.

A special type of concept development is the rapid evaluation (Smith et al. 1999), which is used for high potential product and process innovations. It considerably shortens the process of drawing up a business plan. This is achieved by relying on a special, experienced innovation assessment team that quickly tests the elements with the highest risks and looks for potential sponsors for the project (Koen et al. 2002).

Testing

An idea is intangible, leaving everything to the imagination. Imagination, even if supported by underlying calculations, is not infallible; more often than not ideas that are convincing in theory fail in practical application, either completely or in some respects. If this revelation comes at a rather late stage of product development, a lot of time and money will have been invested in vain. To avoid this disappointment, the task at hand has the specific aim to try out illustrative material for innovative ideas before they enter the stage of mass production.

To find out if an idea really works in practice, it is necessary to create a physical working model, the prototype, mock-up, or dummy (Hallbauer 1997). This physical embodiment of an idea in whichever form – from its first vague origins to the final concrete concept – helps engineers study critical issues of functionality and design and determine the feasibility of and options for serial production (Wheelwright and Clark 1992). In addition, it makes possible or at least facilitates the testing of market reactions.

Prototypes vary according to the degree of the respective idea's development. Working models of product parts, built after a short investigation phase only, are naturally less specific than models representing the concrete final product. The first types are created in a rather informal way

(Sandmeier 2006) with the main focus on speed – hence the name "rapid prototyping". They serve to clarify certain issues of the envisaged idea and are "thrown away" when this aim is achieved (Crinnion 1991). The second types are the result of careful investigation pertaining to all aspects of the future product. The respective development procedure – called evolutionary prototyping (Crinnion 1991) – is more structured because these prototypes form the heart of the new system or product line and will not be thrown away, but kept and stored (Sandmeier 2006).

The testing of these prototypes, rapid as well as evolutionary ones, can take place in various ways. The process of testing prototypes internally, either exclusively by company staff or together with customers on the company's premises, is termed alpha testing. Originally, this term was used in the software branch only, but it is now common among most other branches as well. It also goes by the name "acceptance testing". Selected users in their familiar environment and on their own carry out the next step of pre-testing an unfinished version before it is released to the general public. This procedure is called beta testing or functional testing and originates in the computer industry as well. Its main aim is to discover bugs or flaws in time, i.e. before the final launching of the product, but under conditions of future general use. A combination of both ways is watching or helping customers use prototypes in their own surroundings.

The task description demonstrates that prototype testing may be necessary or helpful at all times within the early innovation phase. It can occur from the first identification/generation of an idea up to the final concept definition. Its methods vary according to the respective state of the underlying idea, to the testers - either company engineers or customers -, and to the kind of product in question. It goes without saying that computer software will be tested in a different way than, e.g. cars, washing-powder, or fuel cells. The common denominator is using the model in the intended way under circumstances as similar as possible to the actual later use.

Knowledge creation management

In a market with countless competitors the "survival of the fittest" company depends on being ahead of the others with regard to knowledge, which is considered a strategic asset (Glazer 1991) and a core competence (Li and Calantone 1998; Lynch and O' Toole 2003). Knowledge is not a constant quantity but grows continually. As described in detail in 2.4, new knowledge has many origins, one of the most important being the combination or systematization (see 2.4.2) of existing knowledge. "Creating" knowledge is a process of extracting and combining knowledge from various internal and external sources (Lynch and O' Toole 2003). Whereas

R&D has been the main source of internal knowledge contribution, external knowledge is gained from universities, other institutions, public databanks etc. and, to a growing extent, from customers. A competent customer knowledge process is deemed a prerequisite of a successful knowledge management (Lynch and O' Toole 2003), which comprises the steps of identification, acquisition, development, transfer, storage, and exploitation of knowledge (Brockhoff 2005b; Teece 1998).

Knowledge creation in the sense of extracting and combining knowledge is a mixture of the first steps of general knowledge management as cited directly above and is inherent in the previously described tasks. New knowledge, whatever its origin, is the necessary and intended by-product, though not the final expressly desired result, of every specific task. This is especially obvious with the identification task: to find a new opportunity, pertinent knowledge of technologies, trends, methods etc. from various sources is required, resulting in the desired opportunity that in itself constitutes knew knowledge. The correlation is even more striking with ideas: innovative ideas are based on knowledge, presupposing scientific and technical competencies and practical know-how. On the other hand, new knowledge is gained by ideas. The process of shaping ideas (see 3.1.1) brings with it a certain amount of surplus knowledge not needed for the realization of the particular idea(s) chosen in the end. This "extra" knowledge is a company's asset to meet as yet unforeseen challenges and needs, enabling it to fall back on a reservoir of scientific skills and practical know-how if and when the need arises. The same applies to technical project development and concept definition as well as to prototype testing, where tacit or explicit knowledge contribution will create new insights that may change the former developments or leave certain aspects for future consideration.

The deeply interwoven existence of knowledge creation and other tasks shows why it is difficult to consider "knowledge creation" a phase or a task of its own. Knowledge creation does not occur at a certain separate phase within the early innovation process but at all times and everywhere. Even the Customer-oriented Concept Development Model (Gassmann et al. 2006a), relying on a circular model with interacting, not necessarily consecutive phases, has to resort to semantics for making up a special phase of knowledge creation that is combined with idea creation but less so with other phases. The following consideration demonstrates why it is not a task either: no innovation manager will say "we must create knowledge", whereas it is certain he will make up his mind to identify opportunities, draw up a business plan, or test prototypes. Knowledge, vital as it is, is not an end in itself but a means to reach an end: innovative products. In order to "keep the idea basket constantly filled to overflowing" (Jonash and Sommerlatte 2000: 43) and to be prepared for tackling future problems that may require so far superfluous knowledge, it is necessary, but sufficient to pick up and store newly gained and "extra" knowledge acquired in the particular tasks.

These considerations back the following proposition:

> **P4:**
> Knowledge creation is an essential element of all innovation activities and not a phase or task of its own.

Still, the collection, distribution, and storage of knowledge must follow a structured, systematic procedure that accompanies all activities in the other tasks. An effective knowledge creation m a n a g e m e n t - which, in contrast, is a task as a part of overall knowledge management – will ensure that new knowledge in all is facets is gathered, combined with existing knowledge, and stored.

The tools and methods of knowledge creation management depend on the respective activities: with gathering knowledge, they mainly consist in listing the knowledge acquired in the various tasks with their pertinent methods (for detailed further descriptions see Enkel 2005). Besides, a "knowledge champion", who must not be confounded with a product or integration champion, might be a good idea. As for storage, company databanks and intranets as well as a company's individual R&D practices will be the methods of choice.

3.2.2 Potential customer contribution

To answer the question of what can or cannot be learned from customers, which refers to the basic possibility of a pertinent contribution and not to the customers' willingness or individual ability, it is necessary to consider what should be learned in the first place. This was explained in 3.2.1.

Identification

In the case of identifying *opportunities* in the sense of need, a company has to find out if the market desires a special type of better or completely new products. It is a matter of fact that customers/users as representatives of the market in question normally know what they would like to see changed in existing products or if, according to them, no product so far can help them with a certain problem. A senior citizen, for example, when asked about his needs or wishes, will complain more or less explicitly that the display on mobile phones is too small for his old eyes, that it is difficult to punch in numbers or letters on tiny buttons or keys, and that the beep or ringing on phones is not loud enough. From these complaints, the conclusion can be drawn that diminishing faculties require special product adaptations. A high tech manufacturer as customer, needing a material for his product that is both supple and stable, will ask his supplier company to create one with just these properties, with the result of, e.g., pliable ceramics. Thus the opportunities "products for the elderly" or "designer materials" (cf. Kausch and Matschullat 2005) are identified.

Customers – who if not they – can provide the desired information about their needs; the question is not if they are basically able to do so, but if the information is correct and reliable. This problem was explained on discussing risks (2.4.2).

The customers can and will be "normal" or lead users: with the first group, as shown in the example of senior citizens, the gained knowledge tends to lead to opportunities for incremental innovations; with the second group, illustrated by the high-tech manufacturer, opportunities for breakthrough innovations are more likely to be discovered.

Learning from customers about their needs will take place within the traditional and newly developed methods of market research. These methods actually depend on cooperation between customers and company staff, either directly, if sometimes passively on the customers' part, or indirectly via siphoning off and interpreting customer contributions gathered with IT-based tools.

The identification of opportunities as new customer/business trends requires a partly different kind of learning. Such a trend encompasses several aspects of life with their respective product range, e.g. "wellness" affects the design of resorts and spas, cosmetics, scents, and so on, or "fitness" applies to sports equipment, food, clothes, or health care among other fields.

Unlike a need, which may, but need not be felt by just one person to constitute an opportunity, a trend is a feeling or an attitude of many people, expressing a current style, vogue, or predominant inclination. A trend evolves simultaneously in various areas, both geographically and topically, and gains momentum in the course of time before giving way to another trend.

Due to this definition of trend, an individual customer is not able to answer the question about a new trend as he could do when asked about a need of his. He can, however, express his preference for a certain product line as compared to others, e.g. for "home-made" or "grandma" ready-to-serve meals with a nostalgic appeal in contrast to brand-new, artificially flavored products or vice versa, thus contributing to discovering a trend. This preference can be uttered directly or deduced from facts, for instance from ordering a special type of products significantly more than others of a similar product line. It is this kind of information that external professional or company-intern IT-based market research, as described in 3.2.1, can unearth. This knowledge contribution, though, is usually not an intentional cooperation with a specific company on the customer's part and therefore at best mere interaction, not integration (cf. Chapter 2.3.2). Besides, a business trend tends to encompass many industries outside a company's special branch; information on a particular customer's likes or dislikes of certain products therefore does not constitute an improvement of the knowledge to be acquired in this trend identification task although it may be relevant in the selection task.

In some cases, a customer's expertise with a certain product or his experience with his own clientele may make him an ideal sparring partner for company employees or external experts in workshops on trend extrapolation and scenario analysis (see above 3.2.1), where the combined knowledge of many is used to identify the desired new customer trend. Lead users will be able to contribute the knowledge in question.

With opportunities based on technology trends or new technologies/procedures, a company has to learn as much as possible about these ways. Knowledge about nano-technology, for instance, is indispensable when wishing to make use of respective manufacturing processes. The pertinent knowledge can be obtained from customers who are already familiar with the technology/procedure, using it for purposes of their own. This will be the case with lead users, but as the development of Open Source software has shown, normal users as well often know a lot about the technological foundations of their private hobby (Piller 2003; Reichwald and Piller 2003, 2005). Not only product know-how, but also know-how pertaining to organizing and even leading the development process can be gathered from customers in this way (Piller 2004). As with trend identification, lead users can contribute their special knowledge in workshops. In addition, focus group discussions, where the aptitude of a certain technology for the company's innovative activities can be established or rejected, constitute a platform for gaining knowledge from customers.

With *ideas*, the potential customer contribution can consist in the complete idea itself. This is the fact in the limited cases when an idea does not need any modification such as tossing up, turning around, combining etc. (cf. 3.2.1) but is the perfect solution for a new product within a specific opportunity. A company may get hold of such an idea via the described methods of market research, in Web-enabled idea banks with links to customers (Belliveau, Griffin and Somermeyer, 2002), in competitions for suggestions on product improvement (Brockhoff 2005a), or in the course of all activities with customer contact, e.g. workshops, trade/technical fairs, or focus groups.

A complete idea, however, is the exception; normally an idea, after being identified in a rough form, needs shaping. R & D personnel will come up with concrete suggestions for a new product, but being experts in a special field, they may overlook practical application problems with their mind fixed on technical challenges and issues, i.e. they lack the naïve view that is necessary as well (Veryzer 1998a). Also, they may have priorities that differ from the wishes they expect in their target group, e.g. they may imagine that housewives will prefer functionality to design in kitchen utensils or vice versa. A customer's contribution can consist in adding his perspective to the engineers', in uttering his preferences, and in informing about his needs, wishes, and problems. This knowledge contribution, which can be summarized as information on better market orientation, is more or less the same as with opportunity identification and requires the same kind of customers (see above). A company can also learn from customers with special skills and know-how pertaining to the desired innovative product. This second type of knowledge gain is useful in workshops on creativity and on envisioning the future with their respective methods and tools. In addition to being workshop participants, customers contribute knowledge in special "creative centers" with the express purpose of furthering collaborative innovations or as managers of core technology units within the central department of corporate technology.

The customers integrated in the idea identification task can be normal or lead users, depending on the method and on the specific questions or problems.

Whereas the observations above have shown what can be learned from customers, it remains to be seen what cannot be learned from them with regard to this particular task.

In the case of opportunities linked with technological developments, customer contribution presupposes a certain technical knowledge. It goes without saying that nothing can be learned from customers who do not have at least a basic technical understanding, which excludes normal users with very few exceptions.

As intimated in 3.2.1, certain identification methods and tools also require a special kind of knowledge that is vital for the job at hand, but normally not to be found with customers. Patent research requires a legal and technical education, and bibliometrics asks for a special training that includes mathematical skills. It would be pointless to expect a knowledge contribution from customers in this area unless they happen to be experts in this field, too.

With the identification/generation of ideas, the same restrictions apply. It normally remains the job of company experts to put together the information pieces that shape the finally emerging idea. It has been noted that product ideas or parts of them, as far as discontinuous innovations are concerned, originate in the firms rather than come from customers (Veryzer 1998a). This limitation, however, is a question of the nature and extent of customer contribution and not an inherent impossibility of customer knowledge contribution.

Selection

The question of what can or cannot be learned from customers in the selection task has to follow the distinction between analysis and actual choice.

The analyzing part, as explained in 3.2.1, starts with determining criteria for assessing and grading opportunities and ideas. As far as these criteria are based on market considerations, customers, as with identification, can provide valuable information via the established methods of market research. With technical/technological considerations, special brainstorming workshops with lead users are helpful to set up the desired criteria.

In the case of *opportunities*, the next step in the selection task, the actual analysis, requires in-depth knowledge of products within comparable opportunities, of pertinent technologies, and of market developments. Only lead users will be able to contribute this kind of knowledge. It can be gained from them in the various workshops on roadmapping etc. that belong to the tools and methods of the selection task. Another recommended way is to invite them as sporadic members of the multifunctional team (see 3.2.1); a permanent membership is not advisable because not all aims and purposes of this task are suited to external participation, e.g. correspondence with the company's strategy or resources.

The evaluation of *ideas* that were generated/investigated with or without the help of customers may be supported by customer knowledge, too, leading to a hierarchy of products with different grades of satisfaction. Lead users will know, for instance, which kind of new drilling tools will be best suited to their particular needs and wishes, and may thus contribute to the grading process prior to the final selection. This can be done in special sessions. Essentially, however, this assessment does not rely on external knowledge but will follow the company's routine as described in 3.2.1.

The final selection process is a company's very own business, with ideas even more so than with opportunities (cf. Koen, Ajamian, Boyce et al., 2002), because it is the company that has to bear the risks and consequences and not the customer. Where opportunities in the form of customer trends are concerned, it may seem advisable to learn the customers' preferences by letting them choose via market research between pre-selected opportunities, e.g. whether they would rather buy "functional food" or "bio" products. This can be done via market research. With ideas, a company may wish to include carefully selected customers – preferably ones who did not take part in the identification task to avoid any bias in favor of their own ideas – in order to overcome any remaining indecisions on market issues.

With regard to the strict selection part of this task, these considerations lead to the following proposition:

> **P5:**
> The selection task is a company's own business; customer integration may add value in exceptional cases only.

Definition

Project definition as the first step of this task entails, among other things, technical feasibility studies. Customers with technical expertise can contribute their pertinent know-how to this task in which concrete production details play an important role. With concept definition, the customers' knowledge contribution can also consist in furnishing information about environmental issues or health/safety risks: external expert knowledge in this field is especially valuable coming from customers with an interest of their own in the project's success. Apart from that, a company can learn from customers with relevant experience what would be the best way to launch the final product in the market.

Empirical studies have shown that customer information is particularly valuable in the project development part but less so in the final concept definition (Gruner and Homburg 2000), which largely depends on a company's internal knowledge and is, again, predominantly its private affair.

With regard to the potential knowledge contribution, customers should be lead users, reference or launching customers, or, in exceptional cases, first buyers. They can be integrated in workshops on detailed aspects of the project or be invited to relevant lectures with following discussions in which their input may lead to concept improvements.

Testing

The task aims, among other things, at assessing the customers' reaction to the envisaged product (Veryzer 1998b). This is a contribution only customers can make: it is only from them that a company can learn how future buyers will use the final product (Gruner and Homburg 2000). Engineers will often be biased when trying out their prototypes: firstly, they will subconsciously tend to see their embodied idea in glowing colors, and secondly "engineers are not real people! They know too much and often think in a way that differs from the people that will be using the product" (Veryzer 1998b: 149). The knowledge customers can contribute will pertain to their overall satisfaction with the product, to possible deficiencies, and to suggestions how to alter product features or production processes (Lynch and O' Toole 2003). This knowledge can be gathered in various ways and from various types of customers:

Focus groups with both "normal" customers and lead users who are given rapid prototypes will clarify open issues when product parts are concerned. Lead users can act as alpha or beta testers; with certain products, so can normal users. Field studies together with lead users as well as Empathic Design market research with normal customers will be helpful to test evolutionary prototypes (all methods from Veryzer 1998b: 141).

Knowledge creation management

As was shown in detail with the other tasks, customers contribute knowledge in many ways, thus helping create new knowledge. Knowledge creation depends to a considerable degree on customer knowledge. Customer integration has the main purpose to integrate their knowledge in order to obtain the benefits depending on it; apart from strategic advantages, all other benefits are more or less related to customer knowledge.

However, as was explained in 3.2.2 above, customers contribute knowledge to the tasks and not to knowledge creation management. A company cannot learn from customers how to organize the process of externalization, socialization, and systematization or how to distribute knowledge internally for further knowledge creation. This is a task that is exclusively a company-intern job, depending on a company's strategy, organization, resources, and appreciation of knowledge as an asset in the innovation race. Besides, even if special customers, e.g. collaboration partners, happen to know from experience of their own how to manage the technical aspects of knowledge creation, a company will not want to serve its entire collected knowledge to outsiders on a platter by including them in the respective management activities.

This is why customers cannot or should not contribute to this task, which leads to Proposition 6:

P6:
Customer integration in knowledge creation management is not advisable.

Without customer integration in this task, assets and liabilities are of no relevance.

3.3 Assets

The concept of customer integration has been widely approved for many years because its beneficial impact on the innovation process is almost taken for granted. The most common benefits resulting from customer integration were described in Chapter 2.4.1 but without differentiation as to sub-phases or tasks. As not all benefits are likely to occur within all tasks - irrespective of individual circumstances -, a risk-benefit perspective ought to consider the potential effects of customer integration in the particular task. This will be done in the section 3.3.1.

Theoretical and empirical research (Campbell and Cooper 1999; Cooper and Kleinschmidt 1995; De Brentanni 1991) has established the existence of several general success factors that will increase the overall value of innovative activities. While primarily pertaining to general New Product Development, these factors also are of special relevance to customer integration, potentially increasing its value. These benefit-increasing factors will be examined in 3.3.2.

3.3.1 Benefits in the various tasks

Identification

Opportunities and ideas for innovative products depend to a very high degree on market considerations. *Better market orientation* as a consequence of customer integration is a desired and frequently gained benefit within opportunity identification (Wilson et al. 1996) and the identification/generation of ideas (Kujala 2003).

As for *reduction of development time*, customer input may shorten the innovation process in the long run (cf. 2.4.1), but it is very unlikely that this benefit will apply to the identification task as such. As far as the identification of opportunities and ideas is based on market research of needs and trends, customer integration within the described research methods is necessary anyway, neither shortening nor extending the process. With customers as participants in workshops, it is not apparent how their collaboration will speed up the task of e.g. brainstorming or roadmapping; their contribution is not per se faster than that of company staff or external experts. However, in a few special cases customers with pertinent knowledge or skills may abbreviate the identification process for both opportunities and ideas, coming up with suggestions that appear to be the perfect solution without further investigation. This illustrates that with the task in question the reduction of time is a chance rather than a definite benefit (as to the distinction cf. 2.4.1).

As with time reduction, the benefit of *cost reduction* is not easily linked with a special task but will apply, if at all, to the entire innovation process. With regard to the identification task, a cost-reducing contribution is not very obvious, except when an already known customer with recognized knowledge about needs or technologies may give the pertinent information directly, thus eliminating the costly selection of other customers for workshops or market research. In the long run, however, a customer's identified opportunity or idea may lead to less expensive production methods. Again, this "benefit" for the identification task is only a slim chance.

The hoped-for benefit of *access to new knowledge* is a very cogent motive of customer integration especially in the identification task. By combining internal and external knowledge sources, companies can discover new fields of innovative activities and create/shape new ideas. New skills and technological know-how are vital for identifying both opportunities and ideas, especially in view of the complexity of many industrial products and of fast-changing technologies. With the appropriate customers, this benefit is a very likely effect of customer integration in this task.

Strategic advantages (cultivating relationships with customers, hoping to find new customers via the integrated ones, improving the company's standing among competitors, cf. 2.4.1) apply to customer integration on the whole and are not linked with special tasks, meaning they are a possible benefit of the identification task, too.

Selection

This paragraph will make a distinction between opportunities and ideas within the selection task only if and when a different perspective is likely or possible.

The selection of opportunities and ideas for innovative products is carried out with one purpose: to further the development of a product that will be successful in the market. In other words, *market orientation* is of the utmost importance. The prospective final profit, depending on how well a product will sell, is the one criterion that, unspoken or not, influences all other criteria on the selection lists. Customers, who are the best links to the market as bearers of its needs and wishes or as prospective buyers, will increase the market orientation by giving their input in the manner that was described above.

Better market orientation, accordingly, is a definite prospective benefit of customer integration in the selection task.

Most of what was said in the context of *reduction of development time* with regard to the identification task (cf. above) applies to the selection task as well: it is not immediately apparent how customers may speed up the selection process. Only in the exceptional case of a few lead users being asked to choose among pre-selected opportunities or ideas, can their input abbreviate or avoid possibly longer discussions among company experts.

Consequently, time reduction is a slim chance and not a likely benefit of customer integration in the selection task.

The observations on *cost reduction* within the identification task fully apply to the selection task as well. However, with regard to ideas, there is a new aspect: Within the selection of ideas, integrated customers may help avoid costly system features that the user does not want or cannot use (Kujala 2003). It is true that such a cost reduction will only become effective, if at all, in the product development process and does not influence the actual money spent on selection, but its foundation can already be laid in the previous selection task.

With *access to new knowledge*, the analysis part of the selection task requires some special knowledge that customers can contribute. Lead users are integrated just because of their pertinent knowledge input, which is a very strong benefit in this task (Campbell and Cooper 1999; Littler et al. 1995).

As explained above, *strategic advantages* are a possible and likely benefit of all tasks, including selection.

Definition

In the final business plan – less so in the project definition – the prospective success in the market plays an important role, making *better market orientation* a highly desired benefit. Customers with corresponding knowledge will further the product's fit with market expectations in this task (Gruner and Homburg 2000), which makes their input a definite chance.

With the concrete technical part of the project development concept, customers – in contrast to the identification and selection tasks – may reduce time in two ways: Lead users/collaboration partners with pertinent technical expertise can add valuable information on how to arrange technical procedures in a faster way, thus shortening the future production. Also, their know-how may abbreviate the time for drawing up the project definition itself, thus reducing the time for the present task. Accordingly, *reduc-*

tion of time is a likely positive effect of customer integration within concept development.

The same arguments as above apply to a possible *reduction of costs* within this task.

As for *access to new knowledge*, technical skills and know-how as well as knowledge about marketing strategies are valuable in the concept definition task, the former predominantly in the project development part, and the latter in drawing up the final business plan. Customers may provide access to new aspects in this respect, which constitutes another chance for this particular task.

The chance of *strategic advantages* is the same as with the identification and selection tasks (see above).

Testing

Contrary to what may have been expected, empiric research has established that customer contribution to prototype testing yields the biggest positive results on new product success, more than any other task (Gruner and Homburg 2000).

Whereas company staff will use prototypes mainly to test technical aspects, customers are primarily integrated to give information on their satisfaction with the product. The resulting increased market orientation is the predominant benefit of customer integration in this task.

With regard to *reduction of development time*, prototype testing with evolutionary prototypes will show possible product flaws at a time when they can be eliminated comparatively quickly. Customers identifying such flaws, e.g. in beta-testing software, will save time in the long term, although the necessary changes will cost time at the moment. Recalling products from the market after launch and changing the product later on will definitely take a much longer time. In rapid prototype testing, customers can speed up the development process in the short term by giving information on product features that are unnecessary or unpractical in their opinion and can be left out in the further development process.

Integrated customers can save costs in more or less the same way as time: product changes are costly, the later the more. The benefit of *cost reduction* applies to the prototype-testing task either immediately or in a long-term perspective.

The benefit of *access to new knowledge* ranks high among the desired benefits in this task. Technically experienced customers are expected to contribute know-how pertaining to technical prototype improvements. Insights in normal customers' ways of using prototypes can lead to new functionalities. Beta testers may add their own experience and creativity to the prototype, suggesting even better solutions. In summary, the chances of gaining new knowledge in this task are very high.

Strategic advantages in testing products with customers will be the same as with the previous tasks. In addition, changes made in compliance with customers' test results will prevent possible embarrassing discoveries of product flaws after market launch when such flaws may ruin or at least damage a company's reputation.

3.3.2 Benefit-increasing factors

Theoretical and empirical investigations have established the existence of numerous generally valid key success factors that will enhance the overall success of innovative activities (Campbell and Cooper 1999; Cooper and Kleinschmidt 1995; De Brentanni 1991). Some of these factors are apt to specifically increase the benefits of customer integration, thus adding to the positive side of a risk-benefit balance.

The primary problem lies in defining success of an integration project. Customer integration may work out well whereas the final product turns out to be a flop, or a prematurely ended unsatisfactory relationship with an integrated customer still yields a beneficial input for the present project or valuable experience for future products (Littler et al. 1995). Bearing in mind that "success" is multifaceted in any case, but especially in collaboration development (Cooper and Kleinschmidt 1987), this thesis concentrates on the recognized factors that increase not only the general success of New Product Development but also and in particular the likelihood of an integration project approved by all parties concerned.

In order to be of special relevance to customer integration, the general success factors have to be adapted to particular needs and issues of customers as well as of integration managers, bearing in mind that successful customer integration relies on certain attitudes and prerequisites on the integrating company's side.

Such benefit-increasing factors are:

Senior management commitment to customer integration

The strong support of senior management has been identified as a major factor for successful New Product Development, especially in the context of collaborative activities (Campbell and Cooper 1999; Littler et al. 1995; Wilson et al. 1995). As customer integration requires extra time, money, and staff, the top management has to agree to the allocation of sufficient respective resources (Littler et al. 1995). In addition, it ought to back the concept of customer integration wholeheartedly by encouraging the implementation of the other recommended success factors described below.

Involvement of both technology and marketing departments in integration activities

Empirical studies have shown that successful integration projects rely to a very high degree on involving managers from R&D as well as marketing (Wilson et al. 1995). Whereas in general New Product Development this recommended factor refers to interdepartmental cooperation only, the benefit-increasing status demands an additional interaction of both departments with customers, exchanging the specific perspectives among all participants. On identifying opportunities, for example, the combined consideration of marketing issues, technological resources and feasibility, and customer input will boost the innovative outcome that a cooperation between customers and either marketing or technical staff alone would not be able to produce. Cross-departmental meetings on a regular company-intern basis, joint analyses, shared expertise, and workshops with staff from both departments as well as customers were given the highest impact factor on successful partnering projects (Wilson et al. 1995).

Clear responsibilities on the customers' and the company's part

This stipulation, which also plays an important role in reducing strategic risks, pertains to customer integration as a whole and is a widely accepted success factor (Farr and Fischer 1992; Littler et al. 1995; Wilson et al. 1995). Whether in relatively simple and short-lived integration projects such as market research via Empathic Design or in continuous workshop sessions on roadmapping, the ground rules, e.g. clearly defined goals, objectives, and responsibilities, should be established (Littler et al. 1995), stating explicitly what is expected from the company and what from the customer. However, such rules are of little use if their observance is not supervised. Accordingly, monitoring the progress via "milestones" – significant points at which progress can be assessed– is a recommended success factor (Littler et al. 1995).

Human factors pertaining to customer integration

Theory and practice agree that success or failure of collaborative activities depend on the individuals involved (Littler et al. 1995; Wilson et al. 1995). If, for example, the personal chemistry among workshop participants is not right, the results will be unsatisfactory, or, as respondents in Littler's empirical studies put it: "it only takes one key individual to block collaboration progress" (Littler et al. 1995: 28). Ensuring harmony, a personal atmosphere, and trust at all levels and among all integration partners does not only save time but is of utmost importance in all respects. These conditions can be achieved by a culture of frequent communication and transparency (Wilson et al. 1995). To reach this goal, a company has to ensure that its own staff backs collaborative activities without mental reservation. It is a well-known experience, called the "not-invented-here syndrome", that R&D personnel often resent external suggestions (Brockhoff 2005a; Mehrwald 1999). Empirical research also established the need for an integration or collaboration "champion" or "mentor" who, besides managing legal and commercial aspects of partnering activities, will smooth over possible disagreements and is committed to making the integration project work (Littler et al. 1995).

Learning from past experience with customer integration

While every integration project is unique with regard to the specific task, a company should make a rule of assessing its experiences with customer integration, preferably by a standard procedure for all projects (Littler et al. 1995; Wilson et al. 1995). Investigating former success or failure will help managers find out what should be repeated, improved, or avoided in future activities with customers, thus establishing "customized" instructions on how to integrate customers in the best possible way.

These benefit-increasing factors, derived from established general success factors for New Product Development (cf. Campbell and Cooper 1999; Littler et al. 1995; Wilson et al. 1995), will be additional assets in a risk-benefit balance, which leads to the following proposition:

| **P7:** |
| Specifically adapted general success factors for New Product Development can increase the overall value of benefits. |

However, integration managers have to bear in mind that there are no mechanistic rules of success because many intangible or unpredictable factors will remain (Littler et al. 1995).

In summary, customer integration may but not necessarily will bring about several benefits that can vary from one task to another and that can be increased by specifically adapted general success factors for New Product Development.

3.4 Liabilities

Certain risks, which were described in detail in Chapter 2.4.2, are apt to be attached to customer integration. As with benefits, they will not always occur in all tasks. The risks that will often turn up in a particular task are aggregated in 3.4.1, showing when a risk-benefit balance of the envisaged integration project within the task at hand may be charged on the debit side.

These risks, however, need not enter such a balance full-scale. Preliminary research has established the existence of various measures by which risks can be reduced or even eliminated. Accordingly, risk-reducing measures, when applied, will lead to a diminished weight of possible risks on a risk-benefit balance. Section 3.4.2 below will touch on ways of risk reduction; a detailed discussion will follow in Chapter 6 when theoretical and empirical investigations of this thesis and own prior research will have come up with comprehensive suggestions for effective risk reduction.

3.4.1 Risks in the various tasks

Identification

As expounded in 2.4.2, the risk of *biased results* has three different forms: biased results due to customers' *views*, *interests*, and *experience*. The search for opportunities and ideas with the help of customers is mainly carried out in the expectation of getting hold of just their views and interests (benefit of better market orientation) and of learning from their experience (access to new knowledge). Apart from demonstrating that benefits have corresponding disbenefits - other examples are reduction of cost/time and increase in cost/time, or access to new knowledge and leakage of knowledge -, this original purpose of customer integration in the identification task implies a strong influence of the customers' expected input, which may be biased. The risk of biased results in all three variations therefore is a likely disbenefit of the investigation task.

The risks of *additional time* and *additional costs* spent on projects with customers (cf. 2.4.2) more or less go back to selecting customers in the first place, to installing elaborate tools for their participation, and to setting up and carrying out workshops with them. All these activities are typical for the investigation task as described in 3.2.1, which makes additional time and costs a frequent and almost certain disbenefit and not only a risk of the investigation task.

The risk of *leakage of knowledge* is combined with the possibility of the customer's gaining company knowledge while contributing his own. This possibility depends to a high degree on the chosen integration method. With Empathic Design, for example, only the company is likely to gain new knowledge by watching the customer use products; a knowledge spillover the other way round is impossible. In contrast, customer integration via workshops where all participants freely discuss relevant topics is certain to transfer new knowledge to the customer as well. Knowledge leakage to the customer is an unavoidable side effect of this integration measure; the risk of the customer's misuse of this new knowledge is closely connected to his personality, i.e. his code of honor and modes of behavior. As these are often incalculable, the pertaining risk must be reckoned with in the investigation task when workshops, focus groups, or similar methods with free discussion are considered.

Strategic risks, like strategic advantages, are not linked to specific tasks or integration methods but may materialize in all tasks, ergo in the investigation task, too.

Selection

The risk of *biased results* is likely to occur in the selection task, though not in all forms (*views, interests, experience*) at the same time and to the same extent.

Everyone who makes a choice will be influenced, either consciously or subconsciously, by his views, no matter if the selection is to be made between persons, concepts, ideas, or specific items. If personal views did not make a difference, any "choice" would be a foregone conclusion relying on objective and verifiable facts; in other words it would not be a choice at all but a logical deduction. That is why an integrated customer's point of view, subjective as it is and welcome for this very reason, will be of special importance in the selection task. If the view, however, is very unusual or limited, relying on it may constitute a grave risk.

The same applies to a customer's *interests*: on selecting opportunities and ideas, he will be influenced by them. The risk of turning down promising opportunities/ideas because of a customer's negative attitude due to his conflicting interests or of selecting future niche products is not to be underrated..

Customers' *experience* may lead to "functional fixedness", as described in 2.4.2, which is an attribute of "normal" customers only. These do not play an important part in the selection task: if at all, they are integrated in big numbers via market research to make a choice between pre-selected opportunities or ideas. This particular risk, therefore, seldom applies to the selection task.

As for *additional time*, all that was expounded on this disbenefit in the identification task applies to the selection task as well, but to a lesser degree because customer integration as a whole is less pronounced in selecting than in identifying opportunities/ideas (see 3.2.1). In summary, additional time will be a disadvantage.

The same applies to *additional costs*: it will cost extra money to integrate customers in the selection task, if less than in the identification task.

In order to help select opportunities or ideas, a customer must necessarily have a certain amount of knowledge about them. This is true no matter if he takes part in the analysis part only or in the actual selection; he will gain a lot of know-how he did not have before and may misuse. With every step forward in the evolution of an innovative product the knowledge will grow, which makes the risk of knowledge leakage in this task even higher than in the identification task.

As mentioned before, *strategic risks* may turn up in all tasks.

Definition

With this *task*, the risk of *biased results* is less likely.

Once an idea has passed the selection process, it is more or less fixed; what remains to be done in this task is laying down the technical and business procedure.

As project definition follows objective technical rules and not subjective opinions, customers' *views* or *interests* are of no importance anymore. As for biased results due to customers' *experience*, this risk only occurs in connection with "normal" customers' functional fixedness and also presupposes a product in the identification or shaping process. Normal customers are unlikely integration candidates in the concept definition task (see 3.2.2), and, as mentioned before, the idea is already shaped, so this particular risk does not exist either.

Within the final drawing up of the business plan, views and interests on e.g. market issues or safety risks may play a certain role, but the risk of biased opinions seams to be minimal.

The risk of *additional time* may turn up if and when customers have to be selected for integration in the project definition task. However, it seams unlikely that a company will only start looking for integration partners when the idea is concrete and the production procedure and business plan are to be discussed. In all probability, only customers who were involved before and are familiar with the idea or who are already known from prior projects will be integrated, which eliminates losing time over customer selection. Apart from that, additional time due to customer involvement is not apparent. Accordingly, this risk is rather small.

Customers taking part in this task are as likely to expect a financial reward as in the previously described tasks (see 3.1.4 and 3.2.4). Besides remuneration costs, however, extra money for integration methods etc. is no more to be expected than extra time (see above). The other possibilities of *additional costs* (cf.3.1.4) are the same as in the previously described tasks.

The risk of *leakage of knowledge* grows in direct relation to the accumulated knowledge. In project and concept definition, customers can gather vital knowledge, which lets this risk appear to be very high.

Strategic risks are identical with those in the previously described tasks.

Testing

Customers testing prototypes may be influenced by particular views or interests, accordingly the risk of *biased results due to customers' views* or *interests* is very likely within this task. Normal customers' possible functional fixedness, however, will be less pronounced than in other tasks because the prototypes they test will demonstrate in which way familiar products can be improved by new ones. "Learning by doing" will mitigate their possibly negative attitude towards novel solutions. With discontinuous new products, however, empirical research has shown that test customers often have difficulties adapting to solutions beyond their experience and intellectual capacity (Veryzer 1998b).

There is no denying the fact that creating prototypes takes time, even rapid prototyping. Still, prototypes would be built anyway for company-intern testing purposes. The *additional time* that will constitute a disbenefit is the time spent on looking for the right customers, on building additional prototypes for them, and on setting up test scenarios. Last but not least, teaching customers how to use prototypes for discontinuous products may take up considerable time (Veryzer 1998b). Additional time will therefore be a certain disbenefit of customer integration in this task.

The comments on the risk of *additional costs* in the context of the other tasks as well as those immediately above on additional time (mutatis mutandis) apply to the prototype-testing task as well.

The risk of *leakage of knowledge* is relatively high with prototype testing: beta testers may show the prototypes to competitors, alpha testers will acquire pertinent knowledge even without knowing construction details because just touching and using prototypes will often convey more information than spoken or written explanations, and they may try to pass on such knowledge.

As for *strategic risks,* the risk of a customers' misuse of power (Brockhoff 2005a) is inherent in prototype testing, too: malevolent customers may intentionally give false information on test results in order to damage the competing company. Also, unsatisfactory test results or disputations about how to arrange tests may lead to conflicts that eventually impair relationships with key customers.

3.4.2 Risk-reducing measures

Whereas the risks pertaining to customer integration have met with growing interest and are relatively well described as shown above (see 2.4.2), the question of their potential reduction has not been answered yet in a comprehensive way. It is one of the main targets of this thesis to establish both scientifically and empirically how risks can be reduced (cf. Chapter 6 below), thus influencing the aspired risk-benefit balance by diminishing the weight of the risks. Such risk-reducing measures, specially adapted to the risks in question, will be more or less the same in all tasks in which the risks may occur.
These measures consist, for example, in

- careful customer selection
- agreements on intellectual property
- good timing of customer integration
- mix of customers,

just to name a few measures of choice.

Contrary to the benefit-increasing factors, which will enhance the overall benefit value and not particular benefits, risk-reducing measures, due to their nature, will influence a special risk only, e.g. a non-disclosure agreement will be relevant to the risk of leakage of knowledge but not to the risk of biased results.

In summary, most risks of customer integration can be downgraded considerably with the help of specific measures, which detracts from the liabilities, just as the assets can be heightened by certain benefit-increasing factors. However, risk-reducing measures cost money and take time, which will increase the disbenefits of additional costs and time, upgrading their weight to some degree. A comprehensive risk-benefit balance therefore has to compare the potential benefits of a particular integration project and the additional positive impact of benefit-increasing factors with the down/upgraded risks following the application of risk-reducing measures.

This is summarized in the following proposition:

> **P8:**
> Risk-reducing measures and their possible effects change the impact of risks.

3.5 Propositions summary

With the focus on risks and benefits of customer integration in the early innovation phase, this study aims at developing concrete recommendations and tools for predicting the overall success of integration measures in various innovation activities. Own theoretical deductions, based on existing research, have led to propositions regarding the general advisability of customer integration (P1), the point of reference for positive or negative effects (P2 and P3), the limits of customer integration (P4 – P6), and the possibilities of influencing the effects of customer integration (P7 and P8).

These propositions will be tested for their validity in the following empirical research, serving as its reference frame and main theme and guaranteeing a close link between theory and practice (Lettl 2004). Having been subjected to empirical examination, they will either be dismissed or turned into respective hypotheses and will serve as a theory-building support for the hypothetical final model (Eisenhardt 1989).

However, the case studies as genuine examples of practiced customer integration will not follow the structure of the analysis model too closely but will report the empirical findings in the chronological and logical context of management practice, paying attention, whenever possible, to all issues raised in the analysis model.

The propositions are listed below:

Table 3.1. Summary of propositions

P1: Customer integration does not necessarily add value to the innovation process but needs a project-oriented risk-benefit analysis.

P2: Certain tasks occur in the course of every innovation process irrespective of the concrete process structure.

P3: Risks and benefits of customer integration pertain to the particular task customers are involved in.

P4: Knowledge creation is an essential element of all innovation activities and not a phase or task of its own.

P5: The selection task is a company's own business; customer integration may add value in exceptional cases only.

P6: Customer integration in knowledge creation management is not advisable.

P7: Specifically adapted general success factors for New Product Development can increase the overall value of benefits.

P8: Risk-reducing measures and their possible effects change the impact of risks.

4 Case studies on early customer integration

As mentioned in the empirical research gap in Chapter 1 and deepened in the review of key problems in Chapter 2, a combined outlook on activities of customer integration and their resulting effects on the outcome of an innovation project has not been the focus of empirical research so far. This thesis therefore resorts to case studies that provide an insight on the relevant aspects of customer integration in the context of practical application, considering as much as possible the issues that were raised in Chapter 3.

4.1 Selection and structure

The cases were selected with the intention of identifying patterns and schemes for successful customer integration and pertinent risk management in the early innovation phase. The predominant selection criterion was the fundamental comparability of the companies' innovative power and the involvement of customers in the innovation process.

The selected companies are all innovation leaders in their respective market and strive hard to maintain this position. A leadership strategy differs considerably from a "follower" strategy, which more or less copies the leaders' results. Leaders, on the other hand, rely on innovative customers as an essential source of information (Schewe 2005; Specht and Zörgiebel 1985). With respect to the industry, all chosen companies are manufacturers because in this way the characteristics of R&D are comparable. Another important selection criterion was the companies' activities in the business-to-business (B2B) market, which means that the customers, too, are companies and not end consumers (the data on those is from other sources). The B2B markets are characterized by the fact that the main buying decisions are made by professionals (cf. Backhaus 2003); the result is a bigger impact on most aspects of customer integration. The geographic location played an important role as well. The innovative output of Switzerland led to the selection of Swiss or Swiss-based companies only. With an R&D intensity of 2.57 % of GDP the country is well ahead of the surrounding EU 15 with 1.91% of GDP or the total OECD with 2.26% of

GDP (OECD 2006). The chosen companies, however, all have international contacts and experience. All case study participants are homogeneous in their business fields. With regard to size, they were expressly selected among big and medium-sized companies.

In summary, the four companies described in the case studies were chosen according to the following criteria:

- Innovation leaders in their market shares
- Manufacturing companies
- Business to business (B2B) companies
- Swiss-based companies
- Homogeneous companies

While these criteria guarantee comparability, the companies' divergent individual branches - printing machines, moving equipment, electrical components, and medical implants - and their different sizes achieve the necessary differentiation for triangulation.

With the express focus on the advisability of customer integration for individual innovation projects and not in general, the case studies each describe a concrete innovation project, termed pilot project, with integrated customers instead of depicting how the companies usually deal with the concept of customer integration. In addition to this main focus, the research also pertains to basic organizational structures that enable the identification of characteristics regarding the assessment of risks and benefits. Accordingly, the case studies concentrate on the company profile with special regard to customers, on the structure of the innovation process which is the basis for answering several issues in Chapter 3, on the pilot project as central unit of analysis, and on the companies' ex post evaluation of both the pilot project and the value added by customer integration.

In accordance with the postulation of research validity and reliability, a variety of tools for gathering data were used, such as interviews, questionnaires, archived data, presentations, internal documents, company websites, and both direct and indirect observation. Interviews were the main and most important source of information. They were based on a semi-structured interview guideline (see Appendix B) that was the result of prior document analysis, preparatory talks, and archived data. The following list contains the interviewees' functions:

- Chief Technology Officer (CTO)
- R&D Manager
- Marketing Manager
- Engineer
- Project Manager of customer integration activities

The analyzed documents mainly comprised annual reports, published articles, presentations, guidelines, and internal documentations, the latter containing important information about customer integration and about the way this information is communicated throughout the company.

Next to the mentioned data, company visits were an important source of information, leading to comprehensive insights into the practical preparation and implementation of customer integration. The pilot projects, accompanied and supported by HSG, required several visits, thus offering many possibilities for in-depth empirical research.

4.2 Customer integration at Gallus

4.2.1 Company profile

Introduction and key data

Today's Gallus group (hereafter Gallus) goes back to the private company Ferdinand Rüesch, Eichmeister, founded in St. Gallen/Switzerland in 1923 by Ferdinand Rüesch-Baur as a scales factory and machine workshop. In 1925, the first Gallus label-printing machine was developed. Since 1974, when the company was converted into a corporation, it has operated under the name of Gallus Ferd. Rüesch AG. The production is concentrated in St. Gallen/Switzerland, also the Gallus headquarters, and in Langgöns-Oberkleen/Germany, the location of the affiliate Gallus Druckmaschinen GmbH.

In 1999, Heidelberger Druckmaschinen AG – a market leader for solutions in the printing and publishing industry – acquired 30% shares in Gallus; the remaining 70% are still held by the Rüesch family. This share acquisition has led to an extensive cooperation in the fields marketing, distribution, and technology. Partly due to combining forces with Heidelberger Druckmaschinen AG, Gallus now operates all over the world.

The Gallus group employs 510 people; its annual turnover amounts to 207 million CHF (positions per 2005).

Table 4.1. Overview of Gallus

Headquarters	St. Gallen, Switzerland
Number of sites	2 manufacturing sites
Number of employees	510
Industry/branch	Machine construction / printing machinery
Products	Printing machines for narrow-web printing suited for various printing processes (offset, letterpress, UV and WB flexography, rotascreen, and hot foil stamping)
Range of technology	High-tech
Position in the market	Innovation leader
Turnover	207 mill. CHF

Products, markets, and customers

Gallus is a producer of printing machines for narrow-web printing, which is mainly employed for printing labels, collapsible cardboard boxes, or foil paper.

The company's printing machines encompass various printing processes: offset, letterpress, UV and WB flexography, rotascreen, and hot foil stamping. Especially the technology of rotary flexographic printing has become increasingly important, making the printing of foil-like materials such as self-adhesive labels or plastic packagings possible at last. This added property of Gallus machines also facilitates the application of gold embossing and color gradients on foils.

Among the many advantages of Gallus machines are their modular structure, allowing an easy adaptation to new technologies, and the open system architecture, enabling different printing and processing operations to be carried out individually or in combination. Gallus is always among the first of its branch to incorporate new technologies; for instance, the company replaced at a very early stage the mechanical main shaft by a multitude of electronically synchronized servo drives. The price of a printing machine, depending on the press type and its configuration, amounts to 0.5 – 2 million CHF.

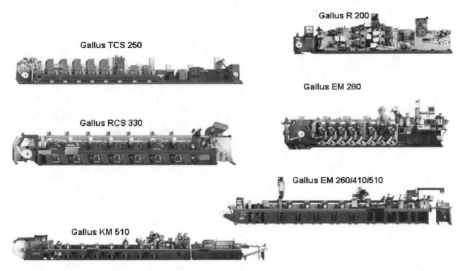

Fig. 4.1. Survey of the Gallus printing machines

Gallus serves the worldwide niche market of narrow-web printing machines, where it is the leader with regard to quality. Internationally known brand producers, such as Nestlé, Henkel, or Procter & Gamble, use labels and packaging printed by Gallus machines.

The direct customers of Gallus are all companies themselves in the label-printing branch. They are mostly family-owned and family-run enterprises with ten to fifty employees. Gallus management has long-standing and close personal relationships with most owners or top managers of these printing companies. So far, only few bigger "industrial" enterprises have been among the customers.

These label printers, being suppliers themselves of companies in the food, beverages, and cosmetics industries, have to mind their respective customers' wishes. In the course of the past ten years, optimization efforts of companies such as Nestlé or Procter & Gamble have led to increasing pressure on the label printers: "just-in-time", flexibility, digitization, quality safeguarding, product safety, and internationalization are just a few examples of the trends and issues printing works have to deal with. Fig. 4.2 illustrates this interdependence in the value chain:

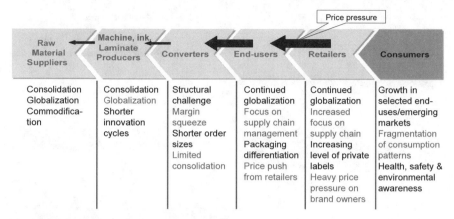

Fig. 4.2. Value chain of the label-printing industry (source: Gallus 2005)

As a supplier in the business-to-business market, Gallus depends to a high degree on its customers' success. Gallus therefore has the vision and policy of promoting this success, offering, in addition to the machines, a comprehensive package for advice, training, and servicing. So far, however, customers have primarily expected Gallus to supply machines and not so much to offer solutions, focusing on the printing machines as such and not on processes and demands pertaining to them. The Gallus strategy aims at broadening their customers' perception of the company as a supplier of not only hardware but also of solutions to demands made on them.

4.2.2 Innovation process at Gallus

Gallus has established a concentrated, unspecific innovation process mainly orientated on technology. The link to market considerations is made by innovation workshops that take place twice a year. These workshops are headed by the R&D manager and include the enlarged management team consisting of representatives from R&D, sales, marketing, and customer service.

One workshop concentrates on the mid-term product and innovation roadmap, taking into account the relevant technological and market-driven innovations as well as the anticipated reactions of the main competitors in the market for narrow-web printing machines.

The second innovation workshop focuses on the R&D development plan for the following year. Its main task is to evaluate and select the most attractive proposals for future development projects and to reconcile them with the available R&D budget of the respective year.

In the course of the year, all projects are monitored periodically and corrective action is taken in case of substantial deviations from the project target or of necessary target adjustments.

4.2.3 Innovation project: Concept for industrializing narrow-web printing

Via fairs, its own distribution channels, and long-term personal relationships Gallus has had good contacts to its customers. In addition to already practiced loose collaboration with customers, Gallus wants to implement new ways and methods of actively including its partners into the investigation of new functionalities for its machines.

The heads of the Gallus development and marketing departments have chosen the trend of industrialization in the printing branch, emerging from the rising requests of the subsequent value chain, for the company's future innovation activities. Gallus wants to develop a novel product concept that adds new functionalities to its machines with special regard to narrow-web printing, thus enabling its customers to meet their clients' demands. In order to get hold of relevant ideas, Gallus has decided to investigate its customers' needs and wishes in a systematic way, hoping to identify new functionalities for the printing machines.

For the pilot project on industrializing narrow-web printing via ideas and functionalities investigated with customers, Gallus has chosen the Lead User approach in the first place. This method's core unit, the workshop with all assembled lead users, would, however, cause a problem in the particular circumstances, because due to the extremely competitive situation in the printing branch and to the employees' strong personal identification with their respective companies an open discussion with constructive contributions cannot be expected. Besides, Gallus wants to learn as much as possible about how its customers actually apply the acquired machines in their printing processes, especially with regard to the interfaces with other machines. This wish has led to combining various integration methods in the pursuit of the innovation goal:

- the Lead User method in respect of its selection criteria
- the Empathic Design method in view of watching customers use Gallus machines on their sites
- semi-structured interviews to identify and prioritize customers' ideas
- the Ulwick method and Quality Function Deployment (see Appendix A) to combine needs and solutions in a correlation matrix.

The final goal of these combined methods is a process analysis at the customers' sites, focusing on the business process along the value chain but leaving aside the concrete machines. This analysis is to identify technical solutions the customers have already found on their own, leading to new functionalities and services, and to discover so far unmet needs.

In a first step, Gallus looks for integration candidates, falling back on its buyer list: customers who ordered the most advanced type of printing machine are considered to be progressive and innovative themselves. Such customers are rated on a regular basis according to four clusters of criteria. In this case, the first cluster containing knockout criteria excludes customers from far away or non-German-speaking countries. Secondly, the progressive buyers have to be potential reference customers, able and willing to check and review the future product concept. The third cluster groups the buyers with regard to their launching qualities: they must be suited to co-develop new product features for novel functionalities. While the interest in the most advanced model has already signaled lead user qualities, the fourth cluster expressly looks for customers with the potential of developing relevant innovative products on their own or who are at least well-known trendsetters.

The different clusters are evaluated. By arrangement with the sales department that knows all listed customers in person, the Gallus development department selects six lead users for the envisaged project.

It is up to the top management to contact the pre-selected customers, thus demonstrating the special interest Gallus has in the respective company's participation. Gallus managers all have close personal contacts with the heads of the predominantly family-run businesses, which leads to all addressed customers' agreeing to join the concept development project. Apart from good personal relationships, this unanimous acceptance is also due to further motivation: as an incentive, Gallus promises to give all participants a report on the visit to their respective printing works, containing the following details:

- a survey with the title "Status and Development of High Quality Label Printing", based on the interviews and on information authorized by the interviewees
- an anonymous benchmark with regard to the cost structure
- feedback on how to realize the explicit individual wishes for improvement.

The next step prior to actually meeting the customers is to prepare the basis for the envisaged process analysis. Gallus staff develops a model of a typical process in a printing plant. This model, which is rather complex, is condensed into a relatively coarse block diagram that is to be discussed with the customers. This way, the respective customer will be able to compare his individual printing process with the model, pointing out in which way the two processes are identical or if and how they differ. The block model is designed in a way to help Gallus identify differences in the various printing processes that have an essential impact on functionalities required of future printing machines and on the machine periphery.

Once the customers are selected and notified and the model is completed, Gallus teams, each consisting of two employees, start visiting the respective companies. Two tasks are waiting for them: to interview company representatives and to watch as well as record the printing process at the sites.

The talks with the customers have to strike a balance between being structured and leaving enough space for individual comments. If the interviews follow too strict a structure, there is the danger of preventing spontaneous, seemingly out-of-the-way contributions that may lead to radically new insights. On the other hand, "open" questions complicate the comparison of the various results and may distract from the focus on industrialization. That is why a semi-structured questionnaire, containing rather vaguely defined questions to the customers, is chosen.

Every Gallus interviewer is given a guideline, listing in six paragraphs the important issues he has to consider:

1. Preparation: This paragraph contains information on the company, which the customer ought not to see, such as a short company profile, current projects, or complaints about the company. This paragraph can be easily removed from the others in case the customer wishes to retain the interview guideline.
2. Preliminary talks: Customers often have questions of their own that they wish to discuss. In order not to burden the envisaged interview with subjects irrelevant for the process analysis, the guideline recommends in such cases to refer the customers to Gallus experts while already trying to extract some useful information.
3. Process analysis: The process at the customer's site has to be recorded, paying special attention to the individual structure and to machine interfaces.
4. Potential for improvement: The interviewer has to question the customer on needs and on suggestions for improvement.
5. Cost structure: This paragraph deals with questions concerning the origin of costs and the most important influencing factors.
6. Future developments and trends.

The process analysis at the various company sites is based on the process model, the guideline, and – with the exception of one company – on an extensive tour of the respective printing works. Watching the printing process and asking for detailed explanation of critical interfaces provide a comprehensive insight into problems and needs/possibilities of improvement. Any remaining unsolved questions are discussed after the tour.

Whereas the respective tour guide's level of hierarchy varies from one company to another, the interview partners are without exception managers or heads of the company, all very well versed in their companies' strategy and processes, mostly in specific technical details, too. Thus, the Gallus team can establish – as a by-product of the interview – which customer would be a good member of a subsequent workshop on co-developing novel printing machines with new functionalities.

The results of each visit, including the interview, are listed in a comprehensive report that is sent to the respective customer. He can cross out critical details he does not want divulged. The approved transcript is the basis for the promised survey on high quality label printing. Gallus employees select pertinent information of general interest, paying special attention to including only such details that will not raise expectations Gallus cannot or does not wish to fulfill. The final survey, together with a letter of thanks, is delivered to the head of each company.

Some customers also receive a benchmark on the costs of printing labels in different quantities and with different printing procedures. The data, which the customers could feed in via Excel, are compared, thus enabling the assessment of where and how processes can or ought to be altered. The anonymous benchmark in the form of a table is sent to the few customers who took part in the benchmark; the limited number of participants is due to the fact that only the bigger printing companies capture data on costs and time and very few are willing to let their calculation be known.

For intern purposes only, Gallus employees combine the gist of the interviews to a "big picture", focusing the information in a structured way. This picture is the starting-point for a company workshop with members of marketing, sales, and services working on identifying ideas for future innovations. In this project, six groups of ideas are identified, each listing the various pertaining needs, e.g. reduction of spoilage, and the respective suggestions made by some or all customers, e.g. using rollers without splices. To support the discussion on alternative solutions and potential new needs the discovered needs and suggested solutions are combined in a correlation matrix with the help of Quality Function Deployment.

Following this procedure, the possible added value for the customers resulting from the possible technical solutions is assessed. A second assessment rates the necessary expenditure in time and costs for Gallus to implement the considered solutions. Both assessments are combined in a portfolio in order to prioritize the ideas with special regard to Gallus' competitive situation and strategic goals.

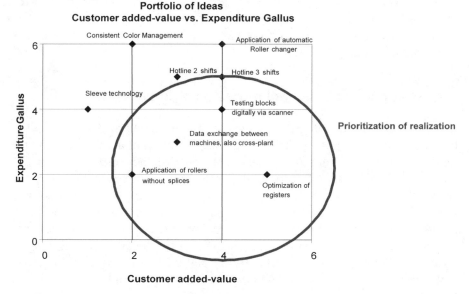

Fig. 4.3. Portfolio of ideas with customer added value vs. Gallus expenditure

4.2.4 Company assessment of the innovation project

The pilot project required 35 man-days and cost about 20.000 CHF.

The immediate result of the pilot project is the identification of six ideas or functionalities within the opportunity of industrializing the printing process. In addition, Gallus has discovered one lead user as a potential participant in an envisaged workshop on developing novel printing machines. The newly developed concept of combining various integration measures, the core element of the pilot project, has proved to be a success. It is going to be checked with reference customers to make sure it offers solutions for a broad variety of customers.

Practical details, however, have caused minor problems: while the strong involvement of Gallus top management increased the customers' motivation for collaboration, the respective involvement of the mostly family-run companies' top managers made data collection outside the on-site interviews and visits a sometimes lengthy and difficult affair. The attempted comprehensive data collection on cost structures could not be achieved via interviews; a separate gathering process via standard tables, carried out with some customers, brought better, if still limited, results. The chosen way of customer integration has turned out to be a very good means of demonstrating to the customers that Gallus does not only offer products but also solutions to problems.

Altogether, Gallus has been very satisfied with the pilot project and considers repeating the procedure.

4.2.5 Company assessment of customer integration

On embarking on the integration of lead users via Empathic Design, Gallus had hoped for several benefits to be gained by their collaboration. A better market orientation, caused by new insights into the customers' special needs, had been high on the company's priority list of expected positive effects. Secondly, access to new knowledge in the form of technical know-how by watching the customers use Gallus and other machines had been another high-ranking desired benefit. A third factor, at least as decisive, had been the hope for strategic advantages in the form of changing their customers' appreciation of Gallus to the better by appearing as a competent supplier of solutions, too, and of discovering potential future cooperation partners.

According to the company, the respective chances have all turned into fully realized benefits.

The company has not commented on prior considerations of risks. In retrospect, the risks of depending on customers' views or interests and of leakage of knowledge have been avoided by the chosen integration method and a careful customer selection. Long-standing personal contacts eliminated the risk of damaged relationships. Extra costs and time, the unavoidable consequence of the pilot project and not fully attributable to customer integration as such, are seen as minor disadvantages that are hoped to be reduced in the future.

A weighing of benefits and disadvantages at the end of the pilot project has led to the company's great and unmitigated satisfaction with the overall success of customer integration.

Summary

The medium-sized company Gallus, a global player in a niche market, has installed an individual innovation process unlike any others. Customer integration is mainly considered as a means of increasing the company's market orientation and of improving its strategic position. The customers, highly specified technical companies themselves, take part in identifying ideas within a company-defined opportunity. In retrospect, Gallus considers the integration of customers in the pilot project a full success.

4.3 Customer integration at Schindler

4.3.1 Company profile

Introduction and key data

The global player Schindler has its roots in a small mechanical engineering company for the production of lifting equipment and various other machines, founded by Robert Schindler and Eduard Villiger in Lucerne/Switzerland in 1874. In 1892, Schindler & Villiger adopted the name "Robert Schindler, Machinery Manufacturer", concentrating its production on elevators. The Schindler Holding Ltd. of today goes back to 1970 when the basic structure of the present group was created. It functions as the holding company for the Schindler Group (subsequently referred to as Schindler), which today consists of two divisions representing its core businesses: Elevators & Escalators and Also, an IT-distributor company of which Schindler has held a majority (now 64.5%) since 1988. Elevators & Escalators, contributing 78% of the group's turnover (per 2005), is still the most important division.

While Schindler's global headquarters is located in Ebikon/Switzerland, it is active in over 130 countries with more than 1,000 offices and 30 manufacturing plants, located in all five continents.

At the end of 2005, Schindler employed 40,385 people; the annual report 2005 reveals consolidated operating revenue of CHF 8.870 billion.

Table 4.2. Overview of Schindler

Headquarters	Ebikon, Switzerland
Number of sites	App. 1000 offices and 30 manufacturing sites
Number of employees	40,385
Industry/branch	Machine construction / moving equipment
Products	Elevators, escalators, moving walks
Range of technology	High-tech
Position in the market	Innovation leader
Turnover	8.870 billion CHF

Products, markets, and customers

Schindler is the largest supplier of escalators and the second largest manufacturer of elevators worldwide; Schindler moving walks contribute to people's mobility as well. The respective machines move more than 700 million people per day. Schindler machines facilitate human mobility in offices, shopping malls, airports, railroad stations, ships, and industrial as well as private buildings. In the freight sector, Schindler provides service elevators for transporting goods as well as people, e.g. beds and patients in hospitals and nursing homes, and freight elevators for warehouses and industrial environments with a lifting capacity of up to 6.3 tonnes.

The company also offers a wide range of services worldwide, comprising the planning, production, and installation of the respective mobility equipment and the subsequent maintenance and refurbishment. The service sector, employing two thirds of the entire Schindler staff, contributes approximately 80% of the company's profit.

Schindler has distanced itself favorably from its competitors (mainly Otis, Mitsubishi, Hitachi, Kone, and Thyssen) by several breakthrough innovations. In 1997, the revolutionary "Schindler Mobile", a self-propelling cabin, was developed, followed in 1998 by the Schindler Smart MRL, an elevator with a driving machine in the hoistway, needing less space and less energy. In 2001, the Schindler Miconic 10 control system, grouping passengers according to their registered destinations, hit the market, and in 2002, SchindlerID, allowing an individualized lift access and excluding non-authorized persons, was launched.

For all its technical achievements, Schindler is also outstanding on the human relations side. The Schindler Award for Architecture, "Access for All", is bestowed on students of architecture for solutions to the removal of barriers to buildings that handicapped people face in everyday life.

The company serves a global market of high-tech mass products (as opposed to niche products). Its numerous worldwide customers vary in type and company size: construction firms, operators of airports or hospitals, architects, individual clients, just to name a few.

4.3.2 Innovation process at Schindler

Schindler's very refined innovation process shows the importance the company attaches to innovative activities:

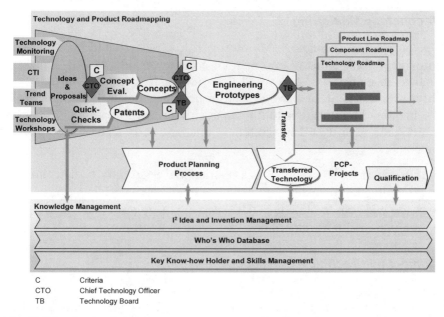

Fig. 4.4. Technology development process at Schindler

Schindler refers to its early innovation phase, illustrated by the funnel in the figure above, as study process. This process aims at providing prototypes of innovative products for the following Product Creation Process (PCP). The study process starts with identifying trends and technologies, continues with generating ideas, and ends with engineering prototypes that are transferred to PCP.

The study process and PCP are separated for two reasons:

- Risk reduction: novel, meaning so far untested, technologies, would greatly increase the risk of missing milestones if applied in a PCP project for the first time. Testing and proving the viability of new technologies within the study process is less risky and much cheaper.
- Time horizon: especially breakthrough innovations take several years of development. This task should be carried out in a separate organizational unit.

The first part of the study process, the identification of new technologies/trends as fields for future innovative ideas, relies on Technology Monitoring, Competitive Technical Intelligence (CTI), Trend Teams, and Technology Workshops.

Technology Monitoring

The purpose of Technology Monitoring is to observe the technological environment for pertinent information. It involves identifying signals of change in embryonic stages and determining its potential impacts. Furthermore, it acts as an alarm system of potential threats. The challenge of Technology Monitoring is to find an appropriate delimitation of the observation area with regard to scope and time and to be open for conflicting outcomes:

- A too narrow observation area restricts the possibility of detecting opportunities from outside
- A too wide observation area ties down too many resources
- Each observation area can be a challenge or a threat.

Competitive Technical Intelligence

The purpose of CTI is to gather information concerning external technology threats, opportunities, or developments that have the potential to affect Schindler's competitive position. It addresses the decision makers' future needs from a uniquely external perspective and supports the strategy and innovation processes as well as tactical decisions. CTI activities are fed by three different kinds of sources:

1. Non-personal information sources: mainly patents, journals / magazines / papers, or internet databases
2. Personal external sources: competitors, universities, conferences, exhibitions, suppliers, customers, consultants
3. Personal internal sources: internal networks in R&D, Product line manager organization.

Trend Teams

Trend Teams, whose job it is to discover relevant market trends, provide the institutional link between technology and marketing. They consist of internal and external members; their work is done in one mixed and one strictly company-intern workshop. On the company side, field engineers and product line managers represent the market side, whereas platform and pre-development experts contribute the technical input. On the external side, customers, consultants, and experts from universities or from other companies reflect the market and technology perspectives.

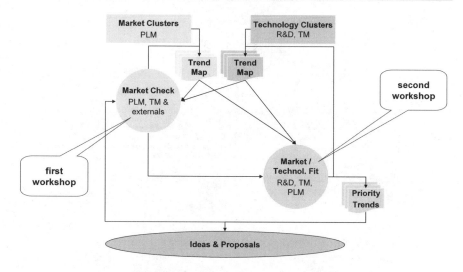

The trend maps record all relevant trends that are
to be updated and improved in the workshop

Fig. 4.5. Trend Team concept at Schindler

Technology workshops

Technology workshops are conducted for each component platform, system platform, and R&D in order to clarify in a comprehensive manner whether a technology is of interest to Schindler. They usually last a day and involve the head of the department and his management team. A technology workshop increases the transparency of technologies and skills. The different portfolios of the departments provide a bottom-up view of the competencies. These can be aligned with the overall R&D competencies by operationalizing the core competencies and analyzing each technology portfolio. The result of the analysis is shown in a radar chart.

The next step in the Schindler innovation process is to generate ideas within the frame of opportunities that were established in the four ways described above. Special idea and creativity workshops in addition to the I2 Idea and Invention database tool support the search for ideas. This database facilitates the creation of intellectual property throughout the company. Innovative ideas must offer either cost reduction due to the improvement or the substitution of a new technology or a new functionality that will increase the present market share. These ideas are evaluated according to a detailed list of criteria before entering the idea pool, from where they are "fished" in the final selection:

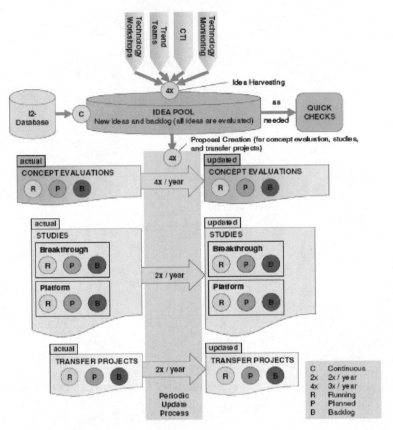

Fig. 4.6. Selection process at Schindler

The ideas in the idea pool are updated and re-evaluated four times a year. Based on these so-called "beefed up" ideas, proposals for concept evaluations, studies, and transfer projects are drawn up. Other biannual updates serve to integrate input from successfully completed studies and from the R&D platform organization.

In order to protect its products, Schindler generates intellectual property as early as possible. Selected ideas are evaluated in a Quick Check, which includes searching for existing patent applications and generating claims for new patents with special attention to patent clusters.

The ensuing concept evaluation aims at creating 3-5 different concepts of how to realize a selected idea. This phase, lasting approximately 3 months, results in simulations, analyses, and drawings.

Promising concepts are transformed into a functional prototype with the help of studies. Schindler has established two different study types:

- Breakthrough studies involve technologies and market applications that go beyond present possibilities. The focus is on creating competitive advantage and increasing market share via new systems and components. Breakthrough studies can last up to ten years.
- Platform studies provide technologies for future product lines. They are to demonstrate that a new technology can be used without intolerable risk in a PCP project. Such studies usually last from six months to a maximum of two years.

Both study types end with a functional prototype that is presented to the Technology Board. Upon its approval, the prototype is transferred to PCP, which means the end of the early innovation phase.

4.3.3 Innovation project: European trends in the elevator branch

Schindler's pilot innovation project centers on investigating European trends in the elevator branch and on identifying pertinent new functionalities with the help of its newly arranged Trend Team concept.

The internal Trend Team members debate upon the customers to be included in the mixed workshop and decide on architects and general contractors in addition to external elevator experts. These possible integration candidates are contacted by phone to find out if they are interested in the first place and, in case they are, which dates would be convenient. In a second step, the interested addressees receive a written invitation containing the exact date, the agenda, the location, and the names of all participants. The fact that a renowned Zurich architect has agreed to take part in the workshop turns out to be an important incentive for the other invited customers who hope to receive new insights from his particular input on top of the general results of the workshop. As Schindler has an excellent reputation in the elevator branch, almost all pre-selected participants appear eager to be part of the pilot project, and all readily sign non-disclosure agreements.

Before the mixed workshop starts, the participants meet for an unofficial lunch where they get to know each other. The official opening begins with introducing the agenda of the day, explaining that the mixed workshop consists of two modules, the first one focusing on market trends, the second one on technology trends. The introduction is followed by a lecture that aims at producing a creative atmosphere. This lecture on future trends explains the basics of trend discovery as well as fundamental issues of the elevator branch in general and the European building branch in particular. The lecture reduces potential opposition to new developments and prepares the ground for the following workshop activities. The participants, thus well tuned in to the subsequent tasks, are divided into small groups of 3-4 members.

Each group discusses and complements the introduced trends; special attention is paid to Schindler experts' exchanging ideas with the customers.

The resulting findings are presented to the plenary session. The multitude of new trends, visions, and ideas constitutes a comprehensive overview of the current and future European trends in the elevator branch.

These trends are allocated to the Schindler Building Matrix (FIf. 4.7. below) and clustered; the combination mid-rise/residential is the most important one in the context of the pilot project.

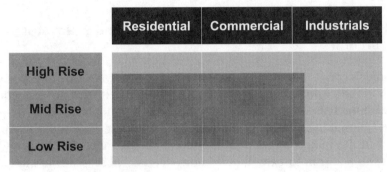

Fig. 4.7. Schindler building matrix

Having compared the newly gathered trends with the original Schindler trend list, the participants start looking for suitable functions to meet these trends. The basis for this task is the handshake analysis (cf. Appendix A) that helps identify product functions in accordance with market needs and technical possibilities.

The plenary session splits into the original small groups, each choosing 2-4 trends from the aggregated pile. The group members start investigating possibilities of new product functions, trying to find the perfect *f*it between *f*unctions and *t*rends (FFT). The questions of market acceptance and technical feasibility can be considered from the very beginning because the group encompasses market and technical experts. With the FFT-approach, the analysis can be completed within a single workshop due to the small size of the group and the composition of its members.

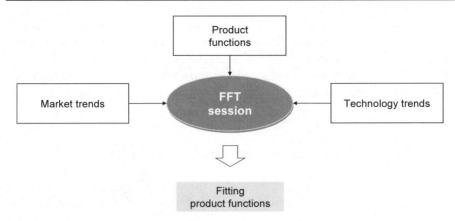

Fig. 4.8. Schindler's FFT workshop

Once again, each group presents its findings, this time the identified product functions, to the plenary meeting. In the following discussion, the findings are analyzed from the participants' point of view. The session ends with each participant receiving a detailed image of priority trends and pertaining product functions.

The results of the first Trend Team workshop are analyzed in detail by Schindler staff on their own in a second workshop of half a day. The trends that were considered important in the mixed workshop are measured against the company strategy in order to find out if this may lead to a different assessment. The final results are used for drawing up product road maps and updating the technology strategy. Product Development and the product line managers receive the listed trends and pertaining functionalities.

4.3.4 Company assessment of the innovation project

The pilot project took up approximately 20 man-days and cost about 5,000 CHF. Schindler expects future workshops to manage on 3 man-days.

The innovation task for the Trend Team had been to discover opportunities and functionalities related to the European elevator branch. Neither new trends nor new ideas/functionalities have been identified; the prior respective suggestions made by company staff and gathered in the trend maps have, however, met with the external participants' approval. This way, the company has gained the assurance that its product strategy is well in accordance with market expectations.

A new leasing concept, which appears promising and will be tested, has evolved as a by-product of the mixed workshop.

The newly developed Trend Team concept as such, tested in the innovation project, has fulfilled Schindler's expectations. Future Trend Team workshops will follow the routine of the pilot project. Especially breaking down the mixed workshop in mini-groups with an internal market and technology expert as well as customers has induced better and faster communication.

4.3.5 Company assessment of customer integration

On considering customer integration via its mixed Trend Team workshop, Schindler had first and foremost hoped to identify so far unknown new opportunities and functionalities with the help of the customers' knowledge input, i.e. the company had envisaged access to new knowledge as the benefit with the highest priority. The second benefit on their mind had been a better market orientation, expressed by the wish to lift the consideration of the market pull on the same level as the existing strong technology push.

The lack of newly identified opportunities and ideas has come as an unwelcome surprise overshadowing the satisfaction that the company's product strategy has been in accordance with market expectations all along. Just looking at the derived benefits, Schindler feels that customer integration has not made any difference to its own innovative efforts.

As for disbenefits, the negligible additional costs and the comparatively short extra time were not considered important. The risk of knowledge leakage, inherent in all workshop activities with customers, has not materialized due to non-disclosure agreements and careful customer selection.

In retrospect, the company does not see an overall success of the concrete customer integration but is not averse to trying out the concept again in the future.

Summary

The large global player Schindler with countless customers in a worldwide sought after market has implemented a very elaborate and detailed innovation process that has been focused on technology. Customer integration is seen as a means to intensify market considerations and to get access to new knowledge. The chosen customers, lead users and indirect customers, take part in identifying opportunities and functionalities in special mixed workshops. In retrospect, Schindler is disappointed with the outcome of the concrete project because it does not differ from mere in-house innovative results.

4.4 Customer integration at Schurter

4.4.1 Company profile

Introduction and key data

In 1933, Heinrich Schurter founded the Schurter AG in Lu-
zern/Switzerland. Since that time, the company has been owned privately
and managed by family members; the president and CEO of today's
Schurter Group (Schurter) is Hans-Rudolf Schurter of the third generation
after the founder.

The Schurter headquarters is in Lucerne. The products are developed
and produced in Switzerland, Germany, and France; other locations are
Czechia, Slovakia, Romania, China, and India. Schurter has corporate offices in 16 countries, sales offices in 34 countries, and distributors in 37
countries (per 2006).
Worldwide, Schurter has 1,118 employees (state: 2005). The sales in 2004
amounted to 156.9 mill. CHF = 130 mill. USD.

Table 4.3. Overview of Schurter

Headquarters	Lucerne, Switzerland
Number of sites	App. 34 offices and 6 manufacturing sites
Number of employees	1,118
Industry/branch	Electrical equipment, appliance, and component manu-facturing
Products	Fuses, connectors, circuit breakers, and input systems
Range of technology	Whole spectrum, from low-tech to high-tech
Position in the market	Innovation leader
Turnover	156.9 mill. CHF

Products, markets, and customers

Schurter operates in the electronic and electrical engineering fields. Its
main products, which also define the four strategic business units, are
fuses, connectors and filters, circuit breakers, and input devices = switches
and keyboards (see Fig. 4.9. below). The product range encompasses more
than 6,000 different items, such as fuseholders, power entry modules, un-

dervoltage protection, touch screens, and voltage selectors, in short almost the whole gamut of electric and electronic devices.

Fig. 4.9. Schurter's product range

Schurter products are developed and produced for specific applications. It is very important for the company to know as much as possible about applications and their potential volume, because the company depends on big volumes and synergy effects on producing electronic components.

Schurter serves a worldwide market of electronic mass products. Its customers – about 30.000 in 45 countries – are mainly manufacturers and suppliers of computers and their peripheral equipment, of technical and medical instruments, telecommunication equipment, control systems, household and gardening equipment, and other technical devices. For these customers, Schurter is a supplier of C-components that they use for their own particular products.

Schurter has the self-imposed mission to "make a leading contribution to the industry worldwide" by maintaining its position as a market leader in the branches defined by its business units. Apart from this economic mission, Schurter follows an ecological vision of environmental protection. Since 1990, when it introduced an environmental management system, Schurter has spent much thought and substantial money on optimum use of resources and minimum ecological risk.

4.4.2 Innovation process at Schurter

The innovation management at Schurter is the result of constant interaction between the sales, marketing, and development departments. Innovative ideas for new products may evolve in each department and in different ways.

The sales department, having a close contact to customers worldwide, contributes a big part of innovative ideas triggered by specific customer demands. These demands are the basis for a special innovation process, called Product Requests. Field Sales Engineers, who are responsible for the regions Europe, Asia/Pacific, and America and who are trained engineers with an additional business education or at least long-standing sales experience, collect and pass on specific customer needs, complaints, and suggestions. Key account managers do the same. Both their information is gathered in a databank for customer requests where it is recorded according to its nature (technical or commercial). Technical requests are passed on to the Development Department of the respective business unit. Within each unit, every product is linked to a special product manager (PM) who is responsible for the technical product care. The PMs have to ascertain if a product pertaining to the customer request exists within the Schurter product range. In case there is no such product, the Sales Department, which is notified by the PM, has to decide whether it ought to be developed. A positive decision leads to passing on the request to the special department Product Change. If it takes more than one month or more than 20,000 CHF to create the desired product, the request is transferred to Product Design. Otherwise, the desired product is developed and handed over to Product Logistics; the customer is informed accordingly and will receive the "customized" product as soon as possible.

Apart from this customer-induced innovation process, Schurter has established a separate one that aims at providing the environment, the methods, and the instruments for gathering and analyzing information on the market and on the competitive situation as well as at developing ideas for new products.

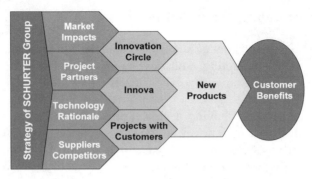

Fig. 4.10. Schurter's special innovation management

The company strategy is the basis for a planned innovation process (PIN). Strategic considerations define the general guidelines for new products or product lines. These considerations are increased by the so-called innovation environment, which consists of market impacts gathered, e.g., via fairs and journals, project partners, company-intern or new extern technologies, and suppliers or competitors. The environment, on its part, influences the decisions of the Innovation Circle, which recommends the further pursuit of existing or the start of new projects. This Innovation Circle consists of members of the Group management, of company managers, and of the Sales and Development departments. It meets once a year. In addition, each strategic business unit holds monthly meetings, called INNOVA, discussing the actual state of the idea pool. The product manager of the Marketing Department and employees of the Development and Sales departments take part in these meeting. INNOVA meetings have the purpose of gathering and developing innovative ideas and of preparing them for the transfer into the product design process. The results of these altogether 48 meetings in the four business units are the basis of the annual discussion in the Innovation Circle.

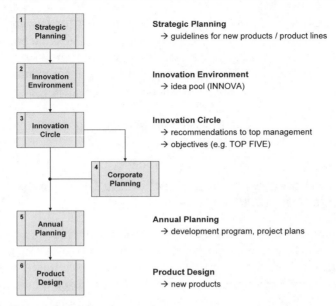

Fig. 4.11. Schurter's product innovation process

The INNOVA meetings are the key element of the PIN process. Several tools are at the members' disposal:

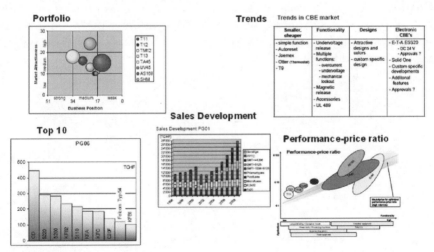

Fig. 4.12. Schurter's INNOVA tool

Having identified and selected innovative ideas, INNOVA / the Innovation Circle transfers them to Product Development where concrete developing plans are worked out. In an initial phase, developing and marketing issues are clarified and the eventual product benefit for customers and/or environment is defined ("book of duties I"). The next step consists in drawing up a concept with mock-ups and a first design review ("book of duties II"). The construction of prototypes follows, accompanied by a second design review and a judgment on fabrication issues ("book of duties III").

With this procedure, Schurter's early innovation phase is over, clearing the way for the actual serial production.

4.4.3 Innovation project: Identification via Customer Application Talks

Schurter hopes to increase the number of radical innovations and fill up its innovation pool, thus strengthening its position as a first mover and staying on top of its competitors. In order to better identify customers' wishes pertaining to electronic components and to create a closer relationship with them, Schurter starts an initiative for a new way of customer integration which aims at increasing, above all, the Development department's application knowledge in the electronic components market. The innovation project to identify new opportunities and ideas basically relies on two customer integration methods, Empathic Design and Lead User approach (cf. Chapter 2.3.2 "methods"), which are combined and modified by the addition of talks with customers on special application issues. Schurter terms this method Customer Application Talk (CAT). The comprehensive concept is depicted in Fig. 4.13. below:

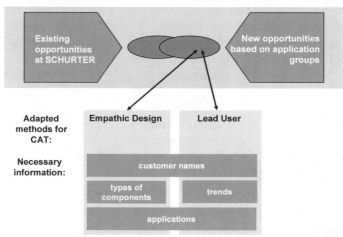

Fig. 4.13. Schurter's CAT concept

A cross-functional team of 6 – 10 persons representing R&D, Marketing, and Sales starts looking for suitable lead users among the company's customers to be watched and interviewed in the course of the CAT project. The first clue to their identification is the list of customers using Schurter components for their own products. All customers are recorded in separate lists for each business unit.

In order to guarantee an objective selection, the team establishes criteria that are given a specific percentage rate according to their significance; this percentage rate facilitates the weighting. Each criterion can be fulfilled in four different ways: -1 (not fulfilled/bad), 0 (perhaps/unknown), 1 (fulfilled/good), or 2 (fulfilled to the highest possible degree/very good).

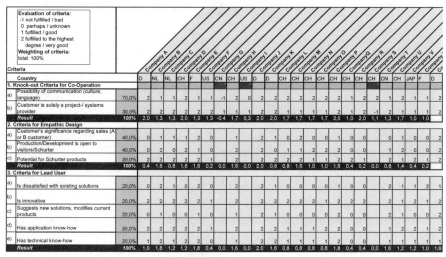

Fig. 4.14. Schurter's customer evaluation table

The "knock-out" criteria are of decisive importance: if there is no possibility of communication with the customer, either with regard to the language or to the culture, or if the customer is not exclusively a supplier of projects/systems, he will not be considered anymore (e.g. Company G or Company I in Fig. 4.14.). Only if both criteria are met, will the evaluation go on; special criteria groups investigate the customer's suitability as a Lead User or partner in Empathic Design.

The weighted grades provide an unbiased answer to the question of good integration candidates, e.g. Company J in Fig. 4.14.

The cross-functional team is well equipped to the grading process: a pure R&D or Sales/Marketing team might come up with very divergent results due to different knowledge of customers or different understanding of technical communication.

The team draws up a portfolio of customers well suited for the envisaged Empathic Design project; the best candidates are those in the right upper field of the portfolio (see Fig. 4.15. below).

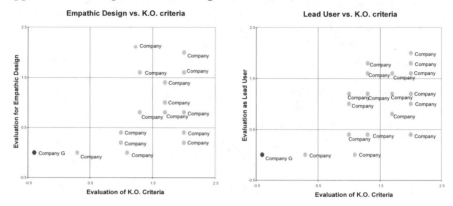

Fig. 4.15. Schurter's customer portfolios

The data leading to these portfolios are stored in a databank and will be updated on an annual basis. Thus, a future evaluation is made easier, and the updating will lead to a comprehensive assessment in the long run.

For each selected customer, a small Schurter team, consisting of at least one member of R&D and one of Marketing/Sales, is put together; this team is responsible for contacting and visiting the customers and for reporting the results. Customers, teams, and the respective business unit that is to benefit from the CAT are listed in a table (see Fig. 4.16. below) in order to prevent a customer being contacted by more than one business unit.

Company	Country	Application	Component	Group	Team
Company A	CH	Medical equipment	PTC, OMF, USF, UMT, 5X20, MGA, OGN, FPG	GS	SE, THU,
Company B	CH	Woodworking, Sawing	USS, TA45, AS 168, TA35	CBE	ABU, BP
Company C	CH	Medical equipment	PTC, OMF, USF, UMT, 5X20, MGA, OGN, FPG	GS	HAA, MER
Company D	CH	Power supply Rack-systems	DC21, DC22, DC11, 4798, DD21, DD22, 20A outlet	GST	SE, HOL
Company E	CH	Power supply	UMT250, SPT, Micro Fuses, OMF 250, OGN	GS	SE, HOL
Company F	CH	Hearing devices	PTC	GS	THU, FI
Company G	CH	Trucks	T13	CBE	ABU, BP
Company H	CH	Telecom base station	OSU, TF600, MSU, FPG, SSU	GS	HAA, MER, THU
Company I	D	Heater controls	T9, FPG	GS	MER, TFL
Company J	D	Eingine steerings	AS168, T9, T11-13, TA35, TA45	CBE	OTH, AN
Company K	D	Medical surgery devices	5220, KFA, 5707, CD, KD, CG	GST	BLU, FI
Company L	D	Medical equipment	PTC, OMF, USF, UMT, 5X20, MGA, OGN, FPG	GS	BLU, FI
Company M	D	Telecom base station	AS168	CBE	HOL, MS
Company N	D	Power supply Rack-systems	DC21, DC22, DC11, 4798, DD21, DD22, 20A outlet	GST	HOL, MS
Company O	D	Mobile IT equipment	0721, 0723, DC22, DC21, 5120, 6100	GST	BLU, MTO
Company P	D	Flat screen	5120, 0721, 0723, 6100	GST	HOL, MTO, MS

Fig. 4.16. Schurter's planned customer contacts

The small respective teams prepare and carry out the application talks within two months. In the case of already existing contacts, these are followed up to arrange a meeting; otherwise, the teams find out on their own who is to be contacted. As these meetings have the express purpose of watching the customer use Schurter components in his production process, it is necessary to involve production managers and engineers as well as technical controllers on the customer's side.

Due to their nature, the individual CAT meetings take place at the chosen customers' sites. A meeting takes up 3 – 4 hours. It starts with an interview on the customer's use of and satisfaction with Schurter products and on possible suggestions or concrete ideas pertaining to new products. In the ensuing tour of the customer's production site, the Schurter team watches the process with special regard to the following questions: What is done? How is it done? What are the interfaces of Schurter products with the customer's production process?

At the same time, the team unobtrusively assesses the customer's or rather his individual staff members' suitability for future collaboration as a lead user in workshops or Tech-Meetings.

After each CAT, the team fills in special standardized forms for component analysis. Each particular Schurter component the customer uses is described with regard to its position in the production process, to the way of interaction, to potential problems and their relevance to the customer, and to suggestions and ideas for solving the problems. This form is stored in an internal databank.

In addition, the CAT teams report their findings to the whole cross-functional innovation team in a steering session. Based on the component analyses, especially on the customers' suggestions and ideas, the innovation team discusses opportunities and ideas for innovative Schurter products. The identified ones are evaluated according to the prospective expenditure for Schurter, the benefit for customers, the profitability, and the prospective turnover in the five years following market launch.

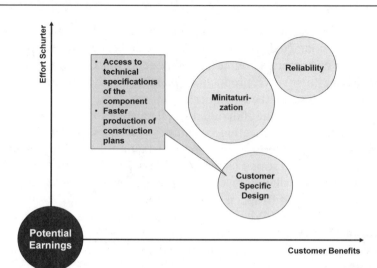

Fig. 4.17. Schurter's evaluation of opportunities and ideas

This evaluation portfolio is spread throughout the company and will be considered in strategy meetings.

4.4.4 Company assessment of the innovation project

The innovation project required 100 man-days and cost 10,000 CHF. The same resources are estimated for follow-up projects.

The pilot project has led to the identification of 7 product ideas in the business unit Fuses & Fuseholders. Two of them are judged to have break-through potential, the other five will lead to incremental innovations. One concrete product development project has evolved, which, at the end of 2005, reached the concept development stage. The resulting new product with 1 million units and an expected turnover of about 0.5 million CHF is going to be launched by the end of 2006.

As for the tested CAT concept, all involved employees were interviewed about the results of the pilot project. 71% assessed the Schurter benefit of the CAT visits as high to very high in comparison to the expenditure; only 4% rated the benefit as very low. The employees' initial skepticism regarding the customers' interest in the application talks was disproved: although Schurter as a C-component supplier does not count among the customers' most important suppliers, 67% of the participating companies displayed a high to very high interest in the visits and the exchange of ideas. There has not been a single case of a customer not being interested at all. In 68% of the visits, the CAT method could be applied successfully in all aspects; with 8% of the visited companies, the focus was on the interview rather than on the Empathic Design part. 46% of the companies have turned out to be potential Lead Users; they will be invited to special workshops in the future.

Altogether, Schurter will continue with the CAT concept.

4.4.5 Company assessment of customer integration

Schurter declares to have had several strong motives for customer integration. In the first place, the company expected a considerable increase in application knowledge regarding electronic components. The second desired benefit was a better market orientation of the development and marketing departments. In addition, Schurter hoped to gain a strategic advantage by improving its reputation as a mere supplier of C-components, rising to the status of a respected and qualified equal for its customers.

All these aspired chances of the particular customer integration project have evolved into benefits to the fullest degree.

Schurter had considered risks as well. The slightly dreaded strategic risk of impaired relationships with customers, professed by some team members, has not become effective. The potential disadvantage of depending on the customers' particular views or interests was mainly avoided by the choice of Empathic Design as part of the integration method but also by a very elaborate system of selecting customers.

The remarkable extra time of 100 man-days as only sizeable disbenefit has not impressed the company unduly: the overall risk-benefit balance from the company's ex post point of view is extremely in favor of the benefits, inducing Schurter to repeat customer integration.

Summary

The medium-sized company Schurter with many customers in a global market for mass products has installed a detailed, classical innovation process. The main reasons for integrating customers are access to new knowledge, better market orientation, and the strategic hope of improving its status among its customers. These, suppliers themselves in the electronics branch, are integrated via Empathic Design into the identification of opportunities and ideas. Schurter is very appreciative of the outcome of customer integration in the investigated innovation project.

4.5 Customer integration at Zimmer

4.5.1 Company profile

Introduction and key data

In 1926, Justin O. Zimmer founded the Zimmer Manufacturing Company in Warsaw, Indiana (USA) as a splint manufacturing business. Today Zimmer Holdings, Inc. (Zimmer) is a worldwide leader in the design, development, and marketing of reconstructive orthopedic implants and trauma products. Whereas the headquarters is located in Warsaw, the head office for the European business has been in Winterthur, Switzerland, since 2003.

In the same year, Zimmer acquired Centerpulse, the leading European orthopedics company. The necessary realignments are expected to be over by the end of 2006, leading to an anticipated synergy effect of 70 to 90 million Swiss Francs.

As a consequence of the acquisition of Centerpulse, Zimmer now operates in 24 countries worldwide; the products are sold in more than 80 countries. The company has a global market share of 25% and employs approximately 6,700 employees. The annual turnover amounts to 3.29 billion US Dollar in the year 2005.

Table 4.4. Overview of Zimmer

Headquarters	Warsaw, Indiana (USA) Head office for the European business: Winterthur, Switzerland
Number of sites	7
Number of employees	6,700
Industry/branch	Health care / medical equipment
Products	Surgical and medical instruments for orthopedics, spine, dentures, and traumatology
Range of technology	Mostly high-tech
Position in the market	Innovation leader
Turnover	3.29 billion US Dollar

Products, markets, and customers

Zimmer's products are designed and developed to improve ill or injured patients' quality of life. In the broad field of orthopedics, the company's core business area, its medical implants restore joint function in knees, hips, shoulders, and elbows, just to mention the most important products. In the spine sector, boosted by the acquisition of *Centerpulse*, the products cover implants for damaged spines and intervertebral disks. In the field of dental products, dental implants and products for teeth regeneration play the main role. In addition, the product range encompasses products related to the treatment of traumata. In all fields, Zimmer has secured a position of prime importance with regard to minimal invasive technology.

The four business fields have influenced the company's structure, leading to the respective four divisions:

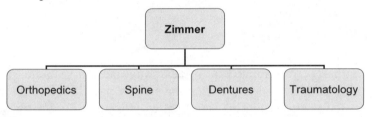

Fig. 4.18. Organization structure at Zimmer

Products are developed at various locations worldwide irrespective of geographical markets but with regard to the particular product demands. Thus, resources can be used in the most efficient way. While this decentralized organization causes higher coordination expenditures, it has the advantages of specializing certain production processes, avoiding redundancies, and making for a well-balanced portfolio.

Zimmer's main markets are U.S.A, Japan, Europe, and Australasia, which is reflected in the corresponding organization of the sales department.

The company's customers are mainly in the B2B sector, e.g large hospitals or health care centers, but also include individual indirect customers, i.e. surgeons who choose implants for their patients.

4.5.2 Innovation process at Zimmer

The entire innovation process at Zimmer follows the life cycle of its products, which leads to a subdivision into eight distinctive phases (0 – 7):

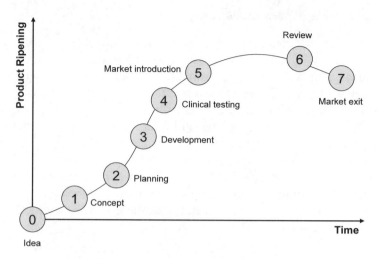

Fig. 4.19. Zimmer's product life cycle

These phases are arranged in a linear way and are separated from the consecutive ones by milestones that have to be passed before the product can enter the next phase. This step-by-step procedure minimizes the risks of new developments and at the same time guarantees product maturity, adequate timing, and cost efficiency. The life span of a product (phases 1 – 7) may extend to 25 years.

The phases "Idea", "Concept", and "Planning" prior to the actual technical New Product Development can be likened to the early innovation phase and will be given special attention.

Phase 0 – Idea: Selecting the best 5 of 100

This phase centers on picking out the best ideas in a specially designed process with the catchword "best 5 of 100".

The phase starts with a person having an idea. This idea, in a written form and, if possible, with a pertinent sketch, is brought to a regional product manager or directly to a manager at the global level. Next, the idea enters an electronic system, the so-called "logbook", where it is given a name. In addition, the author, the date of registration, and the position of the idea within the company's divisions are listed. In a short summary, market potential and possible geographic regions for future use are put down, together with possible risks, necessary resources, and estimated costs for Phase 1. This logbook is the same for Warsaw and Winterthur to ensure identical information for both headquarters and avoid double listing.

The head of the Development department decides on the technical feasibility and possible commercial realization of the registered idea. If he rejects it, it will remain in the logbook. This way, "incoming" ideas can be matched against existing entries to avoid a renewed entry of the same or a very similar idea. The reasons and the date of the rejection will be listed as well. The original provider of the idea will be informed of the rejection within eight weeks, which should encourage him to come back again with new ideas. By this procedure, Zimmer hopes to reach a place among the first three to five enterprises that externs approach with new ideas. In case the idea is accepted, it will be assessed according to its compatibility with the company's strategy.

With a positive respective decision, the idea leaves the definition process and turns into a project. Before this project can enter the following Phase 1, a core team has to be formed with the task of further developing the project. It comprises a product manager, a project leader, and an engineer. As in most cases the project will consist in an implant or a surgical technique with the pertaining instruments, it is imperative to include in addition employees from the departments manufacturing, regulatory, quality, clinical affairs, and logistics as well as medical experts.

Phase 1 – Concept: feasibility investigation

This phase centers on drawing up a "business brief" that ascertains feasibility and realization of the original idea and investigates the prospective gain for the group.

At the beginning, the core team works out detailed project analyses in the fields marketing, development, and production. The product is described with regard to its composition, properties, intended use, and necessary activities.

In the market analysis, the core team investigates which needs the new product will meet and how they are satisfied at present, which market segment will be affected, in which markets the product is to be sold, what will be the actual market size and which market share Zimmer will be able to reach, which competitive advantages will result from the product launch, if comparable products already exist, and how the product will fit with the portfolio.

With the mentioned regard to competitors, the business brief must contain information on their position in comparison to Zimmer, stating if, when and with which technology they will launch competing products.

All information has to state explicitly whether it is based on facts or on assumptions.

The business brief also lists the necessary functional support pertaining to the techniques to be applied, to intellectual property issues, to external expert medical authors, to the division going to be the final producer, and to design control. Additional information is given on cooperation with supervising authorities, stating if clinical tests are necessary and, in case they are, where they will be carried out. With regard to financial aspects, the production plan informs on additional financial investments, standard production costs, and requirements for raw materials. The financial part also presents the most likely scenario with the resulting overall project costs.

The business brief ends with a primary risk analysis, investigating and grading possible risks and relating them to the affected divisions. The very last point is a target - performance analysis of the course the project has taken so far.

The Project Review Board decides on the future fate of the described project. If it is approved, the core project team will be reinforced by suitable experts and will guide the project through the following Phase 2.

Phase 2 – Planning: Detailed planning, description and virtual development

This phase centers on drawing up the final business plan.

It starts with a kick-off meeting of the enlarged project team. Based on the business letter prepared in Phase 1, further investigations with the focus on research, development, prototyping, clinical tests, production, and packaging are carried out. They lead to drafting and designing the product, ending in printouts and mock-ups. A second refined risk analysis, considering the new findings and the models, follows next. The team lays down in which way the product is to be tested, especially if clinical tests are necessary. In case they are, they have to be planned and prepared. If such tests are unnecessary, this has to be documented and recorded. Former clinical tests on identical or similar product types can serve as sufficient proof.

Next, the actual drawing up of the business plan begins.

The business plan is a more comprehensive, more refined and better supported version of the business brief. It contains an additional plan for market introduction and information on preparatory activities with the sales organizations, on training courses for employees and customers, and on necessary time resources.

The business plan also answers strategic questions, e.g. whether Zimmer has to develop new technologies on its own or if it can adopt external ones. Legal conditions – license agreements, intellectual property issues, and contracts with physicians – have to be described as well. In the area of operative strategy, the business plan lays down the exact sales channels.

The business plan, too, ends with a target-performance analysis of the project up to the present.

The final business plan is presented to the Project Review Board that will take the next decision on the project's future before it leaves the early innovation phase. This decision consists in either a logbook entry in case of rejection or in passing the project on to the development phase.

4.5.3 Innovation project: Opportunities for the "female empowered patient"

As with most companies in the medical technology market, Zimmer's customers have primarily been medical companies or surgeons who choose implants and use them on their patients. Widespread information on medical issues - not least due to the Internet – as well as the patients' growing self-confidence and wish to decide on their own on questions pertinent to their health have led to a gradual change in both customer types and product prerequisites. This change is going to become even more pronounced. The "end customers", meaning patients, will have a growing power of decision concerning the selection of implants, doctors, and hospitals. Health insurance companies will influence medical treatment such as the choice of instruments and the type of implants to be used. To meet these future demands and thus keep its strong position in the market, Zimmer tries to adapt at a very early stage to new trends and to a changing environment.

Internal studies have established that self-confident and knowledgeable (="empowered") female patients will play a key role in the future knee and hip implant business, because women are apt to reach a very old age while suffering increasingly from bone problems, e.g. osteoporosis. In addition, it is mostly women that make decisions on health issues for the whole family. Zimmer therefore has decided to investigate opportunities related to female empowered patients.

A project team, consisting of 6 R&D employees doing this job alongside their day-to-day business, is set up under the guidance of a senior director of Development whose presence guarantees the necessary attention and support of the Zimmer management. During their first sessions, the team members study trend analyses and scenarios of the future pertaining to related branches and compare them with the company's strategy and internal studies.

The project team agrees on establishing special trend scenarios with the help of the Pictures of the Future tool (PoF; cf. Appendix A), which is modified according to the special Zimmer situation. For its core element, the workshop with customers, the following specific question is chosen:

"How will female empowered patients experience the process of liberation from pain and from restrictions in the musculoskeletal system in the year 2015?"

This question allows focusing on pain relief and improved mobility from a woman's perspective, paying attention to the dominant role of female patients according to existing trend surveys.

In order to fuel prospective workshop participants' interest in the topic and lead them in the right direction, the project team works out a list of so-called shaping factors that emphasize already known trends. These shaping factors are gathered in trend surveys and scenarios of the future in the course of the starting sessions.

Table 4.5. Shaping factors for Zimmer

• Our population over 65 years is going to increase disproportionately	• Widely globalized and transparent markets give the consumer unprecedented power
• People will spend more money on wellness and beauty	• Focusing on the individual allows and requires responding to the respective patient with all his/her advantages and disadvantages
• Due to their biological structure, women are apt to make disproportionate use of Zimmer's services and products	• It is mostly women that take consumer decisions. Supporting the life-work balance and reducing double taxation is important
• The body mass index (BMI) of our population will increase disproportionately	• In a globalized economy it is imperative to offer services and products worldwide
• Physical and sporting activities are becoming more and more important, especially for older people	• Information on patients and hospitals is mostly digitalized and thus ready to be accessed by anyone anywhere and any time
• Our community is interested in patients staying in hospital as shortly as possible	• The patient-surgeon relationship is based to a high degree on the patient's trust in the adviser.

Having compiled the shaping factors, the project team decides on the time frame for the scenario analysis. Whereas it is comparatively easy to predict developments in the near future, it is difficult for Zimmer to size up trends in ten years' time, especially with regard to market issues. That is why a time focus of 10 years, ending 2015, is chosen.

The exclusive concentration on female patients suggests a respective restriction in the selection of workshop participants, resulting in looking only for women as suitable candidates. In order to consider not only the perspective of patients as end customers but also of indirect customers, the project team decides to include in addition doctors and entrepreneurs wishing to influence their employees' future decisions on health. Furthermore, it is agreed to look for experts such as nurses, physiotherapists, journalists of health magazines, and sociologists. For reasons of manageability and active discussions, the number of participants to be invited to the PoF workshop is limited to 15.

The project team chooses to set up an international but German-speaking group. This way, a possible limitation of future results due to a single national perspective is avoided while all participants can converse in a familiar language on a topic both difficult and partly rather intimate.

As a consequence, it is agreed that the workshop shall consist in equal parts of Austrian, German, and Swiss female participants.

Before actually issuing invitations to the workshop, the project team decides to allocate the future participants to three different groups with the intention to strengthen especially the patients' expression of opinion and to guarantee an equal representation of different perspectives. Accordingly, the invitees are categorized as follows:

Table 4.6. Grouping of workshop participants

Patient	Doctor	Environment
• 4 Patients	• 1 General physician	• 2 Entrepreneurs
• 1 Nurse	• 3 Orthopedists	• 1 Sociologist
	• 1 Physiotherapist	• 1 Journalist

In order to generate objective results, the project team abstains from addressing doctors working with Zimmer on a contract basis. Team members' personal contacts lead to first unofficial meetings with prospective candidates who are asked if they are willing on principle to take part in a workshop. A positive answer is followed by an official invitation. Especially with entrepreneurs, Internet research provides possible candidates as well. In all cases, the personal incentives for the potential participants are stressed: patients are mostly interested in exchanging ideas and getting to know Zimmer, doctors in learning about their patients' needs and about the changes in medical technology, and entrepreneurs in trying out the PoF process. The official invitations purposely do not offer much information on the workshop in order to keep the invitees thrilled; they entail an individual cover letter, a one-page project flyer, and the promise of settling expenses for the journey and the "day off". In addition, participants are asked to sign a non-disclosure agreement.

The night before the official opening of the workshop, the participants are invited to a reception and subsequent dinner, which enables guests and employees to get to know each other, creates a free and easy atmosphere, and gives a first orientation on things to come. This information is kept rather vague to maintain the suspense and avoid a biased start.

Four consecutive modules structure the first workshop day with the external participants. The first module, aptly called "Intro", serves to introduce the goals of the day and the detailed agenda. Modules A and B, concentrating on issues before and during/after treatment, form the middle part, and Module "Closure" constitutes the end of the day, culminating in a visiting tour of Zimmer Winterthur.

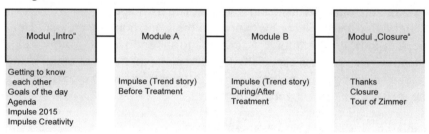

Fig. 4.20. Structure of Zimmer's first workshop

At the beginning of Module "Intro", a Zimmer representative gives a speech on possible trends in 2015 ("impulse 2015"), which are illustrated by large posters with the shaping factors. In order to boost the participants' creativity, the workshop moderator - an extern professional - has them play creativity games.

For the following modules A and B, the participants split up according to the three prearranged categories patient, doctor, and environment. Two Zimmer employees as well as a presenter and a graphical recorder, whose job it is to convert the various contributions to the discussion into pictures, complement each group.

Module A focuses on trends and visions of patients before medical treatment of hips, knees etc., Module B concentrates on trends and visions of patients during and after treatment, both referring to the year 2015. Each module starts with the presenter telling a so-called "impulse" story, which describes a possible scene in 2015. The stories slightly vary in each group according to the participants' respective backgrounds, but basically, they are identical. In Module A, the story contains pre-treatment elements, e.g. Web-based information on therapies and costs, whereas in Module B it is about issues such as hospital rooms or hotels specifying in physiotherapy.

After the story, the participants are asked to write down their spontaneous thoughts on small cards prior to the following discussion. During this discussion, Zimmer employees keep in the background and intervene only if the discussion strays too far away from the topic. The graphic recorder transfers the various contributions into pictures that he pins on a large board in the course of the discussion.

Table 4.7. Example of group contributions

• Supply	• Demand
• Catalogues	• Risk
• Own cell structure	• Implants
• Readiness	• Bedding
• Safe storage of jewelry	•

Modules A and B are interrupted by a lunch break. When Module B is over, the three groups convene and present their respective results – 20 minutes are allowed for each presentation – to the plenary meeting. A discussion of about 15 minutes leads to a cross-comparison of the various findings, ending in a picture that combines the three perspectives.

The final module "Closure" summarizes the preceding modules and acknowledges the customers' and experts' contributions. It ends with Zimmer employees giving a tour of the company's production site before the participants leave with a small gift for their efforts.

The second company-intern part of the workshop takes place the following day. This timing makes sure that memories of the group discussions are still fresh so no important details get lost. The external presenter who headed the first workshop also guides the staff through this day, supported by a graphic recorder. In addition to the R&D members who have taken part in the first workshop with customers, members from the marketing department join this session.

At the beginning of the analysis workshop, the goals of the day – identification of relevant trends and ideas based on the results of the previous day – are presented in the form of a big poster.

The Zimmer employees explain the various group pictures, add small notes of their own, and give reasons why the participants set great store by particular issues and why some points were not included in the final picture. In addition, they describe the atmosphere in the group and its profile.

Based on the thus amended group results of the day before, a new picture incorporates the most interesting aspects (Fig. 4.21. below), leading to an in-depth discussion.

Fig. 4.21. Details of interesting themes

The results of this discussion are clustered; subsequently small groups work out the details of a final graphic presentation. The analyzed possible new business fields are given a graphic form and are integrated into a final Picture of the Future. In this way, the PoF contains both the customers'/experts' original ideas and the employees' identified and analyzed business fields. This PoF is published throughout the worldwide Zimmer group, serving as an input for strategic management and for strategy development and strengthening Zimmer's lead over its competitors. In case more in-depth information is required, Zimmer Winterthur has detailed reports on all developed pictures.

4.5.4 Company assessment of the innovation project

The pilot project has taken up approximately 35 man-days and cost about 60.000 CHF, mainly spent on the external moderator, the graphical recorders, and the participants' expenses for hotel, restaurant, etc.. Future PoF projects are expected to manage with 15-20 man-days.

Zimmer has identified seven new business fields in the context of specially female-orientated medical products, the potential of which cannot be gauged completely and is estimated slightly differently by different company managers. The modified PoF project has served its purpose as an excellent method of customer integration to the company's fullest satisfaction and will be used again in follow-up innovation projects with customers.

4.5.5 Company assessment of customer integration

Zimmer had three benefits of equal importance in mind when embarking on customer integration: getting to know the specific needs of female "empowered" patients (better market orientation), gaining new insider knowledge mainly from doctors and nurses (access to new knowledge), and being first in the race with its competitors to serve this particular market (strategic advantages). According to the company, the first two goals have been reached to a high degree. As for the third, only the future will show if competitors have not been faster; at least the ground for such an advantage has been prepared.

The risks of leakage of knowledge had been taken seriously; due to recognized reducing measures it has not materialized as far as Zimmer can tell. The unavoidable disbenefits of additional time and costs are of minor importance for a company of Zimmer's size.

Altogether, a juxtaposition of risks and benefits leads to Zimmer's positive assessment of customer integration in the innovation project.

Summary

The large medical company Zimmer with numerous customers of various types serves a specialized global market. It possesses a very refined innovation process considering both technical and marketing issues. Customer integration is undertaken with an emphasis on so far not included end customers, i.e. patients. Its main goals are better market orientation, access to new knowledge, and the strategic advantage of keeping ahead of competitors. The integration takes place in mixed workshops. Zimmer considers the integration concept in the particular project as successful.

5 Characteristics of successful early customer integration

The cases presented in chapter 4 have demonstrated how various companies have dealt with customer integration in particular projects that do not necessarily reflect their general procedure regarding this issue. On the contrary, the attribute "pilot", which all investigated companies have bestowed on their projects, indicates that at least the way of including customers was a novel experience.

The empirical insights gathered in the case studies serve a dual purpose: to test propositions and to build new theories (cf. chapter 1.4), relying on the methods recommended by Eisenhardt (1989). In order to answer the research questions with the exception of the last one (c.f. 1.3.1), they will be analysized by way of a cross-case comparison, thus validating or refuting the propositions of chapter 3 (cf. 3.5). Second, they will serve to extend existing theory on the value of customer integration. For the first purpose (5.1 below), the analysis model developed in chapter 3 will guide the evaluation of the empirical results; the second goal (5.2 below) is to be reached by looking for determinants that influence the value of customer integration. Both research goals are to be attained by reflecting theoretical constructs not only against the outcome of the case studies but also against empirical findings within mini-cases.

Finally, the theoretical implications of combining existing theory and newly gathered empirical insights (cf. Eisenhardt 1989; Yin 1994) will be discussed, shaping a conceptual model of a risk-benefit assessment that may predict the success or failure of an envisaged integration project.

5.1 Cross-case analysis

As mentioned above, the case studies were presented in a chronological and logical order that still tried to consider the issues raised in the analysis model. These will be analyzed under the additional perspective of overall valid characteristics of advisable, i.e. probably successful, customer integration, thus meeting the demands on internal validity and possibility of generalization (cf. Eisenhardt 1989). The propositions will be tested in the course of the cross-case analysis, following the structure below:

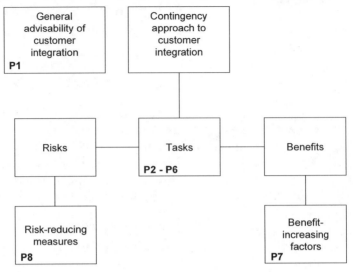

Fig. 5.1. Inducing hypotheses from propositions via cross-case analysis

5.1.1 General advisability of customer integration

The concept of customer integration as a foregone conclusion or a general strategic decision can only be upheld if projects with customers always compare favorably, if to varying degrees, to in-house innovation projects or projects with external experts.

To put it differently: customer integration is generally advisable if it automatically guarantees success, a prevalent belief that is summarized in the words of a *Buechi* manager: "The reason why we integrate customers into innovation projects is simple: success" (cf. Sandmeier 2006: 101).

In order to analyze the case studies with regard to this particular issue, the companies' individual assessments of the integration success are compared, forming the basis for future general or particular integration projects.

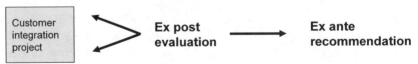

Fig. 5.2. Conclusion on the advisability of customer integration

Gallus, according to its ex post assessment of customer integration, is highly appreciative of the customers' input into the innovation project; they helped identify six new ideas or functionalities and did not cause any problems or undue expenditure in the process.

From an outsider's impartial perspective, too, customer integration proves to be successful. A future integration project, already envisaged by Gallus, indicates that customer integration is an advisable option for the company.

Schindler is disappointed with the outcome of the company's particular integration project, not having gained any new insights or other benefits. Compared to mere in-house identification of opportunities or ideas, customer integration does not make any difference: the customers only confirmed what Schindler had identified before. Irrespective of the reason(s) for this failure to come up with innovative contributions, it remains to be stated that customer integration, while not causing disbenefits worth mentioning, has not automatically added value. However, Schindler has expressed the wish to go on integrating customers in Trend Team workshops.

Schurter, having discovered seven new product ideas with their customers' help and seeing itself in a better position and reputation among its clients, is extremely satisfied with the outcome of customer integration, even in view of considerable time costs. External evaluation of Schurter's customer integration in the particular project backs the company's intention to repeat customer integration in future projects because for Schurter the concept paid off.

Zimmer looks back on the integration project with satisfaction. In retrospect, the concept appears successful, having led to the identification of various new business fields, if of unforeseeable value. The benefits are higher in comparison to the disbenefits, which consist in rather impressive additional costs and time. With a positive risk-benefit balance in the pilot project, Zimmer will go on integrating customers in future innovation projects.

Table 5.1. Overall satisfaction with customer integration (c.i.)

Companies:	**Gallus**	**Schindler**	**Schurter**	**Zimmer**
Characteristics:				
Satisfaction with c.i.	++	0	++	+

++ = very high,   + = high,   0 = indifferent

In summary, the analysis shows that the positive aspects of customer integration do not always prevail: in one case (Schindler), customer integration had neither positive nor negative overall results. Whereas this comparison does not back the general, unrestricted recommendation of customer integration as best practice, it does not appear conclusive, either, to disprove the general advisability just because of one exception. That is why further empirical evidence via mini-cases is necessary to validate or refute Proposition P1 on the general advisability of customer integration.

Throughout the year 2004, ten companies (BASF, Getzner Werkstoffe, Helbling Technik, Henkel, Infoterra, KABA, Merck, Schindler and SIGallCap) met for consecutive workshops on issues related to early customer integration. The companies had all had vast experience with the concept but had more or less all met with negative integration results at one project or another. Their partial dissatisfaction with customer integration was a major trigger for this research. Some companies (e.g. Henkel, Merck, Infoterra, and SIGallCap) complained of major disadvantages such as leakage of knowledge that questioned future integration projects; others had minor misgivings about follow-up integration projects because of prior disappointments with the concept.

While for many companies integrated customers increased the success of innovative activities, for others customer integration did not make a change compared to company-intern innovation or even proved to have overall negative results. This last outcome occurred at SIGallCAP:

The Swiss company SIG offers solutions for the packaging of solid and liquid foods worldwide. SIGallCAP, part of the business unit Combibloc, develops systems and material for the production of beverage boxes. It integrates randomly chosen B2B customers in workshops on generating ideas and on developing concepts for innovative packaging. Such a customer, after jointly identifying a very promising idea and developing the respective business plan, took the acquired know-how to a competitor of SIGallCAP's. The two of them developed the final product together before SIGallCAP could do so, thus strengthening the competitor's market position at SIGallCAP's expense and destroying the company's own innovative success.

These empirical findings, in addition to the ambiguous results of the case studies, demonstrate that the involvement of customers in the innovation process does not automatically lead to success in comparison to in-house activities, it may even lead to worse results than innovation with company staff only.

Thus, the case studies and the mini-case back Proposition P1, transforming it into a hypothesis:

H1:
Customer integration does not necessarily add value to the innovation process.

5.1.2 Tasks

In the following section, the Propositions P2-P6, all related to tasks, will be validated or refuted by way of the cross-case analysis.

Innovation process

The case studies have revealed that innovations are essential for all investigated companies as the means of maintaining a leading position in the respective branches. The importance the four companies attach to innovations is reflected in the mostly very detailed and refined innovation processes they have implemented.

Gallus is the one exception within this group, having an undocumented individual process model that is only remotely similar to established process structures. The identification of both opportunities and ideas is concentrated in one workshop per year, whereas the respective selection and concept definition is the subject of a second yearly workshop. Contrary to the other investigated companies' innovation processes, the Gallus model has no special testers/"gate keepers" or test procedures at various points in time or at different development stages; it is the same management team that makes biannual decisions on the innovation project. However, milestones have to be met by the innovative product in its early form. Prototype testing is not included in the early innovation phase.

In comparison, Schindler's technology development process is very elaborate, regulating in pictorial and written instructions every technical and temporal detail of the early innovation phase, called "study process" (cf. 4.3.2). The process resembles the Development Funnel by Wheelwright and Clark (see 2.2.2) not only in the graphic representation but also in the way it is structured. Opportunity identification and selection take place in Technology Monitoring, CTI, Trend Teams, and Technology workshops; ideas are identified in special workshops, and their final selection as well as the pertaining concept definition is allocated to high-ranking managers.

The engineering of prototypes, which includes testing, is also part of this process structure.

Schurter has installed an innovation process that can be likened to the Front End Model by Khurana and Rosenthal (cf. 2.2.2). Just as in their model, two input streams feed the Schurter process: Product Requests, which represents the external, market-induced stream, and PIN, the company-intern innovation motor (cf. 4.4.2). These two streams cover the activities of identification, selection, concept definition, and prototype building/testing.

Zimmer, like Schindler, relies on an innovation process that regulates every step down to the smallest detail. The Zimmer process structure is almost a perfect copy of Cooper's Stage Gate Process (cf. 2.2.2), having distinct, consecutive stages (Zimmer's phases) that are separated from each other by gates (Zimmer's milestones, cf. 4.5.2). Each phase contains in itself various stages and gates. The different Zimmer phases comprise idea identification and selection as well as concept definition; opportunity identification, not mentioned in the written model, has been newly introduced into the innovation process by the pilot project, the modified PoF. Prototypes, in a medical branch, necessarily take on other forms than mock-ups etc.; the respective testing is replaced by clinical tests according to general regulations.

Table 5.2. Characteristics of the different innovation processes

Companies:	Gallus	Schindler	Schurter	Zimmer
Characteristics:				
Innovation process	Individual arrangement: biannual workshops on innovation issues and monitoring/corrective actions in between	Development Funnel (Wheelwright and Clark)	Front End Model (Khurana and Rosenthal)	Stage Gate Process (Cooper)

The comparison of the four innovation processes shows that all investigated companies have structured their individual processes in completely different ways: there are not even two cases with similar process structures. However, all companies, in one way or another, perform the tasks of identifying and selecting opportunities and ideas, of defining a pertinent concept, and, within or after their early innovation phase, of building and testing prototypes.

The qualitative empirical research of the case study analysis therefore supports Proposition P2, creating the following hypothesis:

> **H2:**
>
> Certain tasks occur in the course of every innovation process irrespective of the concrete process structure.

Investigated tasks and customer integration

The case study research at Gallus encompassed the company's activities from opportunity identification to idea selection. Gallus has identified and selected the trend of industrialization in the printing branch without external support. The pilot project centers on identifying innovative ideas with customers via Empathic Design and interviews, whereas the final analysis and selection of ideas to be pursued are carried out within the company, relying on QFD (cf. 4.2.3).

With Schindler, the case study research comprised the tasks of opportunity and idea/functionality identification and of selection (cf. 4.3.3). The identification of European trends in the elevator branch is combined with the identification of suitable functions to meet these trends; both activities rely on the integration of customers in workshops with the additional methodological support of the handshake analysis. As with Gallus, the final selection of trends and pertinent functionalities is, as with Gallus, up to the company management.

The Schurter case study also contains empirical research on the identification and selection of opportunities and ideas. Schurter integrates customers via Empathic Design (CAT) in both identification tasks (cf. 4.4.3); the respective analysis and selection is the job of CAT teams and top management.

The Zimmer case study is the only one where research and results were restricted to the identification and selection of opportunities, leaving aside ideas / functionalities. Zimmer includes customers into its trend investigation with the help of workshops and the technical support of the modified PoF method (cf. 4.5.4). Analysis and selection of the thus identified trends are left, once again, to company staff.

Table 5.3. Characteristics of tasks and methods

Companies:	Gallus	Schindler	Schurter	Zimmer
Characteristics:				
Investigated tasks and customer integration	O. Identification – O. Selection – I. Identification + I. Selection –	O. Identification + O. Selection – I. Identification + I. Selection –	O. Identification + O. Selection – I. Identification + I. Selection –	O. Identification + O. Selection –
Integration methods	Lead User method Empathic Design (Process analysis)	Workshops Trend Team model	Empathic Design Lead User method CAT	Workshops Modified PoF

The common denominator for all investigated tasks and pertaining integration activities is that the companies have not integrated customers into the innovation process as a whole but into a specific task or, at most, into two ones (identification of both opportunities and ideas with Schindler and Schurter). Accordingly, the risks and benefits of customer integration can only become effective in the respective task and do not influence "the" early innovation phase altogether. This finding supports Proposition P3, again creating a hypothesis:

H3:

Risks and benefits of customer integration pertain to the particular task customers are involved in.

The cross-case comparison of innovation tasks with customer integration has brought another result: all investigated companies, while integrating customers in various identification projects, refrain from doing so when the analysis/selection of opportunities or ideas is concerned. This qualitative finding validates Proposition P5 and leads to the hypothesis below:

H5:

The selection task is a company's own business.

Knowledge creation management

Within all four companies, knowledge creation in the sense described in chapter 2.4 is not a particular issue. They are all interested in concrete results in the form of opportunities or ideas and not in knowledge for knowledge's sake.

The management of the newly gained or already existing knowledge differs from one company to another:

Gallus, as far as could be established, does not have a special knowledge management.

Schindler has implemented a refined knowledge management system that is separate from the innovation process. It consists of an Idea and Invention Management platform, a so-called "Who's Who" Databank, and a "Key Know-how Holder and Skills Management" (cf. 4.3.2).

With Schurter, knowledge management is part of the INNOVA/ idea pool process (cf. 4.4.2); newly gained knowledge is stored in a special internal databank (cf. 4.4.3)

Zimmer, for knowledge management purposes, has installed a very elaborate electronic system called "logbook" that stores down to the tiniest detail ideas (= knowledge) in whichever form, from the first embryonic suggestion past rejected ideas, which may prove useful later on, to the accepted ones. This management, although closely linked to the innovation process (cf. 4.5.2), is a separate unit, being the first and last place for ideas.

The cross-case analysis shows two things: First, knowledge creation is an immanent part of the investigated innovation task, and second, the way knowledge management is implemented suggests that customers are not even remotely considered useful for this task.

These findings back Propositions 4 and 6, giving them the status of hypotheses:

H4:
Knowledge creation is an essential element of all innovation activities and not a phase or task of its own.
H6:
Customer integration in knowledge management is not advisable.

5.1.3 Benefit-increasing factors

Theoretical research has suggested that various established success factors pertaining to New Product Development in general also have an additional

positive effect on customer integration in particular when specifically adapted to this issue
(cf. 3.3.2):

With Gallus, the recommended *strong support of senior management* applies not only to the company's innovation activities as a whole but also to customer integration. The top managers all have *close personal relationships* with the comparatively few customers and even actively participate in contacting them, which increases the customers' motivation to be integrated into the envisaged innovation project. In addition, the management support leads to the employees' identifying themselves with the integration activities to a very high degree.

Gallus also involves *employees of both technology and marketing departments* in jointly selecting the trend of industrialization in the printing branch for its innovative activities with customers and in picking out progressive buyers/lead users as customers for the Empathic Design scrutiny.

Learning from past experience consists in falling back on constantly updated special customer lists. An individual success factor for the New Product Development at Gallus is the *strong orientation on the economic benefits for the customers* and an *analysis of the needs along the whole value chain*, which furthers a fruitful cooperation between company and customers. While not having a detailed process structure, Gallus measures progress against *milestones*.

At Schindler, the so-called *human factors* play an important role. An unofficial lunch before the actual start of the workshop induces a friendly atmosphere and furthers a good "chemistry" among workshop participants; in addition, an introductory lecture prepares the ground for creative thoughts and associations. Special attention is given to Schindler's staff conversing with customers in the workshops (cf. 4.3.3). The Trend Teams, guiding the workshops with the customers, provide a perfect example for the *collaboration of marketing and development departments* because they have the express purpose of combining both views via respective staff members.

With its detailed process structure, Schindler has specific rules on *monitoring and reporting the progress* of innovation / integration activities.

Schurter has perfected the success factor of close *collaboration between technology and marketing departments*. It starts with innovation management being the result of constant interaction between the respective departments (cf. 4.4.2), goes on with the joint compilation of application portfolios by cross-functional teams, and ends with mixed company teams for the CAT visits at the customers' sites. *Senior management commitment* primarily consists in pushing innovative activities with customers by granting the necessary resources.

Learning from past experience can be seen in updating the customer portfolios for future use. As for *monitoring progress*, Schurter employees have to fill in special forms for analyzing their findings on particular components (cf. 4.4.3).

Zimmer has displayed *senior management commitment* by appointing a senior director as head of the project team, thus showing the importance the top management attaches to the envisaged activities with customers. *Human factors* are given high priority: the choice of only German-speaking participants to facilitate conversations in their native language among each other and with experts about intimate details displays sensitivity, and a special night with reception and dinner before the official opening helps create a familiar atmosphere. The *involvement of both technology and marketing departments* is reduced to the last company-intern workshop; up to that point, R&D members have carried out the integration project.

That attribution of clear *responsibilities / milestones* to monitor progress is perfected in the very elaborate Zimmer process structure.

Table 5.4. Benefit-increasing factors of the case study companies

Companies: Characteristics:	Gallus	Schindler	Schurter	Zimmer
Senior management commitment	++	++	-	++
Involvement of both R&D and marketing	++	++	++	+
Human factors	+	++	-	++
Learning from past experience	+	-	+	-
Clear responsibilities / monitoring progress	+	+	+	+
Focus on customer benefits and on needs along the whole value chain	+	-	-	-

All case studies have revealed that certain general success factors, adapted to the special demands of customer integration, help induce or increase the success of innovative activities with customers, going beyond technical aspects such as integration method or customer type.

Thus, the empirical findings validate Proposition P7, leading to Hypothesis H7:

> **H7:**
>
> Specifically adapted general success factors for New Product Development can increase the overall value of benefits.

5.1.4 Risk-reducing measures

Gallus pays special attention to a *careful customer selection*. Customers are listed in a buyer list that indicates which ones have ordered the most advanced types of printing machines and therefore can be considered as progressive lead users. In addition, these customers are rated in a regular basis according to various criteria. The choice of the "right" customers among the thus established possible integration candidates is influenced to a high degree by the long-standing and close relationships with the owners of the customer companies.

As for the risks of *biased results* and *leakage of knowledge*, Gallus chooses the Empathic Design method of integration, which, due to its nature, minimizes the customers' influence on the company-drawn conclusions from the watching process and leads to a one-way knowledge spillover from customer to company.

Schindler *selects its customers*, as far as possible, with regard to existing personal contacts, which are considerably less close than the respective Gallus contacts. A mix of customers with different backgrounds avoids *the risk of biased results due to special views or interests*, which is a common potential consequence of customer integration in workshops. Schindler chooses architects and contractors for its Trend Team workshops, thus preventing a domination of particular interests and views. Architects as indirect users and the involved customers' general qualification as lead users reduce the risk of *biased results due to limited experience*.

Schindler has all integrated customers sign non-disclosure agreements, which reduces, but not always prevents, the *risk of leakage of knowledge*.

Schurter, comparable to Gallus, relies on a very elaborate system of *customer selection*: special customer evaluation tables and customer portfolios (cf. 4.4.3) that are updated annually lead to the choice of customers best suited to Lead User or Empathic Design projects.

As with Gallus, the chosen integration method of CAT is predominantly a variation of the Empathic Design method, which means that *leakage of knowledge* is avoided. As far as *biased results* are concerned, the interviews – which unlike watching the customers at their sites might reflect personal views, interests, or experience – comprise so many different companies that a possible bias is minimized by comparatively big numbers (cf. 3.3.2).

Zimmer, similar to Schindler, does not have a special procedure of evaluating and selecting customers/patients. Personal contacts are a preferred selection criterion, but the company also resorts to Internet research on finding entrepreneurs as indirect customers. In comparison to the other investigated companies, the *careful selection of customers* is less pronounced. With the special project of identifying female-oriented opportunities, possibly "biased" results due to peculiar views and interests appear more desired than unwanted. Again, the careful mix of workshop participants with different backgrounds prevents a particular participant's too strong influence. As far as the integrated patients can be likened to "normal" customers, their limited experience ("functional fixedness") is counteracted by the inclusion of doctors and nurses as experienced "indirect" customers.

Leakage of knowledge is reduced by non-disclosure agreements that work as long as the workshop participants honor them.

Table 5.5. Risk-reducing measures within the case study companies

Companies: Characteristics:	Gallus	Schindler	Schurter	Zimmer
Risk-reducing measures	Careful customer selection Empathic Design method	Careful customer selection Mix of customers Lead user integration Non-disclosure agreements	Careful customer selection CAT-method Comparatively big numbers of integrated customers	Personal contacts Careful customer selection Mix of customers Non-disclosure agreements

In summary, all investigated companies adopt, though in various ways and to various degrees, several recommended risk-reducing measures. In all cases, the respective risks have not materialized into disadvantages (however, leakage of knowledge is difficult to establish in a short time frame).

Altogether, the empirical findings of the case studies back proposition P8, creating the final hypothesis H8.

> **H8:**
>
> Risk-reducing measures and their possible effects change the impact of risks.

5.2 Determinants for successful customer integration

The cross-case analysis of the previous section 5.1 has validated all propositions of Chapter 3: Hypothesis 1, claiming the change of paradigm from customer integration as a generally recommendable concept to a situational concept based on contingency factors, and Hypotheses 2 – 8, related to just these factors.

Still, a further analysis of the findings in the case studies may yield patterns that indicate archetypes of companies for which customer integration is likely to be advisable, leading, if not to a generally valid concept, to predominantly valid typologies or at least to contingency factors. Again, the companies' ex post assessment of the integration projects serves as basis for respective conclusions.

5.2.1 Size of the integrating company

The four investigated companies were chosen for the case studies with special regard to their divergent size (cf. 4.1).

Table 5.6. Size of the case study companies

Companies:	Gallus	Schindler	Schurter	Zimmer
Characteristics:				
Employees	510	40.385	1.118	6.700
Turnover	207 million CHF	8.870 billion CHF	156.9 million CHF	4.15 billion CHF

Schindler and Zimmer are both big companies with considerable human and financial resources; Gallus and Schurter both belong to the upper section of small businesses, the first one having fewer employees, but higher turnover than the other.

The two smaller businesses Gallus and Schurter are very satisfied with their respective customer integration, as is Zimmer, if a little bit less so. Schindler, by far the biggest company, does not see an overall positive effect of its integration activities. These findings seem to imply that small companies tend to profit more by customer integration than bigger ones.

However, as Zimmer and Schindler share the characteristic of big size, but differ in the outcome of customer integration, this dimension does not appear conclusive for the advisability of including customers. Besides, Schindler has had prior positive experience with customer integration in other projects and therefore is willing to try the concept again, which also indicates that size is not a determinant of successful customer integration.

Empirical research outside the case studies backs this conclusion:

Infoterra, a small start-up company with 25 employees (per end of 2004) and a prospective turnover of 30-40 mill. € per 2006, operates in the branch of geoinformation. The company, a participant of

a workshop on customer integration (cf. 5.1.1), has had negative ex-
periences with customer integration. BASF, a very large global
company in the chemical industry and another participant, is overall
satisfied with the integration results.

These additional findings seemingly link small size with dissatisfaction
and big size with success, which does not agree with the results of the case
studies and with common sense. The expressly chosen divergent characteristic of size on compiling the selection criteria for the case study participants therefore does not determine the outcome of customer integration.

5.2.2 Identical selection criteria as determinants

The identical characteristics, apparently relevant determinants of possibly
successful customer integration that influenced the case study participants'
selection (cf. 4.1) cannot explain the mixed results either. Schindler and
Zimmer with almost identical typical parameters such as global status, innovation leader, B2B integration, and manufacturing industry, come to a
very different assessment of their innovation projects with customers. Further externally recognizable factors – integration method or type of integrated customers – are similar as well: both companies have included lead
users and indirect customers in workshops without having comparable results.

Mini-cases point in the same direction, but from a different perspective:

Ravensburger Spiele GmbH, a medium-sized producer of all kinds
of games (puzzles, card games, parlor games etc.), integrates all
kinds of customers – parents, teachers, nursery school staff, ran-
domly chosen consumers, and children (the latter mostly via Em-
pathic Design) – in selecting a type of game among a set pre-
selected by the company (idea selection), in choosing a title (a typi-
cal customer contribution during concept definition), and in test-
ing=playing with prototype games. Ravensburger's main purposes,
better market orientation and access to new ideas, have so far been
reached to the company's full satisfaction.

BMW, a large car manufacturer, tests cars via Empathic Design
with a company employee accompanying and watching a normal
user on test-drives. In addition, the company integrates lead users
via IT-based tools and in workshops and relies on both B2B and
B2C integration. This company, too, has been satisfied with cus-
tomer integration.

While partly differing, partly agreeing in parameters of integration, both companies come to similar results. This backs the empirical finding of the case studies that there are **n o   a r c h e t y p e s** of companies that per se indicate a lower or higher advisability of customer integration. Just as Hypothesis 1 suggests that customer integration is not generally advisable, these findings suggest that every company has to consider on its own, irrespective of general attributes it may share with other companies, if customer support will be advisable or not. The same company may find customer integration worthwhile in one project and useless or even detrimental in another one. Accordingly, it remains to be investigated whether the case studies at least yield some patterns that help predict the success of customer integration for a particular project.

5.2.3 Contingency factor of dependence on customers

While there are no dimensions defining typologies of companies for which customer integration generally appears advisable or not, some other characteristics may serve as contingency factors for successful customer integration in single cases.

Table 5.7. Customers and markets of the case study companies

Companies: Characteristics:	Gallus	Schindler	Schurter	Zimmer
Customers	Comparatively few, mostly family-owned companies	Construction firms, architects, operators of airports or hospitals	Manufacturers and suppliers of technical products and computer equipment	Hospitals, health care centers, surgeons
Market	Global niche market for high quality machines	Global market for high-tech mass products	Global market of electronic mass C-components	Global market partly for niche, partly for mass medical products

Gallus serves a niche market for very specialized high quality machines. As the number of buyers is comparatively limited, Gallus depends to a very high degree on the customers' satisfaction with its products and, as a consequence, on the knowledge of its customers' needs and wishes. Also, the customers' know-how regarding the Gallus machines and their interfaces with other printing machines and equipment is vital for the company's search for innovative ideas. With regard to the identification task, the dependence on customers' knowledge is extreme; with the envisaged collaboration with one customer in technical project definition, for example, or in prototype testing it may be less crucial.

Schindler is a supplier of a huge market of high-tech moving equipment with numerous customers of all kinds. With an almost immeasurable amount of actual and potential customers, Schindler is able to get a basic access to customer needs and wishes via normal market research and the usual trend investigation means (cf. 3.2.1). In respect of the identification task, the company's dependence on customer knowledge is moderate; with prototype testing, for example, it is likely to be more pronounced.

Schurter, according to the company's own assessment, is a rather low-ranking supplier of C-components in a mass market for electrical and electronic equipment. Most of its customers do not consider Schurter as an equal partner in the supply chain. In order to improve this standing by gaining special insight of the customers' needs and wishes, Schurter, as much as Gallus, depends on its customers' information and cooperation, at least as far as the identification task is concerned. It is unlikely that this dependence is as high in other tasks.

Zimmer, compared to the other companies, serves a mixed kind of market: its numerous varied medical implants for B2B/indirect customers can be considered as mass products, whereas the envisaged products for female patients with their special needs will be niche products at least at present and in the near future. In the context of this niche market, Zimmer depends to a high degree on its customers', especially the direct customers' = female patients' knowledge, above all with regard to identifying pertinent business fields and respective ideas.

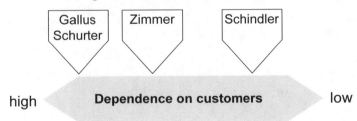

Fig. 5.3. The case study companies' dependence on customers in the identification task

The different degrees of dependence on customers (very high with Gallus and Schurter, high to very high with Zimmer, and moderate with Schindler) are possibly reflected in the benefits the companies have derived via customer integration:

Table 5.8. Benefits for the case study companies

Companies:	Gallus	Schindler	Schurter	Zimmer
Characteristics:				
Derived benefits				
Better market orientation	++	0 = confirmed own assessment	++	++
Access to new knowledge	++	-	++	+
Strategic advantages	discovery of future cooperation partners improved status with customers	-	customers' interest in future cooperation	competitive lead

In comparison, both Gallus and Schurter have gained many benefits by their respective projects with integrated customers, Zimmer slightly less, and Schindler none but for the confirmation of its own judgment of market orientation.

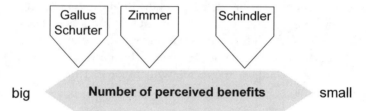

Fig. 5.4. Positive results of the companies' customer integration

A combination of Fig. 5.3. and Fig. 5.4. shows the following correlation:

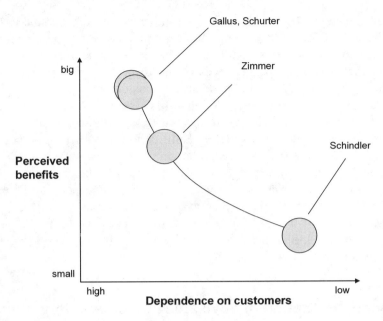

Fig. 5.5. Perceived benefits versus dependence on customers

This leads to an additional hypothesis, created by the combination of the empirical case study research and own theoretical deductions:

H 9:

The more companies depend on their customers' knowledge, the more benefits they tend to gain by customer integration.

The contingency factor of dependence on customers for certain innovation tasks therefore is a decisive characteristic of successful customer integration with regard to the benefit side of a risk-benefit balance.

As for the perceived disbenefits, all companies have listed additional time and costs for their innovations with customers; other possible risks have not come true.

Table 5.9. Additional time and costs for the case study companies

Companies:	Gallus	Schindler	Schurter	Zimmer
Characteristics:				
Additional time	35 man-days	20 man-days	100 man-days	35 man-days
Additional costs	20.000 CHF	5.000 CHF	10.000 CHF	60.000 CHF

The difference in these disbenefits (Schindler has by far the smallest in size, Schurter and Zimmer have the highest ones, if in different characteristics, and Gallus takes up a middle position) can only be attributed to the particular methods and circumstances of the respective pilot projects (cf. 4.2-5) and not to the degree of dependence on customers.

From an ex ante position, the possible other risks (cf. 2.4.2), e.g. biased results or leakage of knowledge, follow customer integration as such: a customer's exotic views may turn the identification into a wrong direction, another one may trade the knowledge he gained in the innovation process to a competitor, or a third one may misuse his power to the company's detriment, no matter if the integration was imperative for reasons of dependence on customers or just an added source of information.

The realization of the risks depends on the success or failure of risk-reducing measures and is not defined in advance by the degree of dependence on customers.

5.3 Conceptualization of advisable customer integration

On building theory from case studies, it is necessary to link determining factors emerging from empirical research to existing theory (Eisenhardt 1989). With the focus on the companies' dependence on customers as the major contingency factor, the Resource Dependence Theory is the obvious choice.

5.3.1 Overview of the Resource Dependence Theory

The Resource Dependence Theory, rooted in the open systems perspective of organization theory (Scott 1992), has influenced scientific research into external influence on organizations (Hatch 1997). It has its origin in Pfeffer and Salancik's by now classic work "The External Control of Organizations", published in 1978. With this provocative title the authors wanted to emphasize their main point that the environment is a powerful constraint on organizational action (Hatch 1997). The organization's dependence on the environment is the result of its need for resources, e.g. raw materials, labor, knowledge, or outlets for its products or services (Hatch 1997). However, organizations need not tolerate this dependence in a passive way (Scott 1992); they will seek to reduce it. The success of this strategy is critical for the organizational survival (Casciaro and Piskorski 2005).

In the effort of successfully "navigating the harsh seas of environmental domination" (Hatch 1997: 78), the organization has to determine the degree of its dependence on a resource. Three factors influence this degree (Gruner and Homburg 2000): The first one is the importance of the resource for the organization's purposes. Resources are estimated critical when they are indispensable for the organization's functioning, e.g. beef is critical for McDonald's but drinking straws are not (Hatch 1997: 80). The second factor is the availability of a resource, depending on alternatives of supply. The dependence grows when a resource is scarce, for example gold or platinum in contrast to air or as yet water (Hatch 1997: 80). The third influencing factor is the extent to which the resource owner has discretion over its allocation and use (Gruner and Homburg 2000): if it is up to the owner to grant access to the resource, the company depends on his good will and has to comply with his demands. It goes without saying that resources that are both critical and scarce and with which the owner can do as he pleases create the highest level of dependence or constraint.

Resource Dependence Theory holds that organizations will develop ways to reduce their dependence on resources with a variety of tactics. The easiest, if not always feasible, strategy, called buffering, is to reduce constraint by increasing a company's tolerance of external resource shortage over a limited period of time (Scott 2003). Reducing the interest in the valued resource (Casciaro and Piskorski 2005) – impossible with critical resources –, cultivating alternative or multiple resources (Hatch 1997) – difficult with scarce resources –, adjusting workflow to minimize variations in input and output requirements, increasing stock levels, and forecasting resource needs in order to adjust the production scale accordingly (Scott 2003) are buffering methods of choice.

In most cases, however, it will be necessary to seek cooperation with the resource owner (Gruner and Homburg 2000), trying to mitigate the constraint and creating, if possible, counter dependence (Scott 1992). Dependence can be lessened or avoided by merger strategies or by competitor strategies. Other strategies include developing personal relationships with the resource owner or establishing formal ties, e.g. taking up membership on the resource owner's board or inviting him to sit on the organization's one (Hatch 1997). All these strategies, in contrast to buffering strategies, have been termed "bridging" strategies (Scott 1992) because they bridge the gulf between organization and resource owner. Constraint absorption is the highest level of bridging strategy: it entails conferring the right to the resource on the dependent actor/organization (Casciaro and Piskorski 2005).

Conceptually, Resource Dependence Theory is viewed as dealing with the problems of uncertainty (Gruner and Homburg 2000) with regard to the flow of needed resources (Casciaro and Piskorski 2005).

5.3.2 Linking Resource Dependence Theory with customer integration

Even at a cursory glance, there is a striking resemblance between the problems Resource Development Theory tries to solve and those concerning customer integration.

The actors

Resource Dependence Theory boils down to investigating conflicts over a resource an organization needs and somebody else owns. Whereas there is no need to explain that a company intent on customer integration is an organization, it does seem necessary to have a closer look at the resource and its owner respectively.

Resources are defined as physical, informational, either tangible or intangible raw materials provided for use in transformation or production processes (De Greene 1973). Natural resources, capital, ideas, and information are examples of such materials (Lengnick-Hall 1996). In the context of this study, customer knowledge in general and information on customer needs and user experiences in particular fit this description (Gruner and Homburg 2000). The customers, as knowledge carriers, are the resource owners in the light of Resource Dependence Theory.

Degree of dependence

For developing innovative products, companies depend to various degrees on customer knowledge and information (as is shown by Gallus, Schindler, Schurter, and Zimmer). This dependence is determined by all three influencing factors (see 5.3.1).

For Gallus, the knowledge its customers can supply with regard to their needs and to technical application is close to critical. As Gallus has relatively few customers, the resource customer knowledge is scarce. The customers, who so far have regarded Gallus as a mere supplier and not as a provider of solutions (cf. 4.2.3), do not have to cooperate with Gallus for reasons of their own – although they will profit from collaboration products – which gives them at least a considerable amount of discretion over their resource "knowledge". Altogether, the influencing factors of Resource Dependence Theory are in accordance with the empirical findings of the Gallus case study in concluding that the company depends to the highest degree on its customers.

For Schindler, customer knowledge in the identification task is welcome, but not to the degree of criticality. Schindler obviously can identify new opportunities without customers; otherwise, the customers' confirmations of the company's own assessment of market needs would not have been possible. With the huge number of customers, the resource is far from being scarce. However, all customers, even if they badly want or need "customized" moving equipments, can easily turn to the comparatively many global competitors (cf. 4.3.3), which gives the resource owners a high degree of discretion. In summary, Resource Dependence Theory backs the deduction from the case study that Schindler only moderately depends on its customers.

Schurter, by the standards of Resource Dependence Theory, is faced by an almost critical need of customer knowledge for strategic reasons: only if it can customize its products according to the clients' wishes can it hope to survive in the competitive race and keep its position as a market leader for C-components. In view of the customer lists (cf. 4.4.3), Schurter seems to be able to choose among comparatively many resource owners, which indicates an at least moderate availability of the resource. In contrast, the customers' discretion is very high: they are free to decline the invitation of integration and or cooperate with competitors. The three influencing factors confirm the empirical deduction of Schurter's high dependence on its customers.

For Zimmer, with its project of the "female empowered patient" customer knowledge is critical as far as female patients are concerned: who but these customers can supply information on typically feminine medical needs? Scarcity of the resource, on the other hand, is not an issue because many women meet the required attributes of well-informed and demanding patients. These women's discretion over the resource, i.e. their free choice to agree or not to agree to customer integration, is unlimited in theory but moderately reduced in practice due to their expected profit from innovative medical products. Altogether, Zimmer's dependence on customers, defined by the theory's influencing factors, is high.

Buffering or bridging strategies

In the perspective of Resource Dependence Theory, customer integration is the perfect example of how to counteract constraint up to the point of total constraint absorption.

Risk-reducing and benefit-increasing measures as well as many integration methods more or less reflect the strategies suggested by Resource Dependence Theory (cf. Hatch 1997: 80). This applies, for example, to "establishing multiple sources of supply" as primary buffering strategy: by relying on many rather than on few customers, companies can lessen their possibly misleading influence. "Developing personal relationships" is also a benefit-increasing factor for integration activities (see 3.3.2), which Gallus, for instance, has perfected. "Establishing formal ties" is done, for example, by appointing lead users to members of the multifunctional team (see 3.2.2), by giving them a long-term function in creativity centers, or by employing them as managers in core technology units.

Special attention ought to be given to a particular aspect of bridging strategies recommended by Resource Dependence Theory: constraint reduction by horizontal or vertical integration (cf. Hatch 1997), which refers to the chosen integration method. Vertical integration, leaving the power of decision on all innovation activities with the company only, is to be found in those integration methods that are carried out exclusively under the ultimate guidance of the integrating company, whereas horizontal integration, to various degrees, leaves certain fields of action to the integrated customers' discretion.

Customer inclusion in workshops (this is what Schindler and Zimmer have done), focus groups, conjoint analysis, and problem analysis, just to mention the most current methods (cf. 2.3.2 "Methods") are examples of vertical integration, whereas collaborative technical project definition on the company's or customer's sites, Empathic Design/Ulwick Method (this, to some degree, is Gallus' and Schurter's approach), or customers' unwatched testing of prototypes shift a distinct amount of responsibility and influence to the customers. There is no general preference attached to either horizontal or vertical integration; both have advantages and disadvantages, sometimes combined in a single method. Empathic Design, for instance, while leading to possibly less constraint reduction than vertical integration methods, has the advantage of avoiding leakage of knowledge.

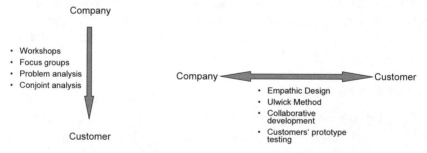

Fig. 5.6. Bridging strategies in the form of vertical and horizontal integration

Constraint absorption (see 5.3.1), giving the dependent company direct control over the resource (cf. Casciaro and Piskorski 2005), can be reached by e.g. agreements on intellectual property conferring all rights to the contributed and newly gained knowledge on the company (see 3.4.3 leakage of knowledge).

Last but not least, "creating counter dependence" (Hatch 1997: 78) can be identified when companies are the only or most able ones to develop a product that meets customers' special needs or wishes. Trading a customized product for pertinent customer experience, know-how, and skills is tantamount to creating or making use of mutual dependence – this applies to the customers of Gallus, Schurter, and Zimmer.

Problems of uncertainty

Another aspect of Resource Dependence Theory, which links it even more closely to customer integration, is the conceptual connection with the problems of uncertainty (cf. 5.3.1).

Risk and chance presuppose uncertainty, probability being one of their determining factors (cf. 2.4). It is the uncertainty of the value of envisaged customer integration activities that makes integration a gamble, at least in the light of the discussed change of paradigm. The risks of customer integration appear tolerable if the chances appear higher. Otherwise, the ultimate answer of Resource Dependence Theory to the question of how to avoid constraint, namely to do without the resource, will suggest relying on company-intern innovation activities without customer participation.

5.3.3 Conceptual model of successful customer integration

The problem of a company's dependence on its customers is closely related to the issue of potential customer contribution (cf. 3.2.2), which restricts the cooperation with customers to a limited area.

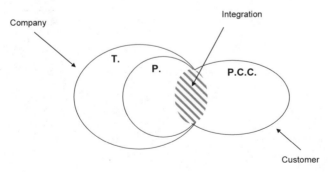

T. = Task, P. = Concrete project, P.C.C. = Potential customer contribution

Fig. 5.7. Area for customer integration

The question of what can or cannot be learned from customers in specific tasks defines their importance for the company with regard to criticality and scarcity. While it is obvious that the integration of customers without pertinent knowledge does not make sense, it is plausible that knowledge easily attainable from other sources diminishes the scarcity of customer input, and if their potential knowledge contribution is only partially useful for the innovation task, its criticality will be lessened, too. This shows that the decision on customer integration must also consider the company's dependence on its customers in the particular project.

In addition, a single-case decision has to take into account the benefits and risks that may turn up in the course of just this project. These potential effects will give an idea of whether the project of integrating customers appears promising or not. In case there are no or only minor benefits, the integration project is likely to be abandoned without further efforts on the company's part. With both benefits and risks worth mentioning, the question of influencing them in favor of the benefits becomes an issue.

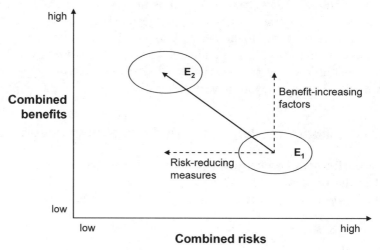

E_1 = Balance of original effects
E_2 = Balance of modified effects

Fig. 5.8. Intended modification of effects

The contingency approach to the project-oriented decision on customer integration leads to the conceptual model below:

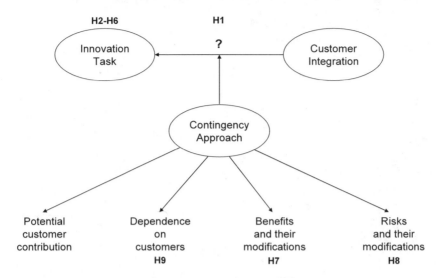

Fig. 5.9. Concept for predicting the potential integration success

This figure contains a seeming paradox: According to Hypothesis H9, a high dependence on customers is likely to bring about more benefits, which would suggest that companies try to increase their dependence on customers and not to reduce it, as Resource Dependence Theory recommends.

The solution is the slight difference in perspective. The *general* dependence on customers for an envisaged innovation task delineates the scope of possible benefits from customer integration, whereas the *particular* dependence on concrete integration candidates is to be reduced by buffering and bridging strategies in the form of pertinent risk-reducing measures.

The final risk-benefit balance, which is the outcome of the applied conceptual model, will constitute the "gate document" for single-case customer integration. This balance prepares the particular strategic go/no go - decision on customer integration, which replaces the prevalent general strategic decision, in the same way as a business plan prepares the final decision prior to the technical development part of the innovation process.

6 Managerial recommendations for advisable envisaged customer integration

With the proclaimed change of paradigm, holding that customer integration can no longer be considered a priori a generally advisable practice, innovation managers are faced with an additional burden of decision-making. They ought to decide in every single innovation task whether customer integration would add value in comparison to mere in-house activities or to innovations with the help of other external sources. The rationale for this decision is simple in theory: customer integration is advisable if the prospective benefits gained by it are higher than the prospective dis-benefits. In practice, however, such a decision presupposes a variety of other, if smaller, decisions on the factors that influence this balance, e.g. the task in question, the likely benefits, or special risk-reducing measures.

This chapter will deal, from a practitioner's point of view, with the issues of task and potential customer contribution (6.1), assessment of benefits and risks (6.2), their modification (6.3), quantification of benefits, risks, and their potential modification (6.4), and a formula for assessing the prospective value of envisaged customer integration (6.5). The objective is to speed up the necessary final single-case decision, which replaces the general strategic one, by preparing a standardized formula for the "gate document" on customer integration.

6.1 Innovation task and potential customer contribution

The first and decisive step an innovation manager has to take, whether considering customer integration or not, is to define as clearly as possible the concrete result he hopes to achieve within the early innovation phase. For this purpose, he has to consider the general task the envisaged project belongs to. This task can be

Identification	Selection	Definition	Testing
of opportunities or ideas (cf. 3.2.1)	of opportunities or ideas (cf. 3.2.2)	of a project or concept (cf. 3.2.3)	of prototypes (cf. 3.2.4)

Fig. 6.1. Tasks within the Early Innovation Phase

A concrete objective will normally cover only a part of a certain task; for example, opportunity identification encompasses more than e.g. finding out new technological developments via roadmapping, which is illustrated in Fig. 5.10.. To delimit the project within a given task, it is recommended to describe in short terms what exactly is the company's goal. This was done by the companies described in Chapter 4: Gallus, having chosen the trend of industrialization in the printing branch within the company, looks for functionalities it can add to its machines in order to enlarge and speed up the printing process for its label-printing customers; Schindler looks for new trends and pertaining ideas in the European elevator branch, just to give an example of this procedure. For other tasks, e.g. definition, it is necessary to define whether a problem of technical project definition or concept definition has to be solved and what it consists in.

The next step is to decide by which means and methods the concrete innovation goal is to be reached. That is where customer integration starts being an issue. Trends, for example, can be identified in several ways (cf. 3.2.1). Whereas scenario analysis and trend extrapolation do not necessarily involve customers but can be carried out by company staff or external experts, Empathic Design, per definition, includes customers. The question of customer integration has to be answered on choosing the method, either as an intrinsic element or an additional support of the company's innovation activities. In this context, a manager ought to state explicitly why customer support may be useful in this particular project, showing in which way the company depends on customer knowledge and what the customers can be expected to contribute – which is the transformation of the theoretical issues of dependence on customers and potential customer contribution into practice.

Gallus managers, in the case study project, might have stated that the company's success depends on its customer's success in the following value chain, which necessitates a close investigation of the particular needs and wishes only customers are able to point out. Their technical skills, too, will be a valuable knowledge input for new functionalities.

Schindler, in comparison, could have listed the general dependence of all producers on their customer's satisfaction as main reason to include them, and would have listed indirect customers', i.e. architects'and entrepreneurs', supposed knowledge of European trends in the elevator branch as potential customer contribution.

As for the issue of potential customer contribution, which may limit the customers' involvement to certain parts of a given task (cf. 5.3.3), managers should consider which particular contribution only customers can make and which parts of a task company staff can carry out just as well or better. Schurter and Zimmer, for example, shaped and defined the results they had identified with customer support on their own, thus finishing the identification task without customers.

6.2 Benefits and risks of the envisaged customer integration

Having stated the possible extent and the technical implementation of customer integration within the concrete innovation project, practitioners are approaching the crucial question of the prospective value customers may add to the result.

As mentioned above, this value depends on the ratio of expected benefits to possibly realized risks.

6.2.1 Benefits for the concrete project

Contrary to the still prevailing attitude that benefits due to customer integration are taken for granted and that only, if at all, risk-reducing measures have to be considered, an innovation manager should expressly investigate what benefits are likely to result from including customers. If they appear negligible, a further pursuit of the concept may appear uneconomic with regard to the human and financial resources customer integration requires.

To support and speed up this investigation, innovation managers can fall back on the list of benefits that, in general, are apt to occur as a result of customer integration in various innovation tasks. This list, compiled on the basis of the analysis model in chapter 3 (cf. 3.3.1), gives an idea of benefits that will often result from customer integration in similar tasks. Some benefits may be excluded in the particular task due to special circumstances/contingency factors only the company is aware of, others, not included in the list, may appear likely nevertheless also because of such factors.

Table 6.1. Generally likely benefits of customer integration

	Identification	Selection	Definition	Prototype Testing
Better market orientation	+	+	+	+
Reduction of time	?	?	+	+
Reduction of costs	?	?	+	+
Access to new knowledge	+	+	+	+
Strategic advantages	+	+	+	+

Strategic advantages, for example, would appear likely for Gallus, Schurter, and Zimmer, whereas Schindler would not include this benefit in a respective list had the company chosen to follow such a procedure.

With a promising amount of benefits to be gained from customer integration, innovation managers ought to continue with the next step.

6.2.2 Risks for the concrete project

The negative side effects of customer integration have so far not met with a sizeable amount of practitioners' attention, with the exception of the rather widespread awareness of possible leakage of knowledge.

As with the possible benefits for the company's concrete innovation project with customers, a list of generally likely risks will help to compile the ones that may apply to the particular task.

Table 6.2. Generally likely risks of customer integration

	Identification	Selection	Definition	Prototype Testing
Biased results due to customers'				
views	+	+	?	+
interests	+	+	?	+
experience	+	-	?	+
Additional time	+	+	?	+
Additional costs	+	+	+	+
Leakage of knowledge	+	+	+	+
Strategic risks	+	+	+	+

Again, the innovation manager in charge will adapt this list to the company's special circumstances.

Gallus and Schurter, for example, could strike the risk of leakage of knowledge from their - assumed - list because with the chosen method of Empathic Design this risk is avoided from the beginning, whereas with other methods (e.g. workshops as with Schindler and Zimmer) this risk is always to be reckoned with due to unforeseeable traits of human nature.

Additional time and costs because of customer integration will also appear on almost every list irrespective of the companies' special circumstances with the possible exception of the definition task (cf. 3.2.1 and Table 6.2. above). As they can only be assessed completely when the integration project is over, at least a rule-of-thumb estimate is necessary, unless former projects can serve to predict these additional resources more accurately (this will be the case with the four investigated companies in similar future projects, cf. chapter 4, 4.2.5 - 4.5.5).

6.3 Modification of benefits and risks

A weighing of the established possible benefits and disbenefits appears to be the obvious next step. With every company's presumed intention of optimizing all its processes in the effort of profit planning, practitioners will or ought to try to influence the balance of benefits and risks in favor of the benefits. This can be done by two means, heeding both empirical findings and theoretical recommendations especially of Resource Dependence Theory:

The first way is to increase the benefits by way of specifically adapted general success factors (see above 3.3.2 and below 6.3.1), the second to reduce the risks by pertinent measures (below 6.3.2). An optimum can be reached by combining both ways.

6.3.1 Benefit-increasing factors

Even irrespective of customer integration, managerial practice, in accordance with scientific and empiric findings, should rely on general success factors for New Product Development. Those being of special relevance to customer integration, increasing the benefits and applying to all tasks, are listed below:

Table 6.3. Success factors of NPD specifically adapted to customer integration

- Senior management commitment to customer integration
- Involvement of both technology and marketing departments in integration activities
- Clear responsibilities on the customers' and the company's part
- Human factors considering the involved persons' personalities and their attitudes to customer integration
- Learning from past experience with integration projects

Again, it is up to the innovation manager to decide which factors apply to the company's special circumstances, i.e. which ones already exist (such as good personal relationships with customers in the case of Gallus) or which ones can be newly established or increased (e.g. the involvement of R&D and marketing in Schindler's Trend Teams). Other benefit-increasing factors not included in Table 6.3. may emerge contingent on a company's particular circumstances, such as Gallus' special and permanent consideration of its customers' value chain.

Such factors, in case they apply to the envisaged project of customer integration, will boost the beneficial impact of the combined benefits and not of special benefits.

6.3.2 Risk-reducing measures

The buffering and bridging strategies recommended by Resource Dependence Theory (see 5.3.2) ought to be considered prior to actual customer integration, leading to specific measures that eliminate or at least reduce the aggregated individual risks of the envisaged integration project.

Choosing the "right" customer

Risk-reducing measures will vary according to the characteristics of each specific risk. Still, as customer integration first and foremost depends on the customers themselves, all risks more or less boil down to having chosen a "wrong" customer: A wrong customer will induce wrong market assessments; will necessitate extra time for harmonizing the atmosphere he damaged in workshops; will "steal" knowledge; will take over undue control, and so on. A careful selection of customers therefore is the general measure to minimize most risks.

The selection of the "right" customer, while pertaining to all risks, still has to consider the special type of risk and the various types of customers that are necessary for the particular method within the identification task.

That is why the details will be discussed in the context of each risk, but certain general rules of how to choose the right customer do exist.

Normal customers, who are the usual target group of conventional market research, are mostly addressed at random or, if specific demands have to be met with regard to e.g. gender, age, or education, are chosen according to the established market research methods. A special selection is necessary with the more refined methods such as Empathic Design (cf. Chapter 2.3.2 "methods"), which depends on the observation of users. In this case, the company has to set up criteria about who is to be watched along with why, where, in which surroundings, and by whom. It goes without saying that people who have never used the product in question before will behave differently from experienced users, so that a mixture of both types of users will produce representative results. With the newly developed IT-based tools, the selection of normal customers can be influenced by the way the toolkits are programmed. Definite configurations will interest only those customers who have a basic understanding of the problem at hand, and certain guidelines will prevent answers completely off the mark. This way, hitherto unknown groups of rather more than "normal" – due to the necessary presupposed interest and understanding – customers can be reached. This "information pump" (Dahan and Hauser 2001) has the added advantage that customers selected in this way will be less shy or reticent on articulating their needs, wishes, and suggestions. In some cases, however, the toolkit method has met with criticism for being too expensive (Jeppesen and Molin 2003), unreliable (Franke and Piller 2004), and unsatisfactory (Franke and von Hippel 2002), and it was suggested that the toolkit method be used with preselected lead users only (Thomke and von Hippel 2002). Each company considering the integration of "normal" users via toolkit selection should make the decision contingent on the complexity of the aspired opportunities and ideas.

The choice of the "right" lead users as a risk-reducing means is even more important. Lead users as participants of workshops will influence the innovation task to a higher degree than normal customers. Their identification has been widely discussed (Herstatt and von Hippel 1992; von Hippel 1986). Several proven selection criteria have been gathered in the course of the research for this thesis (see Table 6.4.below): Lead users ought to be either trendsetters or market leaders; have an excellent reputation in the market; be competent; have complementary skills and interests; have a high PR and sales potential, preferably also for selling off the result of the collaboration, and, if possible, be known to the company from former, if minor collaboration projects.

Table 6.4. Selection criteria (from Gassmann et al. 2005a)

• Technology leader	• Multiplicator
• Market leader	• Minimization of costs via geographic proximity
• Trendsetter	
• Opinion leader	• Benefit for the Lead User
• Codes setter	• Top 1-4 performer
• Reputation	• Assessable risk
• Revenue potential	• Win-Win situation
• Innovation culture	• Innovativeness
• Trust / positive experiences	• Representative of branch
• Ability to communicate	• Complementary competencies
• Availability of infrastructure (geographic, strategic)	• Capability / product competence
	• No exclusivity agreements expected
• Sensitivity for the problem	• Competitive risk
• Concrete demand	• Sustainability

Many practitioners' burning question is where to find lead users who meet the above-mentioned demands. In addition to the by now established concepts of screening a great number of users and of networking, i.e. asking few well-known customers about other users known to them, trade fairs and sales conferences open up ways of identifying lead users. Seminars held by companies in search of lead users are a good way of discovery, too: among the participants, suitable co-developers and lead users can often be discovered.

As a precautionary step, companies should consistently monitor the "quality" of their "customer resources" (Lengnick-Hall 1996: 799), which means checking if an initially "right" customer goes on being one.

By choosing the right customers, most risks will be reduced; the degree of the reduction will, however, be contingent on the specific circumstances.

Measures to reduce biased results due to customers' views

In so far as "normal" customers within market research may be biased by strongly individual views, this risk can be countered by big numbers of interviewed people: the more customers are asked, the more easily extraordinary views of particular persons will be counterbalanced.

Lead users in workshops are generally chosen just for representing specific tastes or perspectives. To avoid being misled into a wrong direction by "one-track-minded" customers with rather exotic views, innovation managers should endeavor to mix lead users with different backgrounds who represent different needs in the market and, if feasible, different branches. The integration of one lead user only ought to be avoided.

Measures to reduce biased results due to customers' interests

With regard to a possible conflict of interests, this risk will mainly occur with lead users who may fear for their own line of production. It can be avoided by providing a mix of lead users in workshops (see measures to reduce biased results due to customers' views). The problem with "normal" customers' potentially conflicting interests lies in gaining insight into their conscious or subconscious interests in the first place. Consumer diaries, home visits, Internet platforms, or the "day of my Life" Empathic Design tool favored by *Henkel* can help with this task.

The other manifestation of this risk, the customers' contribution to later niche products only, requires a different risk-reducing procedure. Empirical investigation recommends integrating customers in two or three different tasks of the innovation process, using different customers in each, e.g. in identification, selection, and prototype testing. This way, different prospective buyer groups can be considered, which will lead to divergent wishes and thus prevent a niche product for a limited clientele.

Measures to reduce biased results due to customers' experience

As mentioned before, mere incremental innovations as consequence of customers' functional fixedness constitute a disbenefit only if a company is interested in nothing but radical innovations. The most effective way of eliminating or at least minimizing this risk is to integrate lead users rather than "normal" customers. In addition, empirical research suggests relying on "indirect" customers, e.g. electrical fitters who install fuel cells for their clients/end customers, because indirect customers, being experts themselves, can pass on their direct customers' experience without the latter ones' functional fixedness. This measure proved to be successful with the company Zimmer. In some cases, mock-ups or prototypes (see 3.2.1) will help normal customers to overcome their functional fixedness by visualizing so far unthought-of possibilities of use (Sandmeier 2006).

Another risk-reducing measure is to rely on as many customers as possible. Toolkits may be helpful, easily reaching big numbers. Potentially incremental inclinations can be compensated by prioritizing the various suggestions, blending them with lead users' or own experts' ideas.

Finally, incremental innovations can be avoided by an intelligent timing of customer integration. An early involvement of customers offers opportunities of counterbalancing limited experience later on and with different knowledge sources.

Measures to reduce additional time

As explained above (3.4.1), additional time caused by customer integration is a sure disadvantage and not only a possible risk. The necessary time for selecting suitable lead users, preparing Web-based tools and so on cannot be shortened by generally applicable measures; the only hope of shortening this preparation time is a certain routine and experience integration managers will develop in the course of consecutive integration projects.

However, an increase of time caused by efforts to harmonize conflicting management styles or to mediate between incompatible workshop participants can be influenced:

As to conflicting management styles, the first step for a company should be to implement an innovation culture that ensures transparency, trust, and easy communication. In a second step, the company should try to learn as much as possible about the envisaged partner company's innovation culture in order to compare the styles. If one or both partners do not have an innovation culture, collaborative activities should be abandoned unless the lack can be remedied in advance.

With "time costs" due to customers' personal traits, it is recommended to fall back on the findings of ergonomics. This science established the importance of recognizing and making use of the different roles employees may play in workshops, e.g. controller, agitator, or visionary (Margerison and McCann 1984). Integration managers should apply these findings to integrated customers as well and should not hesitate to exchange participants in workshops, customers as well as employees, if the roles are not distributed evenly or if the "personal chemistry" between the major players does not fit.

With the last two measures, the disbenefit of additional time caused by customer integration can at least be reduced to some extent.

Measures to reduce additional costs

Costs for preparing and running customer integration projects are unavoidable in all tasks. The costs incurred by remunerating customers usually cannot be negotiated either. If a company is interested in a customer who wants to be paid for his efforts, it has to pay or let him go; the question is not if the costs can be avoided but if the customer's expected contribution is worth the money.

Only with opportunity costs does a reduction appear possible: once a company realizes that the means, i.e. customer integration, has become more important than the end, i.e. the desired result of the innovation task at hand, it will take care to get its priorities right. By doing so, opportunity/transaction costs can be cut down.

Measures to reduce leakage of knowledge

The legal means to protect company knowledge is to draw up specific agreements on intellectual property rights. Such written contracts should include non-disclosure agreements, detailed lists of who contributes which know-how, and agreements on the ownership of the prospective innovative result. This measure, which appears effective and easy to handle in theory, is rather problematic in practice. Conflicting interests have to be considered: with regard to protecting company knowledge, the rules should be detailed and strict, but the desired knowledge spillover from the customer to the company, which is the main reason for customer integration, could be impaired by comprehensive restrictions. Secondly, innovative activities require entrepreneurial discretion and flexibility, leaving the necessary space for creative work on both the company's and the customer's side. Thirdly, the very wish to draw up agreements can offend the prospective collaboration partner because it questions the degree of trust on which collaborative relationships ought to be founded (Wilson et al. 1995). Still, legal protection is a must.

Even the best agreements are of no use if the integration partner does not keep his side of the obligations. Choosing the "right" customers is of utmost importance, meaning in this respect the selection of honest and trustworthy ones. The best way of finding such customers is to "test" them in minor projects before embarking on a more important one where leakage of knowledge could be disastrous.

Another measure is to subdivide the task in question as much as possible, both topically and personally, using different customers for different limited jobs. If a customer only gains insight into a part of the task, e.g. trend extrapolation for a certain technology, while another one is integrated in extrapolating environmental trends, he may not be able to figure out what the company is trying to identify. In this case, too, a balance has to be struck, this time between telling a customer enough to perform the task he is supposed to do and not betraying too much company knowledge.

The choice of the right moment heads into the same direction. Customers ought to be integrated as early as necessary but as late as possible, so that the customer contributes his ideas when they still have big leverage while learning as little as possible himself. If it is feasible with the project in question, customers – for reasons of knowledge protection – ought to be integrated for a limited time only.

With all these measures, it is possible to reduce the risk of knowledge leakage to some degree, but due to the uncertainty of choosing the "right"/trustworthy customer a certain risk will remain.

Measures to reduce strategic risks

Taking care of good personal relations among the parties concerned can prevent the strategic disadvantage of a damaged relationship with a key customer caused by an integration project gone wrong. A project may fail for a number of reasons, e.g. the global crisis in the markets following the attack of 09/11/01 or an unexpected flaw in a new technology. Such a failure need not have a negative effect on the customer-company relationship as long as no on is personally blamed for such external failure factors. Even if a key customer's representative or a company employee did not behave or perform as expected, it ought to be easy to solve such a problem on a high level, preventing a permanent alienation.

The risk of losing power to either the collaborating partner or to competitors can be countered by clearly defining the spheres of influence (Littler et al. 1995). If there is even the slightest possibility of ending up as the customer's subcontractor, the company ought to abandon the project, preferably before it is started. In case this danger turns up in the course of a running integration project, exit provisions - a must! - have to make a quick termination possible (Das and Teng 1999).

With these measures, strategic risks ought to be prevented. However, in view of customers with the unspoken intention of damaging their competitor in the course of the integration project (see Brockhoff 2005a), this risk cannot be excluded completely.

The following table lists the possible measures against the various risks for the practitioner's choice contingent on the company's circumstances:

Table 6.5. Possible risks and pertinent reducing measures

Risks	Reducing Measures
Biased results due to customers' views:	
a) Normal customers	Careful selection
	Big numbers
	Integration in different tasks
b) Lead users	Careful selection
	Mix of users with different backgrounds
	Integration in different tasks
Biased results due to customers' interests:	Careful customer selection
	Mix of users with different backgrounds
	Good timing/different tasks
	Consumer diaries, home visits
	Integration platforms
Biased results due to customers' experience: (functional fixedness)	Integration of lead users and/or indirect users only
	Mix of normal and indirect customers with lead users
	Good timing
	Big numbers
	Integration in different tasks
	Careful customer selection
	Mock-ups
Leakage of knowledge:	Intellectual property agreements
	Careful customer selection
	Good timing
	Integration in different tasks

Table 6.5. (cont.)

Strategic risks:	
a) Damaged relationships	Taking special care of good relations
	Clear ground rules
b) Losing power to customers/ competitors	Careful prior research
	Exit provisions
c) Malevolent/unrealistic customers	Careful customer selection
Additional time:	Harmonizing management styles
	Mediating among workshop partici-pants
	Scientific findings of ergonomics
	Comparison of innovation cultures
Additional opportunity costs:	Paying more attention to innovation goal
	Getting the priorities right

In case innovation managers want to adopt certain risk-reducing meas-ures, these will lessen the weight of the respective risks on an imagined risk-benefit balance. However, as risk-reducing measures require time and money, they will slightly increase the disbenefits of additional time and costs.

In theory, an ex ante evaluation of the prospective value of customer in-tegration would appear possible after the compilation of possible benefits, risks, and their modifying factors. In practice, a weighing of risks and benefits presupposes a standard of comparison, which will be developed in the following section.

6.4 Quantification of benefits, risks, and their modifications

With the change of paradigm regarding customer integration, the inherent risk of an integration project going wrong can no longer be shifted to a general strategic decision of top management. The particular overall risk involved in a concrete innovation project with customers ought to be cal-culated in advance to avoid, if possible, the disappointment Schindler, for example, had to experience on finding out that in-house activities would have brought the same result, or, more important, a total failure of the in-tegration.

Resource Dependence Theory, being linked with the problems of uncertainty (cf. 5.3.2), provides the clue for establishing a standard of comparison with regard to the possible effects of customer integration.

6.4.1 Basic considerations

The uncertainty surrounding the resource "customer knowledge" is not related to its access but to its prospective value. This uncertainty requires a conscious decision of the managers in charge whether to integrate customers or not.

With decisions concerning uncertainty, the first step to reach a conclusion is to identify chances and risks (Baird and Thomas 1985; Rowe 1977).

The next step is to analyze/assess the established risks and chances (WLA 2001). As literature on the pertinent techniques mostly refers to "risk" assessment and not to "chance" assessment (exceptions: Link 2001; Muessig 1997), the following text will use the term risk assessment for both types of uncertainty unless expressly mentioned otherwise.

The techniques of risk assessment are numerous and vary according to the related field, for example health/drugs or safety/machines, and with regard to the general approach, i.e. quantitative or qualitative/descriptive (cf. 2.3). Both qualitative and quantitative techniques usually rely on the same definition of risk: risk = impact multiplied by probability (Muessig 1997), which is termed mathematical definition (for other definitions cf. Link 2001: 12 ff). They calculate risk by assigning values to the variables of the risk formula, but this is done in different ways.

In quantitative assessments, presupposing scientific studies and measurements, risk and its components are expressed as a mathematical statement that is typically based on complex statistical and probability calculations. The probability of death in a road traffic accident, for example, would be described as .0001 or 1 in 10.000 (Joy and Griffiths 2005: 53ff.). Quantitative assessments rely on a multitude of pertinent documented data and are the preferred risk assessment tools for health, safety, and ergonomics risks (Covello and Merkhofer 1993).

Qualitative risk assessment uses verbal descriptions of impact and probability and also of the final risk output. The probability of death in a road traffic accident would be described as "remote". The scales can be adapted to suit the circumstances, and different descriptions may be used for different risks. This technique relies on the expertise, judgment, and knowledge of a risk management team (VWA 2006), which makes the outcome very subjective. It is based on an analysis of risks identified in a semi-scientific or non-scientific way (Covello and Merkhofer 1993) and is useful when reliable data for quantitative approaches is not available (Joy and Griffiths 2005: 48ff.). Qualitative risk assessment is often used for management or strategy risks in day-to-day tasks, which normally applies to customer integration projects.

A combination of both assessment techniques is the semi-quantitative approach, which is sometimes considered a variant of qualitative risk assessment (Ring 2002). The initially verbal descriptions of impact and probability are given numerical values, which allows the assessment of cumulative risks (VWA 2006) and reduces personal and individual biases (Ring 2002). It is less refined than the quantitative technique but more expressive than the strictly qualitative one.

Risks and chances of customer integration, as mentioned before, are contingent on a company's individual situation with regard to size, resources, branch etc., which excludes a scientific data collection of a multitude of similar cases. In addition, assessing chances and risks of innovation projects is a highly subjective affair anyway (Link 2001). This applies to the company as a whole, which has developed, tacitly or explicitly, a so-called specific "risk culture" or "propensity to take risks" (Bozeman and Kingsley 1998: 110), and to the individual innovation managers who tend to "view their world through the lens of their organization's culture" (Sitkin and Pablo 1992: 21). Customer integration as a part of innovation projects will depend on such subjective decisions as well. That is why qualitative assessment is basically the most appropriate technique in this context. However, with the purpose of developing a model for weighing many risks and benefits, a cumulative risk/chance assessment, which requires numerical values, is necessary. Accordingly, the semi-quantitative technique appears most appropriate.

6.4.2 Quantifying benefits and risks

An overall value of the benefits and risks possibly resulting from customer integration can only be established if the respective effects are each expressed by a numerical value.

This so-called quantification (Muessig 1997) presupposes, in a first step, a categorization of each benefit and each risk into different groups, and, in a second step, an assignation of a distinct numerical value to each group, for example classifying a benefit as belonging to the category "medium" with the assigned numerical value of 2. On doing so, innovation managers must always bear in mind that with quantifying benefits, the question is **not** what the effect of the innovation activity or the ultimate innovative product will be but what value customers may possibly add to the innovation task, and with quantifying risks, which impact negative side effects of customer integration may have on the envisaged innovation task.

A multitude of very refined methods for establishing categories (cf. Link 2001; Muessig 1997) are at hand, suggesting extensive impact and probability levels. The second step, the assignation of numerical values, usually relies on a semi-quantitative benefit/risk assessment matrix (cf. VWA 2006). Such elaborate measures are necessary on calculating risks or benefits in warfare or in health care, but with normal projects of customer integration, the priorities of innovation problems would be wrong if the issue of customer integration took up the considerable amount of time these measures require.

Still, an assessment of the prospective benefits and risks is necessary, relying on the involved innovation managers' experience and feeling and on fixed criteria each company ought to develop according to its individual needs and empirical deduction from former projects with customers. It is true that such an assessment will be subjective to a considerable degree, but this personal influence can be reduced by involving several managers and by a set of pre-established evaluation criteria.

Just as the grading of ideas in the selection task (cf. 3.2.1), this categorization of benefits and allocation of numerical values is a decision that will influence the final strategic decision on the subject, i.e. idea selection in the first example and customer integration in the second one.

Carried to the extreme, a rule-of-thumb assessment would lead to a qualification of benefits and risks as either big or small. With a little more differentiation, an assignation of these effects to the categories high, medium, or low ought to meet the requirements of day-to-day customer integration.

In order to find the numerical values for a rough estimate of benefits and risks, it is sufficient to make the following connections:

- High benefit/risk   = 3
- Medium benefit/risk = 2
- Low benefit/risk   = 1
- No risk   = 0

This way, it is possible to add up the likely benefits and risks of an envisaged customer integration project. Gallus, for example, might have considered the benefit of better market orientation as high = 3, of access to new knowledge as high = 3 as well, and of strategic advantages as medium = 2, coming to a total of unmodified benefits of 8. Zimmer, in case it had made such an ex ante calculation, might have rated the risk of leakage of knowledge as medium = 2, of additional time as medium = 2, and of additional costs as medium = 2, coming to a total of unmodified risks of 6.

A juxtaposition of the cumulative benefits and the cumulative risks can be made at this point, but as was pointed out above (6.3), a company will try to maximize its profits by optimizing all its processes, including customer integration, and therefore will or ought to consider the influence of general success factors and of risk-reducing measures.

6.4.3 Quantifying benefit-increasing factors and risk-reducing measures

General success factors, as described in 3.3.2, are apt to increase the overall success of New Product Development in general and of customer integration in particular. However, they do not directly influence specific benefits but can only be seen to increase the sum of all benefits expected with customer integration. That is why their quantified numerical value has to be added to the combined benefit values on the final risk-benefit balance.

This quantification once more requires experience and special feeling and will be based on the actual number of the success factors for general New Product Development that are implemented in the company. Contingent on the respective situation, additional 3 value points for full-scale installation, 2 for medium installation, and 1 for basic installation can be added to the combined benefits. Installation refers to both the extent and the number of implemented success factors, e.g. "clear responsibilities" (see 3.3.2) can exist in a rudimentary form or in an established process with a monitoring system, and it can be the only general success factor or one among several.

The four case study companies, for example, all have established various success factors, which, in the case of Schurter, would justify 2 extra value points to be added to the cumulative benefit values, in the case of the other companies 3.

With risk reduction, the quantification is not quite as simple.

Having established the risks, i.e. the potential scope of disbenefits following customer integration, innovation managers have to decide how to deal with them. A risk evaluation, apart from quantifying the risks, will group them according to their acceptability in intolerable, tolerable, or broadly acceptable (Joy and Griffiths 2005; Link 2001). This distinction must take into account that there is no situation without risk; all actions, decisions, or situations involve some level of risk, although in most cases it is very low (Joy and Griffiths 2005).

Basically, there are no risks in customer integration that are intolerable per se. However, specific circumstances can lead to classifying a risk as unacceptable, for instance leakage of knowledge in a breakthrough innovation project. Besides, the risk tolerance level will vary from one company to another. Small companies with few financial resources will view risk differently from large-scale enterprises (Link 2001), and different risk cultures, meaning the propensity to take risks, also influence the distinction between tolerable and intolerable. Still, it seems a safe assumption to classify high risks (values of 3) as intolerable for almost any company, whereas medium risks (2) and low risks (1) will appear as tolerable and broadly acceptable respectively.

In traditional risk management, this classification indicates if and when risk-reducing measures have to be taken. Projects involving intolerable risks must either be abandoned or the risk has to be reduced to acceptable levels, whereas with tolerable or broadly acceptable risks a reduction is not absolutely necessary, though perhaps desirable (VWA 2006). An exception has to be made with the "risks" of additional time and costs. Strictly speaking, they are not risks but definite disadvantages because their occurrence is not probable but certain. High costs and considerably more time may be very inconvenient and cause abstention from an integration project – that is why they have to be included in a risk-benefit balance –, but even a "risk" value of 3 does not necessarily mean that the project must be abandoned by all means if the risk cannot be reduced.

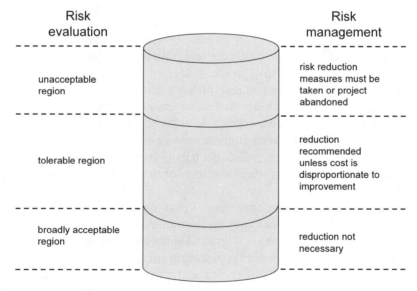

Fig. 6.2. Risk cylinder

With a risk-benefit perspective on customer integration, however, all risks should be reduced as far as possible with the intention of tipping the scales in favor of the benefits. Possibly disproportionate costs of reduction measures in comparison with the improvements to be gained by them are a question to be considered later.

In the case of intolerable risks, there are two options: to abstain from the integration project or to eliminate/reduce the risk. The first way would be in accordance with the final solution of Resource Dependence Theory if all else fails: abandon the resource (Hatch 1997). The second way is what risk management is about: eliminate, reduce, or pass on risks, which corresponds with the theory's buffering and bridging strategies.

In view of the partly inaccurate use of the terms "risk avoidance" and "risk elimination" (cf. Link 2001: 39), it is appropriate to clarify the difference: a risk is avoided when the risk-producing situation is abandoned, e.g. Gallus and Schurter avoiding leakage of knowledge by relying on the integration method of Empathic Design, whereas risk elimination totally abolishes either the cause or the effect of an established risk in a forthcoming or ongoing situation, e.g. Gallus eliminating the strategic risk of damaged relationships by excellent personal contacts. Risk reduction is achieved by partly abolishing the causes/effects or by reducing the likelihood of risky incidents (VWA 2006). The risk of developing unwanted incremental products, for example, can be eliminated by relying on lead users only rather than on "normal" customers with their possible "functional fixedness", thus removing the cause; it can be reduced by relying on big numbers of "normal" customers or by integrating additional "indirect" customers, thus reducing probability or impact in the risk formula (cf. 3.4.2). However, with the risks of customer integration it is difficult at times to make a clear distinction between the reduction of probability and of impact, easy as it is in theory: on integrating a multitude of normal customers, for example, the probability that all or many of them will have biased or limited views/interests/experience is reduced considerably, and at the same time the impact of such impairments is counterbalanced or at least vastly diminished by untampered contributions of fellow customers. A combination of various risk-reducing measures can lead to minimizing or even eliminating risks.

The third tool of risk management – pass on the risk to collaboration partners/customers or transfer it to an insurance company – is almost nonexistent in customer integration. Again, it is necessary to keep in mind that the risk at hand is not a product flaw causing financial or bodily harm but a negative effect of customer integration activities. It is hard to imagine that a customer will agree to bear the consequences of realized integration risks, especially disbenefits that exist only in the eyes of the integrating company but not in his own eyes, e.g. increase in costs due to a customer's financial remuneration or knowledge spillover from company to customer. An insurance against such risks, short of Lloyd's, is also inconceivable or at least disproportionate in costs.

That leaves the risk-reducing measures described in this chapter as the only means of risk management but pertaining to all risk levels.

The problem is to develop a mathematical formula for downgrading the risks. With the purpose of finding a workable day-to-day tool for innovation managers, such a formula should not be too detailed and scientific.

Again, feeling and experience will help integration managers to gauge how risk-reducing measures will influence the possible impact of a risk; such measures, at a rough estimate, may lead to a total, a major, or a minor reduction of the original risk value. The numerical expression of this rule-of-thumb assessment is:

- Total reduction   = 0
- Major reduction   = reduction to ¼ ⎤
                                                    ⎬ the original value
- Minor reduction   = reduction to ½ ⎦

Zimmer and Schindler, for example, can reduce the risk of leakage of knowledge in the workshops by non-disclosure agreements to half the original value; a higher reduction does not appear justified because it is never absolutely certain that customers will keep to the agreements.

In summary, most risks can be downgraded both practically and mathematically. However, before embarking on the respective measures a company has to decide on their efficiency (Link, 2001), which means establishing whether the potential risk reduction is worth the extra costs. As mentioned before, this decision is due only with tolerable and broadly acceptable risks; with intolerable ones, the project must either be abandoned or the risks be reduced irrespective of costs.

With the typical risks of normal risk management, complicated limit value calculations and models have been developed in order to investigate the efficiency of risk reduction measures (Chapman 2000; Farny 1989). However, the extra costs of customer integration do not require an overly scientific investigation. Once again, the arguments for qualitative risk assessment in customer integration (see above 5.3.1) suggest relying on the judgment, experience, and good sense of the integration managers involved. Falling back on prior projects with customer integration, they will be able to decide whether risk-reducing measures are generally worth the money or not.

In case the measures appear cost-efficient, the estimated extra costs and extra time have to be converted into mathematical values and added to the established values of additional costs and time. General rules for this upgrade cannot be given; a company will know best how to estimate the costs for risk reduction.

For Schindler and Zimmer, extra time and costs for non-disclosure agreements reducing the risk of leakage of knowledge appear negligible to the point of non-existence.

The reduction/elimination/upgrade caused by such measures applies to the respective risk and not to the sum of all risk values.

6.5 Towards a formal decision model

The numerical expression of risk and benefit values and their respective modifications allows the establishment of a risk-benefit ratio that gives an indication of the prospective success of customer integration. Once more, it is necessary to point out that the derived mathematical value does *not* constitute or replace the particular strategic single case decision on customer integration. It helps, though, to prepare the strategic decision in about the same way a rating of opportunities or ideas prepares the final decision in the selection task or a business plan prepares the final go/no go-decision prior to the development phase. It is true that a risk-benefit balance in favor of the benefits will prejudice a favorable decision on customer integration, but so will a business plan with high predicted profits with regard to the decision on developing the innovative idea, and an idea graded with 9 on a scale of 10 is far more likely to be selected than one with a grade of 4.

The ultimate aim of this dissertation is to find a way of calculating if customer integration in whichever project within the early innovation phase will be advisable. The advisability depends on the prospective success of the intended integration measures.

The actual success of customer integration can only be established ex post when risks and chances have turned into definite disadvantages and benefits, which may be difficult to assess exactly. At that moment, success is the difference between the combined benefits and the combined disadvantages; with any value above zero customer integration was successful, with a value of zero, it was useless, and with a value below zero, it was a failure. Gauging the success ex ante means considering chances and risks, and because of their inherent uncertainty, a simple subtraction is not possible. As with all risk-benefit calculations, the risk-benefit ratio, i.e. the quotient of risks and benefits, will have to answer the question of advisability (VWA 2006): customer integration appears advisable when the prospective risks are lower than the possible chances, leading to a risk-benefit ratio of <1.

A ratio of 1 is the result of identical modified cumulative risk and benefit values, which means they neutralize each other and therefore have no different outcome than in-house innovations without customers. With a risk-benefit ratio of >1, the risks outweigh the chances, suggesting failure of the concept in the particular case.

A formula predicting the success of an envisaged customer integration project can only calculate the *prospective* outcome; positive or negative surprises when the project is finished and the success can be established with the help of concrete facts are always possible. With the quantified effects and their modifications, a mathematical calculation will at least increase the likelihood of good or bad results.

Based on the theoretical and empirical deductions of the previous chapters, the formula has the following form:

$$pO = \frac{(mR1 + mR2 + mR3 + ...)}{(B1 + B2 + B3 + ... + SF)}$$

with

pO	=	prospective outcome
mR	=	modified risk
B	=	benefit
SF	=	adapted general success factors.

With Gallus, for example, the formula might have come to the ex ante assessment below:

Example Gallus:			
Risks:	Value:	Reducing Measures:	Modified Value:
Leakage of knowledge	2	Empathic Design	0
Biased results due to customers'			
views	2	Empathic Design	1
interests	2	Empathic Design	1
experience	0	Lead Users	0
Strategic risks	1	Personal relationships	0
Additional costs	1	-	1
Additional time	2	-	2
Overall modified risk value:	5		
Benefits:	Value		
Better market orientation	3		
Access to new knowledge	3		
Strategic advantages	2		
General success factors	3		
(cf. Table 6.3.)			
Overall modified benefit value:	11		

$$pO = \frac{5}{11} < 1$$

Such an ex ante calculation would have supported the Gallus managers' decision to integrate customers in the pilot project.

With Schindler, the respective considerations might have led to the following assessment:

Example Schindler:			
Risks:	Value:	Reducing Measures:	Modified Value:
Leakage of knowledge	2	Non-disclosure agreement	1
Biased results due to customers'			
views	2	Mix of customers	1
interests	2	Mix of customers	1
experience	2	Lead Users	0
Strategic risks	1	-	1
Additional costs	1	-	1
Additional time	1	-	1
Overall modified risk value:	6		
Benefits:	Value		
Better market orientation	2		
Access to new knowledge	1		
Strategic advantages	0		
General success factors (cf. Table 6.3.)	3		
Overall modified benefit value:	6		

$$pO = \frac{6}{6} = 1$$

With such an ex ante calculation, Schindler may have abstained from the pilot project with customers unless superordinate considerations, e.g. the wish to test the new Trend Team concept, would have led to a positive decision on customer integration irrespective of the indifferent outcome. This example also shows that the formula does not make the final strategic decision redundant but is one among several influencing factors, although an important one.

In any case, the formula will help with the decision process, showing what should be considered on integrating customers. The main focus ought to be on risks and on risk-reducing measures that influence the risk-benefit balance to a considerable degree in favor of an overall positive answer to customer integration. The formula, presupposing many partial decisions, e.g. on integration methods or selection and type of integrated customers, can support managers by providing a quick survey of the factors that predict the potential success of an envisaged integration project.

As for the main research question of whether customer integration is advisable (again, advisability does not mean that customers *have to* or *must not* be integrated), it can be answered in the following way:

Customer integration is not always advisable. It is advisable in a particular innovation project if its prospective positive effects outweigh its prospective negative effects.

7 Conclusion

This chapter answers the research questions and sums up the hypotheses that were derived in the course of this thesis. In addition, it discusses managerial implications, also indicating likely future management trends, and implications for the theory of innovation management, summarizing the contributions to science. Finally, the chapter points out open issues by indicating where further research is necessary or desirable.

7.1 Results

The foremost results are the answers to the questions that started the theoretical and empirical research in the first place, i.e. the main research question and its sub-questions.

7.1.1 Is customer integration in the early innovation phase advisable?

The trigger for this research question was the clash between the majority of supporters and the growing minority of opponents of customer integration, which has resulted in numerous practitioners' uncertainty on facing this issue. The research of this thesis has not supported either position; the alternative unconditional answers "yes", indicating that customer integration should go on being considered best practice, or "no", implying that innovative activities without customers are preferable to involving them, cannot be given. However, the prevalent belief that customer integration will automatically add value to innovative activities has been shattered; customer integration may, but need not have overall positive results. In other words: this is the typical case of an open question where the answer is not yes or no but "it depends".

The answer consists in defining on what exactly success or failure of customer integration depend. The best way of doing this is the contingency approach, which suggests itself for two basic reasons:

Theoretical and empirical research (Chapters 3 and 4) has established that customers are hardly ever integrated throughout the entire early innovation phase. In most cases, they are involved in limited parts only, irrespective of what these may be termed, and not from the very first beginning of the early innovation phase to its end. Any answer pertaining to customer integration in this phase therefore has to be given with regard to the special restricted period of actual customer involvement, which prevents a general statement on the prospective positive or negative result of integration activities in the early innovation phase.

Secondly, even with such a sub-division, the research has come up with many conflicting results, forbidding a simple yes or no in answer of the question about the advisability of customer integration. The special circumstances, e.g. moment, duration, specific object, or involved persons, will influence the prospective outcome. Customer integration may be successful in one company whereas another one, choosing the same integration methods and departing from identical parameters, may find customer integration (not the final product!) a disappointment or even a total failure.

The decisive criterion for the distinction between success and failure is a balance of the risks and chances of customer integration. Customer integration is likely to be successful – and therefore advisable – if the chances or benefits outweigh the risks or disadvantages.

Accordingly, the resulting answer to the main research question is:

> **Customer integration is not always advisable. It is advisable in a particular innovation project if its prospective positive effects outweigh its prospective negative effects.**

This answer as yet does not yield any concrete recommendations on how to go about this weighing process. The final answer depends on the answers to the sub-questions that were put in support of the main research question.

7.1.2 Can customer integration be investigated irrespective of different individual process structures?

A comprehensive investigation of customer integration in the early innovation phase presupposes an exact definition of the period to be examined. In accordance with the scientific majority, this phase has been delimited as the time from the very first appearance of an opportunity to the final decision on serial production, including building and testing prototypes (cf. Chapter 2.2.1). Within this entire phase, various theoretical models have been developed, structuring and subdividing the early innovation phase according to specific criteria (cf. Chapter 2.2.2). Empirical research, too, has established that companies have developed different process structures with sometimes strictly consecutive, sometimes parallel, and sometimes interacting sub-phases; a generally valid model that might have served as reference frame for the investigation of risks and benefits could not be deduced or discovered.

In order to find such a reference frame nevertheless, this thesis has made use of the fact that no matter how a company has structured its innovation process within the early innovation phase it has to fulfill certain tasks along the discovery and shaping of the desired innovative product. These tasks may, but need not coincide with the sub-phases some models have developed, e.g. Koen's New Concept Development Model (Chapter 2.2.2), and do not necessarily occur at consecutive points in time. The identification task aims at discovering opportunities as well as ideas, both activities being very much alike, though not completely identical. The selection task, too, covers choosing opportunities as well as ideas to be pursued, each activity normally taking place at different moments within the early innovation phase but requiring almost identical measures and integration methods. The definition task prepares and draws up the business plan, and prototype testing is carried out to confirm the technical feasibility and market suitability of the envisaged product. Knowledge creation management is a rather new task the importance of which is just emerging.

Attaching the research on customer integration to tasks instead of subphases makes for a generally applicable result and also allows the quick investigation of only a minor section within the early innovation phase if so desired.

The answer to the first sub-question of the main research question therefore is the following:

> **Irrespective of individual process structures customer integration in the early innovation phase can be investigated by resorting to generally valid tasks: identification, selection, definition, prototype testing, and knowledge creation management.**

7.1.3 Which possible effects of customer integration have to be taken into account?

The thesis has focused on the effects of customer integration that determine its overall value. The positive results of customer integration, i.e. its benefits or chances (for an exact definition cf. Chapter 2.4.1), are the intended effects that have made the inclusion of customers into the innovation process such a widely acclaimed procedure. Naturally, the negative effects, while often unavoidable, are not intended but mere undesired side effects. These negative side effects (or risks/disbenefits, cf. Chapter 2.4.2) may detract from the value of customer integration and sometimes even outweigh the positive effects.

The positive and negative effects that are likely to accompany customer integration may vary from one task to another, which has made their separate investigation with regard to each task imperative (cf. 3.3.1 and 3.4.1). The predominant effects with all their possible forms and ramifications - in view of the focus on practical management recommendations rare or untypical effects or scientific effects of socio-economics and psychology were not included - form the basis of a risk-benefit balance.

These effects may be modified by factors not necessarily related to their origin. While the benefits may be increased by specially adapted general success factors of New Product Development, the risks may be reduced or totally eliminated by pertinent risk-reducing measures.

Altogether, an evaluation of customer integration has to take into account:

- Benefits (better market orientation, time reduction, cost reduction, access to new knowledge/skills, strategic advantages; cf. Chapter 2.4.1)
- General success factors for New Product Development specifically adapted to customer integration (senior management commitment, involvement of both technology and market departments, clear responsibilities, human factors, learning from past experience; cf. Chapter 3.3.2)
- Risks (biased results, additional time, additional costs, leakage of knowledge, strategic risks; cf. Chapter 2.4.2)
- Risk-reducing measures (choice of the right customers, integration of many customers instead of only one or very few, a mix of customers with different views/interests, relying on lead users/indirect customers, intellectual property agreements, innovation culture, findings of ergonomics; cf. Chapter 6.3.2)

The final answer to this sub-question, summing up the explanations above, is:

> **On assessing the overall value of customer integration, benefits, benefit-increasing factors, risks, and risk-reducing measures have to be taken into account.**

7.1.4 Can the potential success of customer integration be predicted?

"Success" of customer integration is the surplus of its resulting benefits as compared to its resulting disbenefits. It must not be confounded with the market success of the product combinedly developed by company and customers: a product can well turn out to be a flop whereas the cooperation with the customer(s) was successful and vice versa.

This success can only be assessed accurately when the integration activities are over; with some effects such as strategic advantages/disadvantages it may take months or even years to find out the precise amount of their impact. Before turning into definite advantages or disadvantages, the respective effects are mere chances or risks; they may, but need not be realized. In order to overcome this uncertainty, which is the main characteristic of risks and chances, to at least a considerable degree, this thesis has developed a model for a calculation that, while still not excluding unforeseeable developments, will be a solid basis for predicting and not merely guessing at the outcome of customer integration projects.

The principles and methods of risk management have supported the development of a basic algorithm for calculating the results of envisaged customer integration activities. By attaching numerical values to the effects that are likely to occur on integrating customers into a special task, integration managers are able to weigh the prospective chances against the prospective risks. The numerical values for each risk (R) or benefit (B) can be established with the help of procedures described at length in Chapter 6.5. The thus gathered risk values have to be modified by the factors of respective risk-reducing measures. These factors, too, have to be translated into arithmetic values (cf. Chapter 6.4.3); their application to the original risk values leads to the modified risk values (mR), which have to be added up for the overall risk value. The sum of the benefit values has to be increased by the numerical values attached to general success factors (SF; cf. Chapter 6.5).

Thus, a formula for calculating the prospective outcome (pO) of a concrete envisaged customer integration activity can be derived:

$$pO = \frac{(mR1 + mR2 + mR3 + ...)}{(B1 + B2 + B3 + ... + SF)}$$

Customer integration appears advisable if pO < 1, meaning that the combined modified risks are smaller than the combined, possibly increased chances; if the risks and chances are of identical value or if the risks outweigh the chances (pO ≥ 1), customer integration in this particular case is not likely to add value to the innovation project.

This formula, however, does not replace the strategic single case decision of integrating customers or not; it is an important assistance in reaching it, as it were a "gate document of customer integration", which may be overruled by other considerations.

7.1.5 Summary of hypotheses

Apart from the answers to the research questions, various hypotheses that were either validated by or built from the empirical findings in Chapter 4 summarize the results of this thesis in a nutshell.

In accordance with Yin's (1994) prescriptions on research methods and with Eisenhardt's postulations on building theories from case study research (Eisenhardt 1989), four case studies and several mini-cases have served as a triangulation basis for testing propositions deduced from theoretical considerations in Chapter 3 and for developing new hypotheses in Chapters 5 and 6.

The hypotheses that originated in propositions have either served to answer the research questions – this applies to hypotheses H1–H3, H7, H8 below – or to restrict the research field, indicating when customer integration is only rarely or never desirable in the first place (hypotheses H4-H6). The impact of this latter restriction will be discussed in the context of the implications for management theory.

H1:	Customer integration does not necessarily add value to the innovation process.
H2:	Certain tasks occur in the course of every innovation process irrespective of the concrete process structure.
H3:	Risks and benefits of customer integration pertain to the particular task customers are involved in.
H4:	Knowledge creation is an essential element of all innovation activities and not a phase or task of its own.
H5:	The selection task is a company's own business.
H6:	Customer integration in knowledge creation management is not advisable.
H7:	Specifically adapted general success factors for New Product Development can increase the overall value of benefits.
H8:	Risk-reducing measures and their possible effects change the impact of risks.

The case study analysis has brought an additional hypothesis on the possible amount of benefits from customer integration:

> **H9:**   The more companies depend on their customers' knowledge, the more benefits they tend to gain from customer integration.

Finally, a new hypothesis or – in accordance with Eisenhardt's (1989) terminology – a new "theory" has been built, answering the last research question:

> **H10:** The potential overall success of customer integration can be predicted with the formula:
>
> $$pO = \frac{(mR1 + mR2 + mR3 + ...)}{(B1 + B2 + B3 + ... + SF)}$$

7.2 Implications for management practice

Theoretical and empirical research in this thesis has confirmed a growing suspicion: contrary to the still predominant belief customer integration is not an asset to innovation activities as a matter of course. It may have overall positive or negative results or lead to the same outcome innovation activities without customers would have brought about. This is true for integration projects of any kind, from extensive B2B customer integration to the smallest projects with end users or just one customer. The main managerial implication therefore is that customer integration should no longer be taken for granted as a means of improving a company's position in the innovation race. Accordingly, the first and foremost managerial recommendation is:

> **<u>Always</u> consider beforehand whether customer integration is advisable, no matter how important the envisaged integration project appears to be.**

The model developed in Chapter 6.5 will help with these considerations, providing a comparatively easy way to gauge the prospective success of customer integration without, of course, guaranteeing it.

The second implication pertains to questions innovation managers will have to ask themselves and their staff in order to prepare the application of the model but also if they intend to integrate customers without using it:

What exactly do we want to establish with the intended project?

This question refers to the concrete task within the innovation process. Opportunity identification, for example, has aims that differ from those of, e.g., concept definition or prototype testing. The special task defines and, to some extent, limits customer integration (see Chapter 3.2.1). At the same time, the type of task is closely connected with the next important question to be put:

What can or cannot be learned from customers?

The prospective customer contribution is a vital factor within the necessary considerations on customer integration. In most cases, this contribution will consist in knowledge of whichever kind that, depending on the task, cannot always be expected from every type of customer (cf. Chapter 3.2.2).

Once the required customer type has been established, the next managerial recommendation is to select individual customers who meet these requirements. The case studies have shown that refined customer lists (cf. Chapter 4.2; 4.4) facilitate the selection. In addition, managers ought to heed the recommendations on choosing the "right" customer described in Chapter 3.4.2.

With the concrete innovation goal and the prospective customers in mind, innovation managers should next consider the following question:

Which effects are generally likely to occur with customer integration in this particular innovation task?

Depending on each task, e.g. identification or prototype testing, different benefits and risks can normally be expected (see Chapter 3.3.1. and Chapter 3.4.1), although some may turn up within every innovation task, such as better market orientation or leakage of knowledge. These general effects may be more or less pronounced or even non-existent for the particular company, contingent on its individual situation. That is why innovation managers have to ask themselves:

Which effects of customer integration may influence this particular integration project?

The next implication for management practice is the advice to consider benefit-increasing factors of New Product Development and risk-reducing measures (cf. Chapters 3.3.2 and 6.3.2).

Having finished all these considerations, innovation managers ought to calculate the concrete prospective success of integrating customers with the help of the model described in Chapter 6.5 in order to obtain a useful support for the final decision on customer integration in the envisaged project.

The model itself needs preparations that may seem lengthy when using it for the first time but will become swift routine with the following applications. In order to standardize the assessment of customer integration projects, managers and the involved staff will have to discuss the criteria for rating risks and benefits, falling back on former experiences as well as on their combined feeling and common sense. In addition, a report on every customer integration project with the express focus on its advantages, disadvantages, and unmet expectations should be written. Such a report will help avoid future problems.

A likely future trend of customer integration that managers may wish to watch is a slight slow-down of its so far growing spread. Not least due to the still mostly unrecognized, but increasing abuse of the integrated customers' position by competitors (cf. Chapter 2.4.2), a reconsideration of its values has begun. In the long run, it may induce managers to reconsider a too close involvement of customers. The overall satisfaction with customer integration, still on the positive side but varying among the case study participants (see Chapter 5.1.1 Table 5.1.), has indicated that customer integration may not go on being unconditionally considered best practice. The model developed in Chapter 6.5 – the main novel contribution to management practice – clarifies the conditions when customer integration still is a recommendable option. The burden of a special decision on customer integration in every project, which the model helps reduce, is a small price to pay in comparison to the additional security such a calculation can offer.

7.3 Implications for management theory

The thesis contributes a broad variety of novel aspects to the theory of innovation management, to science as well as to teaching.

Change of paradigm regarding customer integration

For over a decade, customer integration has been considered as a highly recommendable means of increasing the companies' innovative power. Acclaimed by management science, the concept of customer integration has been widely accepted as "best practice" in R&D management, leading to an almost general strategic decision for actively involving customers in the early innovation phase. The question in the context of this concept has not been "if" customers ought to be integrated but only "how" this should be done. While the positive effects of customer integration have been taken for granted, supposedly leading automatically to added value, negative effects have been neglected. This thesis has taken the few, but increasing critical voices as an opportunity to question the existing paradigm of generally advisable customer integration. From a novel risk-benefit perspective, the concept is investigated with all its ramifications. Based on theoretical deductions and backed by empirical research, the thesis develops a new paradigm of single case assessment of customer integration, judging the overall value no longer a priori but viewing it as contingent on the prevailing conditions within the individual companies.

First comprehensive investigation of risk modification

Apart from the significance that risk-reducing measures have for management practice, management theory, too, will profit by the contributions to the research of risk modification in the context of customer integration. The growing awareness of risks, preceding and inducing the change of paradigm in customer integration, will take on a different dimension when risks are discussed in the light of possible reduction or even elimination. Specific risks ask for specific measures (cf. Chapter 6.3.2). As the same kind of risk is apt to occur in different, but not in all tasks (cf. Chapter 3.4.1), an investigation of risk modification that is attached to the risks and not to the tasks avoids repetition and allows, if desired, a quick information on particular issues. Management theory will want to discuss special ways of risk reduction and their foreseeable impact on risks, thus creating a counterweight to the extensive theoretical research on benefit-increasing factors. Risk management in New Product Development, so far mainly discussed with regard to the innovative product, will gain a new meaning by encompassing as well the issue of customer integration and its negative side effects.

Model of a risk-benefit calculation

The model developed in Chapter 6.5 is not only a major contribution to management practice but also to management theory, constituting an entirely novel approach to customer integration by calculating its prospective risks and chances and weighing them against each other.

For the first time, a comprehensive list of factors influencing the success of customer integration has been translated into mathematical terms. In this way, a standard of comparison for benefits and risks based on theoretical insights and empirical findings has been found, showing when the integration of customers is likely to be more advantageous than innovation without them. The model will rekindle the ongoing scientific debate on the merits of customer integration by providing an objective instrument that neither glorifies nor vilifies the concept a priori.

New perspective on Research Dependence Theory

So far, customer integration has not been given a comprehensive scientific basis. If at all, certain positive effects have been backed by a cursory reference to Resource Dependence Theory (Brockhoff 2005a; Gruner and Homburg 2000; cf. Chapter 5.3.1), whereas negative effects and other aspects of customer integration were up to this thesis uncharted scientific regions.

The novel contribution lies in the fact that for the first time customer integration with all its implications is examined in the light of a recognized organization theory. In fact, after being mirrored in the Resource Dependence Theory, customer integration can be said to be its perfect example.

The starting-point of Resource Dependence Theory is that organizations depend to various degrees on the environment due to their need of resources (cf. Chapter 5.3.1). Companies as organizations and customers as carriers of the resource "knowledge" are the actors in this relationship of dependence. The thesis points out in detail in which way the problems pertaining to customer integration can be explained and solved with the help of scientific recommendations, for example by seeing risk-reducing measures as an expression of buffering or bridging strategies (cf. Chapter 5.3.2). With the focus on a model of a risk-benefit assessment model, the thesis finds theoretical support for its research on risk management in the theory's link to the problems of uncertainty (cf. Chapter 5.3.1; 6.5), which is the main characteristic of risks and chances.

Novel approach to subdividing the early innovation phase

Management science has produced a variety of models describing the early innovation phase in its different stages or sub-phases (cf. Chapter 2.2.2). These models, mostly widely recognized in scientific circles, are almost all idealized ones that seldom appear in practice in their pure form, even if they are based on practical implementation discovered by empiric research. This fact, together with the plethora of divergent structure models encountered in the practice - e.g. the four case study companies each use a different model for structuring their innovation process in the early innovation phase - , has led to attaching the research on the effects of customer integration to tasks instead of sub-phases or stages. Innovation tasks have to be carried out in the course of whatever concrete form of innovation process, such as identification (of opportunities and ideas), selection (among the established opportunities and ideas), definition (of project and concept), and prototype building/testing (cf. 3.2.1). By using tasks as reference frame and starting-point, it is ensured that the respective results are generally applicable. Another advantage is that repeated examinations of almost identical activities can be avoided: Former investigations on side effects – as far as there have been any at all – had to carry out very similar studies twice when resorting to e.g. Koen's New Concept Development Model or its modified version (see Chapter 2.2.2) because the identification and selection of opportunities and ideas follow more or less the same rules but, with these models, take place in different respective sub-phases.

The new approach in this thesis will contribute to the scientific debate on this issue.

New perspective on knowledge creation

Knowledge has entered the limelight of scientific attention. Its importance for companies in the ever-growing competition in the market, especially with regard to the development of innovative products, is widely recognized (cf. Chapter 2.5). This thesis underlines the role knowledge plays in the context of customer integration, holding that customer integration, in essence, is predominantly the integration of customer knowledge. Customers are integrated – with few exceptions for strategic reasons – with the one and only intention of adding their skills, know-how, and both technical and economic expertise, whether explicit or implicit, to the company's own knowledge; most expected benefits of customer integration can be traced back to this knowledge inflow.

In whichever task customers take part, they mingle their knowledge with the company's own knowledge pool. New knowledge originates this way, often leading to new product ideas, to amendments of existing products, or to an abstention from an idea shown to be infeasible. In other words, customer integration is knowledge creation in its purest form, just the same as cooperation with external experts or cross-departmental research. This novel perspective forbids to consider knowledge creation as a distinctive sub-phase or task of the early innovation phase: knowledge is created throughout the entire innovation process, whether with or without customers, and not in a single separate phase/stage/task, even if such a subdivision is thought to be closely related to the others.

The resulting repudiation of respective models does not pertain to knowledge management. Newly gathered and already existing knowledge must be "managed" in order to guarantee quick access and facilitate new developments (for a perfect example of such knowledge management see the case study on Zimmer, Chapter 4.5.2).

7.4 Suggestions for further research

Although the research questions, as shown above, have all been answered, some answers will need further scientific and empirical support, and some new aspects have turned up that could not be investigated in detail.

Quantitative research on the model

The central goal of this thesis, the model for gauging the prospective success of customer integration, relies to a high degree on theoretical deductions and to a lesser degree on qualitative case study research. The model needs testing in practice, being so far only a theoretical construct that has not been tried out. The necessary quantitative empirical research ought to pertain to all listed elements that are part of the derived mathematical formula: benefits, risks, risk-reducing measures, and benefit-increasing factors.

Negative side effects of customer integration

The negative side effects of customer integration, while meeting with growing interest, need further research in particular. The thesis has compiled and investigated all negative side effects with practical relevance, deduced from a certain theoretical and empirical frequency of occurrence. However, other negative side effects are likely to exist, or the better-known ones may take on special forms that have not been covered by research as yet. In the context of negative side effects, further investigation of pertinent risk-reducing measures, both theoretical and empirical, seems desirable.

Potential customer contribution

The question of what can or cannot be learned from customers has emerged in the course of this thesis, leading to the investigation of potential customer contribution. This problem, which at first glance does not seem to be of much importance, may turn out to be a major open issue in the wide field of customer integration, because it is a decisive factor for the ultimate use of integrating customers. Involving customers who cannot contribute new knowledge for whatever reasons does not make sense. The pertinent research ought to comprise the objective and subjective prerequisites for such a knowledge contribution.

In summary, this thesis is highly relevant to management practice – whose demands triggered the research – as well as to management theory, serving as a practical guideline for managers and providing a broad field of discussions among management scientists.

8 Appendix

A Special innovation tools

Quality Function Deployment

The concept of Quality Function Deployment (QFD), developed by Mizuno and Akao in the 1960s, was first presented to the public in 1983 (Kogure and Akao 1983). QFD is a structured approach to defining customer needs or wishes and translating them into specific production plans for products that will meet those needs (Crow 2002; Johnson 2003). It presupposes the capturing of explicit or unstated customer requirements, which are referred to as "voice of the customer" (Crow 2002). This "voice" is "listened to" (Johnson 2003) in various ways, e.g. empathic design, focus groups, discussions, interviews, etc., and is then summarized in a product planning matrix or "house of quality". The QFD matrices combine customer needs – the "what" – with product requirements – the "how"- (Crow 2002; Saatweber 1997).

QFD is an extremely useful method to facilitate communication, planning, and decision-making within a product development team (Crow 2002). Among its various benefits the most outstanding one is the fast production of outcomes (Johnson, 2003). A typical (simplified) matrix is shown below:

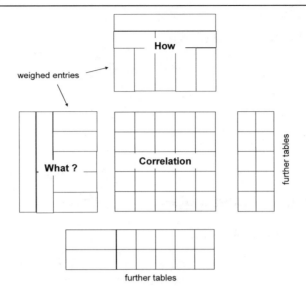

Fig. 8.1. Quality Function Deployment matrix

Handshake Analysis

The term handshake in a transferred sense has its origin in the information technology where it describes the contact between a transmitter and a receiver. This contact, desired as it is, has to be brought about by a special action and does not exist on a permanent basis.

A parallel situation exists in technology-orientated companies that are normally faced with the following problems:

- Identified customer needs cannot be transformed into successful products
- New fields of application for company-owned technologies cannot be found
- The decision-making process regarding the use of technologies is not transparent ("layer of clay effect").

To overcome these problems, Birkenmeyer, Brodbeck and Tschirky (1996; 1995) developed the Handshake Analysis (HSA), which helps combine technology push and market pull – bring about the contact or handshake - while clarifying the pertinent decision process.

The HSA normally starts with systematically listing present and, if possible, future customer needs. At the same time, product functionalities that may satisfy these needs are traced. Needs and functionalities are matched against each other in a matrix where corresponding ones are marked.

The actual "handshake" takes place in a second step when listed company-owned product technologies are matched against the marked results of the first step, the desired product functionalities. The respective second matrix identifies in a transparent way the recommended fields of innovative activity in technology-driven branches.

The HSA process can also start from the technology side instead of being initiated by market considerations; in this case, a company will look for new functionalities that its own technologies and know-how can provide.

Brainwriting

Brainwriting, a tool of creativity techniques, is a way of collecting ideas and suggestions. The name is due to the method's decisive characteristic: "brainwaves" are "written" down on cards.

Brainwriting usually takes place in a special workshop. The question or problem to be solved is explained in detail to the participants. A big card with the question is pinned on a board, and the participants, by themselves or in twosomes, write down their spontaneous suggestions/problem solutions on small cards, an extra one for each new idea. These cards are pinned on the board in a random fashion. The participants regard the cards and clarify possibly misleading or inexact formulations (see Higgins and Wiese 1996).

The main step consists in regrouping or categorizing the cards according to pertaining themes. This can be done in two ways: either the participants develop among themselves certain groups of themes, and the workshop leader attaches one card after another to the respective card with the chosen theme name, or the cards are pinned on a board with previously arranged themes according to the participants' decision. If there is a doubt as to where a card ought to be fixed, the author of the card has the last word on the matter.

Experts evaluate the resulting clusters. (For further details and references, see Schlicksupp 1989).

Pictures of the Future

The "Pictures of the Future" (PoF) are a tool of technology forecast, developed and thus termed by Siemens.

In order to identify technologies with high growth potential as well as technical breakthroughs and future customer needs, the PoF combine two contrary methods and perspectives: the extrapolation from the "world of today" and the retropolation from the "world of tomorrow".

The extrapolation is identical with the so-called roadmapping that projects forward presently known technologies and product families and portrays them as a succession of generations. The idea is to assess as precisely as possible when necessary components will be available and when they will be needed. The great advantage of this method is its certain and reliable starting-point; the disadvantage is its inability to predict discontinuities and development leaps.

This deficiency is balanced out by the complementary scenario technique. With the help of "strategic visioning", the scenario technique propels its users into the future – by five, ten or even more years depending on the field of work. For the respective point in time a comprehensive scenario is drawn up, including as many influencing factors as possible, e.g. the development of social and political structures, environmental pollution, globalization, technical trends, and new customer needs. By way of retropolation back into the present, problems and tasks can be identified, indicating what has to be tackled today in order to be prepared for the future.

The combination of extrapolation and retropolation leads to consistent pictures of the various fields of work – the PoF. They not only point out visions but also and in the first place serve to illustrate in a qualitative way future markets, track down continuities, anticipate future customer needs, and identify technologies with high growth potential and widespread effect. The foremost advantage of the PoF is that in addition to describing the future they help find a way to get there successfully.

(Based on Stuckenschneider and Schwair 2005; for further details see ibid.)

B List of abbreviations

AG	Public company (German: Aktiengesellschaft)
B2B	Business to business
BU	Business unit
CAT	Customer application talk
CEO	Chief Executive Officer
CH	Switzerland
CHF	Swiss Franc(s)
CTI	Competitive technical intelligence
CTO	Chief Technology Officer
EU	European Union
FFE	Fuzzy front end
GDP	Gross domestic product
HBS	Harvard Business School
IP	Intellectual property
IT	Information technology
ITEM-HSG	Institute of Technology Management, University of St. Gallen
NCD	New concept development
NPD	New Product Development
OECD	Organization for economic co-operation and development
PCP	Product creation process
PIN	Planned innovation process
PLM	Product line manager
PM	Product manager
PoF	Picture of the Future
QFD	Quality function deployment
R&D	Research & development
SMEs	Small and mid-sized enterprises
USA / US	United States of America /
USD	US-Dollar

References

Achilladelis, et al. (1971) Project Sapho. A study of success and failures in industrial innovation. Center for the Study of Industrial Innovation

Achtenhagen L, Müller-Lietzkow J, zu Knyphausen-Aufseß D (2003) Das Open Source-Dilemma: Open Source-Software zwischen freier Verfügbarkeit und Kommerzialisierung. Schmalenbachs Zeitschrift für betriebswirtschaftliche Forschung - zfbf, 55(August):455-481

Adamson RE, Taylor dW (1954) Functional fixedness as related to elapsed time and to set. Journal of Experimental Psychology, 47(2):122-126

Alam I (2002) An exploratory investigation of user involvement in new service development. Journal of the Academy of Marketing Sciences, 30(3):250-261

Alba JW, Hutchinson JW (2000) Knowledge calibration: what consumers know and what they think they know. Journal of Consumer Research, 27:123-156

Albach H (1994) Culture and technical innovation. A cross cultural analysis and policy recommendation. Walter de Gruyter Verlag, München

Altshuller G (1984) Managing the flow of technology - Technology transfer and the dissemination of technological information within R&D organizations. Cambridge, London

Altshuller G (1999) Innovation algorithm - TRIZ, systematic innovation and technical creativity. Technical Innovation Ctr

Anderson JR (1983) A spreading activation theory of memory. Journal of Verbal Learning and Verbal Behavior, 22:261-295

Arthur DL (2004) Innovation Excellence Studie - Mit Innovation gegen Stagnation. Arthur D. Little GmbH, Wiesbaden

Athaide GA, Stump RL (1999) A taxonomy of relationship approaches during product development in technology-based, industrial markets. Journal of Product Innovation Management, 16(5):469-482

Atuahene-Gima K (1995) An exploratory analysis of the impact of market orientation on new product performance: A contingency approach. Journal of Product Innovation Management, 12(4):275-293

Backhaus K (2003) Industriegütermarketing. Vahlen

Bacon G, Beckman S (1994) Managing product definition in high-technology industries: A pilot study. California Management Review, 36(3):32-56

Baird IS, Thomas H (1985) Toward a contingency model of strategic risk taking. Academy of Management Review, 10(2):230-243

Baker GA, Burnham TA (2002) The market for genetically modified foods: consumer characteristics and policy implications. International Food and Agribusiness Management Review, 4:351-360

Barney JB (1991) Firm resources and sustained competitive advantage. Journal of Management, 17(1):99-120

Barney JB (2001) Is the resource-based "view" a useful perspective for strategic management research? Yes. Academy of Management Review, 26(1):41-56

Battarbee K, Mattelmäki T, al. e (2000) Design for user experience - method lessons from a design student workshop. NordiCHI2000, Stockholm, 1-2

Bech-Larsen T, Nielsen NA (1999) A comparison of five elicitation techniques for elicitation of attributes of low involvement products. Journal of Economic Psychology, 20:315-341

Belliveau P, Griffin A, Somermeyer S (eds) (2002) PDMA Toolbook for New Product Development. John Wiley and Sons, New York

Berger PL, Luckmann T (1966) The social construction of reality. A treatise in the sociology of knowledge. MacMillan, New York

Biemans WG (1991) User and third-party involvement in developing medical equipment innovations. Technovation, 11(3):163-182

Biemans WG (1992) Managing innovation within networks. Routeledge, London

Birch HG, Rabinowitz HJ (1951) The negative effect of previous experience on productive thinking. Journal of Experimental Psychology, 47(2):121-125

Birkenmeier B, Brodbeck H, Tschirky H (1996) Die Handshake Analysis: eine neue Methode des Technologie- und Innovationsmanagements. IO New Management, 11:19-23

Bleicher K (1991) Das Konzept Integriertes Management. Campus Verlag, Frankfurt / New York

Bollen J, Luce R, Vemulapalli SS, Xu W (2003) Usage analysis for the identification of research trends in digital libraries. D-Lib Magazine, 9(5)

Bonner JM, Walker OC (2004) Selecting influential business-to-business customers in New Product Development: Relational embeddedness and knowledge heterogeneity considerations. Journal of Product Innovation Management, 21(3):155-169

Bossink BAG (2002) The development of co-innovation strategies: stages and interaction patterns in interfirm innovation. R&D Management, 32(4):311-320

Boutellier R, Gassmann O, von Zedtwitz M (2000) Managing global innovation. Springer, Berlin

Bower JL, Christensen CM (1995) Disruptive technologies: Catching the wave. Harvard Business Review, 73(1):43-53

Boynton A, Zmud R, Jacobs G (1994) The influence of IT management practice on IT use in large organizations. MIS Quarterly 18:299-320

Bozeman B, Kingsley G (1998) Risk culture in public and private organizations. Public Administration Review, 58(2):109-118

Brockhoff K (1997) Wenn der Kunde stört - Differenzierungsnotwendigkeiten bei der Einbeziehung von Kunden in die Produktentwicklung. In: Bruhn M, Steffenhagen H (eds) Marktorientierte Unternehmensführung. Gabler, Wiesbaden, pp 352-370

Brockhoff K (1998) Der Kunde im Innovationsprozess. Vandenhoeck und Ruprecht, Göttingen

Brockhoff K (2003) Customers' perspectives of involvement in new product development. International Journal of Technology Management, 26(5/6):464-481

Brockhoff K (2005a) Konflikte bei der Einbeziehung von Kunden in die Produktentwicklung. Zeitschrift für Betriebswirtschaft ZfB, 75(9):859-877

Brockhoff K (2005b) Management des Wissens als Hauptaufgabe des Technologie- und Innovationsmanagements. In: Albers S, Gassmann O (eds) Handbuch Technologie- und Innovationsmanagement Strategie - Umsetzung - Controlling. Gabler Verlag, Wiesbaden, pp 61-80

Brodbeck H, Birkenmeier B, Tschirky H (1995) Neue Entscheidungsstrukturen des Integrierten Technologie-Managements. Die Unternehmung, 2:107ff.

Bruce M, Leverick F, Littler D, Willson D (1995) Success factors for collaborative product development: A study of suppliers of information and communication technology. R&D Management, 25(1):33-44

Bruseberg A, McDonagh-Philp D (2002) Focus groups to support the industrial/product designer: a review based on current literature and designers' feedback. Applied Ergonomics, 33(1):27-38

Buchholz W (1998) Timingstrategien - Zeitoptimale Ausgestaltung von Produktentwicklungsbeginn und Markteintritt. Zeitschrift für betriebswirtschaftliche Forschung, 50(1):21-39

Buckler SA (1997) The spiritual nature of innovation. Research Technology Management, 40(2):43-47

Buggie FD (2002) Set the "Fuzzy Front End" in concrete. Research Technology Management, 45(4):11-14

Cai J (2006) Knowledge management within collaboration processes: A perspective modeling and analyzing methodology. Journal of Database Management, 17(1):33-48

Calder BJ (1977) Focus groups and the nature of qualitative marketing research. Journal of Marketing Research (JMR), 14(3):353-364

Callahan J, Lasry E (2004) The importance of customer input in the development of very new products. R&D Management, 34(2):107-120

Campbell AJ, Cooper RG (1999) Do customer partnerships improve new product success rates? Industrial Marketing Management, 28(5):507

Carroll JD (1972) Individual differences and multidimensional scaling. In: Shepard RN, Romney AK, Nerlove SB (eds) Multidimensional scaling: theory and applications in the behavioral sciences. Seminar Press, New York, pp 105-155

Casciaro T, Piskorski MJ (2005) Power imbalance, mutual dependence, and constraint absorption: A closer look at resource dependence theory. Administrative Science Quarterly, 50:167–199

Chapman CB (2000) A desirable future for technology risk management. International Journal of Risk Assessment and Management, 1(1/2):69-79

Chesbrough H (2003a) The logic of open innovation. California Management Review, 45(3):33-58

Chesbrough HW (2003b) The era of open innovation. Sloan Management Review, 44(3):35

Chesbrough HW (2003c) Open innovation: The new imperative for creating and profiting from technology. Harvard Business School Press, Cambridge

Chesbrough HW (2003d) Reinventing R&D through open innovation. strategy+business news:1-5

Chesbrough HW (2004) Managing open innovation. Research Technology Management, 47(1):23-26

Christensen GL, Olson JC (2002) Mapping consumers' mental models with ZMET. Psychology & Marketing, 19(6):477-502

Christiano JL, Liker JK, White CGI (2000) Customer-driven product development through quality function deployment in US and Japan. Journal of Product Innovation Management, 17:286-308

Claeys C, Swinnen A, Vandeen Abeele P (1995) Consumers' means-end chains for "think" and "feel" products. International Journal of Research Marketing, 12:193-208

Cockburn I, Henderson R (1998) Absorptive capacity, co-authoring behavior, and the organization of research in drug discovery. Journal of Industrial Economics, 46:157-183

Cohen WM, Levinthal DA (1990) Absorptive capacity: A new perspective on learning and innovation. Administrative Science Quarterly, 35(1):128-152

Collins AM, Loftus EF (1975) A spreading-activation theory of semantic processing. Psychological Review, 82(6):407-428

Conner KR (1991) A historical comparison of resource based theory and five schools of thought within industrial organization economics: Do we have a new theory of the firm? Journal of Management, 17(1):121-154

Conner KR, Prahalad CK (1996) A resources-based theory of the firm: knowledge versus opportunism. Organization Science, 7(5):477-501

Conway S (1995) Informal boundary-spanning communication in the innovation process: An empirical study. Technology Analysis & Strategic Management, 7(3):327ff.

Coombs CH (1964) A theory of data. Wiley, New York

Cooper RG (1983) A process model for industrial new product development. IEEE Transactions on Engineering Management, 30(1):2-11

Cooper RG (1988) Predevelopment activities determine new product success. Industrial Marketing Management, 17(3):237-247

Cooper RG (1990) Stage-gate-systems: A new tool for managing new products. Business Horizons, 33(3):44-56

Cooper RG (1994) Third-generation new product process. Journal of Product Innovation Management, 11(1):3-14

Cooper RG (1996) Overhauling the new product process. Industrial Marketing Management, 25(6):465-482

Cooper RG (1997) Fixing the fuzzy front end of the new product process: building the business case. CMA magazine, 71(8):21-23

Cooper RG, Kleinschmidt EJ (1987) Success factors in product innovation. Industrial Marketing Management, 16(3):215-223

Cooper RG, Kleinschmidt EJ (1990) New products: The key factors of success. American Marketing Association, Chicago, IL

Cooper RG, Kleinschmidt EJ (1993) Stage gate systems for new product success. Marketing Management, 1(4):20-29

Cooper RG, Kleinschmidt EJ (1994a) Determinants of timeliness in product development. Journal of Product Innovation Management, 11(5):381-396

Cooper RG, Kleinschmidt EJ (1994b) Screening new products for potential winners. Institute of Electrical and Electronics Engineers IEE, Engineering Management Review, 22(4):24-30

Cooper RG, Kleinschmidt EJ (1995) Benchmarking the firm's critical success factors in new product development. Journal of Product Innovation Management, 12:374-391

Cordero R (1991) Managing for speed to avoid product absolescence: a survey of techniques. Journal of Product Innovation Management, 8(4):283-294

Coulter RA, Zaltman G, Coulter KS (2001) Interpreting consumer perceptions of advertising: an application of the Zaltman Metaphor Elicitation Technique. Journal of Advertising, 30(4):1-21

Covello VT, Merkhofer MW (1993) Risk assessment methods. Approaches for assessing health and environmental risks. Kluwer Academic / Plenum Publishers

Crinnion J (1991) Evolutionary systems development. Pitman Publishing, London

Crow KA (2002) Customer-focused development with QFD. DRM Associates, Palos Verdes

Dabholkar PA, Bagozzi R (2002) An attitudinal model of technology-based self services: Moderating effects of consumer traits and situational factors. Journal of the Academy of Marketing Sciences, 30:184-201

Dahan E, Hauser JR (2001) Product development - Managing a dispersed process. In: Weitz BA, Wensley R (eds) Handbook of Marketing. Sage, London, pp 179-222

Dahan E, Hauser JR (2002) The virtual customer. Journal of Product Innovation Management, 19(5):332-353

Danskin P, Englis BG, Solomon MR, Goldsmith M, Dave J (2005) Knowledge management as competitive advantage: lessons from the textile and apparel value chain. Journal of Knowledge Management, 9(2):91-102

Das TK, Teng B-S (1999) Managing risks in strategic alliances. Academy of Management Executive, 13(4):50

Davenport T, De Long DW, Beers MC (1998) Successful knowledge management projects - Eight key factors can help a company create, share, and use knowledge effectively. Sloan Management Review, 39(2):43-57

Davenport TH, Prusak L (1998) Working knowledge: How organizations manage what they know. Harvard Business School Press, Cambridge, MA

Davis S, Botkin J (1994) The coming of knowledge-based business. Harvard Business Review, 72:165-170

De Brentanni U (1991) Success factors in developing new business services. European Journal of Marketing, 15(2):33-59

De Greene KB (1973) Sociotechnical systems: Factors in analysis, design, and management. Prentice Hall, Englewood Cliffs, NJ

Dehne T (2003) Innovation insider - the corporate culture and customer-inspired innovation. R&D Magazine, (5):11-13

dos Santos A, Specht G, Bingemer S (2003) Die Fallstudie im Erkenntnisprozess. Technische Universität Darmstadt, Darmstadt

Drazin R, Van de Ven AH (1985) Alternative forms of fit in contingency theory. Administrative Science Quarterly, 30(4):514-559

Dürrenberger G, Behringer J (1999) Die Fokusgruppe in Theorie und Anwendung. Rudolf-Sophien-Stiftung GmbH, Stuttgart

Ebert G, Pleschak F, Sabisch H (1992) Aktuelle Aufgaben des Forschungs- und Entwicklungscontrolling in Industrieunternehmen. In: H.G. G, Pleschak F (eds) Innovationsmanagement und Wettbewerbsfähigkeit. Gabler Verlag, Wiesbaden

Eisenhardt KM (1989) Building theories from case study research. Academy of Management Review, 14(4):532

Eliashberg J, Lilien GL, Rao V (1997) Minimizing technological oversights: A marketing research perspective. In: Garud R, Nayyar P, Praveen R, Shapira ZB (eds) Technological innovation: Oversights and foresights. Cambridge University Press, New York, pp 214-230

Engelhardt W, Kleinaltenkamp M, Reckenfelderbäumer M (1993) Leistungsbündel als Absatzobjekte: Ein Ansatz zur Überwindung der Dichotomie von Sach- und Dienstleistungen. Zeitschrift für betriebswirtschaftliche Forschung (zfbf), 45(5):395-426

Enkel E (2005) Management von Wissensnetzwerken - Erfolgsfaktoren und Beispiele. Deutscher Universitäts-Verlag, Wiesbaden

Enkel E, Kausch C, Gassmann O (2005) Managing the risk of customer integration. European Management Journal, 23(2):203-213

Enos JL (1962) Petroleum progress and profits: A history of process innovation. MIT Press, Cambridge, MA

Ernst H (2004) Virtual customer integration - Maximizing the impact of customer integration on new product performance. In: Albers S (ed) Cross-functional innovation management. Perspectives from different disciplines. Gabler Verlag, Wiesbaden, pp 191-208

Farny D (1989) Risk Management und Planung. In: Szyperski N, Winand U (eds) Handwörterbuch der Planung. C.E. Poeschel, Stuttgart, pp 1750-1758

Farr C, Fischer WA (1992) Managing international high technology cooperative projects. R&D Management, 22(1):55-67

Fornell C, Menko RD (1981) Problem analysis: A consumer-based methodology for the discovery of new product ideas. European Journal of Marketing, 15(5):61

Förster A, Kreuz P (2005) Different thinking! Redline

Foxall GR, Tierney JD (1984) From CAP 1 to CAP 2: user initiated innovation from the user's point of view. Management Decision, 22(5):3-15

Franke N, Piller F (2004) Toolkits for user innovation and design: exploring user interaction and value creation in the watch market. Journal of Product Innovation Management, 21(6):401-415

Franke N, Shah S (2003) How communities support innovative activities: an exploration of assistance and sharing among end-users. Research Policy, 32(1):157-178

Franke N, von Hippel E (2002) Satisfying heterogenous user needs via innovation toolkits: The case of apache security software. # 4341-02, MIT Sloan School of Management, Cambridge, MA, 1-32

Freeman C (1968) Chemical process plant: Innovation and the world market. National Inst. Economic Review, 45:29-57

Freeman C (1991) Networks of innovators: a synthesis of research issues. Research Policy, 20:499-514

Frewer LJ, Howard C, Hedderley D, Shepherd R (1997) Consumer attitudes towards different food-processing technologies used in cheese production - the mediating influence of consumer benefit. Food Quality and Preference, 8:271-280

Fuld LM (1994) The new competitor intelligence: The complete resource for finding, analyzing, and using information about your competitors. John Wiley and Sons, New York

Ganesan S (1994) Determinants of long-term orientation in buyer-seller relationships. Journal of Marketing, 58:1-19

Garud R, Nayar PR (1994) Transformative capacity: Continual structuring by intertemporal technology transfer. Strategic Management Journal, 15(5):365-385

Garvin DA (1988) Managing quality. Free Press, New York

Gary L (2003) The customer as product developer. Harvard Management Update, 8(9):3

Gassmann O (1999) Praxisnähe mit Fallstudienforschung: Nutzen für das Technologiemanagement ist gegeben. Wissenschaftsmanagement, (May/June):11-16

Gassmann O (2001) E-Technologien in dezentralen Innovationsprozessen: Empirische Untersuchung unter besonderer Berücksichtigung von Internet-basierten Innovationsprozessen. Zeitschrift für Betriebswirtschaft, (Ergänzungsheft 3/2001):73-90

Gassmann O (2006) Opening up the innovation process: towards an agenda. R&D Management, 36(3):223-228

Gassmann O, Kausch C (2005) Den Technologietrend nicht verschlafen: Strategische Unternehmensführung mit Suchfeldanalyse. Wissenschaftsmanagement, 11(2):25-30

Gassmann O, Kausch C, Enkel E (2005a) Einbeziehung des Kunden in einer frühen Phase des Innovationsprozesses. Thexis, 22(2):9-12

Gassmann O, Kausch C, Enkel E (2005b) Integrating customer knowledge in the early innovation phase. The Sixth European Conference on Organizational Knowledge, Learning and Capabilities (OKLC), Boston, MA

Gassmann O, Kausch C, Enkel E (2006a) Negative side effects of customer integration. International Journal of Technology Management, (forthcoming):1-38

Gassmann O, Kausch C, Wolff T (2006b) Virtual customer integration in the early phase of the innovation process. ITEM Working Paper,

Gassmann O, Sandmeier P, Wecht CH (2004) Innovationsprozesse: Öffnung statt Alleingang. io new management, (1-2):22-27

Gassmann O, Zedtwitz Mv (2003) Innovation process in transnational companies. In: Shavinina LV (ed) International Handbook on Innovation. Elsevier Science, Oxford, pp 702-714

Gebert D, von Rosenstiehl L (1981) Organisationspsychologie. Kohlhammer, Stuttgart

Gebert H, Geib M, Kolbe L, Brenner W (2003) Knowledge-enabled customer relationship management: integrating customer relationship management and knowledge management concepts. Journal of Knowledge Management, 7(5):107-123

Gemuenden HG (1981) Innovationsmarketing: Interaktionsbeziehungen zwischen Hersteller und Verwender innovativer Investitionsgüter. Mohr, Tübingen

Geschka H (1993) Wettbewerbsfaktor Zeit: Beschleunigung von Innovationsprozessen. Moderne Industrie, Landsberg

Geschka H (1995) Methoden der Technologiefrühaufklärung und der Technologievorhersage. In: Zahn E (ed) Handbuch Technologiemanagement. Schäffer-Poeschel Verlag, Stuttgart, pp 623-644

Gibbert M, Leibold M, Probst G (2002) Five styles of customer knowledge management, and how smart companies use them to create value. European Management Journal, 20(5):459

Glazer R (1991) Marketing in an information-intensive environment: Strategic implications of knowledge as an asset. Journal of Marketing, 55(4):1

Grant R (1997) The knowledge-based view of the firm: Implications for management practice. Longe Range Planning, 30(3):450-454

Grant R (2002) The knowledge-based view of the firm. In: Choo CW, Bontis N (eds) The Strategic Management of Intellectual Capital and Organizational Knowledge. Oxford University Press, New York

Grant RM (1991) The resource-based Theory of competitive advantage - Implications for strategy formation. California Management Review, 33:114-135

Grant RM (1996) Towards a knowledge-based theory of the firm. Strategic Management Journal, 17(Winter Special Issue):109-122

Grant RM, Baden-Fuller C (1995) A knowledge-based theory of inter-firm collaboration. Academy of Management Journal:17-21

Green PE, Carmone FJ (1969) Multidemnsional scaling. An introduction and comparison of nometric unfolding techniques. Journal of Marketing Research, 6:330-341

Green PE, Krieger AM, Wind Y (2001) Thirty years of conjoint analysis: reflections and prospects. Interfaces, 31(3, part 2):56-73

Green PE, Srinivasan V (1978) Conjoint analysis in consumer research: issues and outlook. Journal of Consumer Research, 5:103-152

Greenbaum TL (1993) The handbook for focus group research. Lexington, New York

Greenhoff K, MacFie HJH (1994) Preference mapping in practice. In: MacFie HJH, Thomson DMH (eds) Measurement of food preferences. Blackies Academic & Professional, Glasgow

Grossmann M (2006) An overview of knowledge management assessment approaches. Journal of American Academy of Business, 8(2):242-247

Gruner KE, Homburg C (1999) Innovationserfolg durch Kundeneinbindung. Eine empirische Untersuchung. Zeitschrift für Betriebswirtschaft, (Ergänzungsheft 1/1999):119-142

Gruner KE, Homburg C (2000) Does customer interaction enhance new product success? Journal of Business Research, 49(1):1-14

Gugler P (1992) Building transnational alliances to create competitive advantage. Long Range Planning, 25(1):90-99

Guinard J-X, Uotani B, Schlich P (2001) Internal and external mapping of preferences for commercial lager beers: comparison of hedonic ratings by consumers blind versus with knowledge of brand and price. Food Quality and Preference, 12(4):243-255

Gutman J (1982) A means-end chain model based on consumer categorization processes. Journal of Marketing, 46:60-72

Hagedoorn J (1993) Understanding the rationale of strategic technology partnering: interorganizational modes of cooperation and sectoral differences. Strategic Management Journal, 14:371-385

Hagedoorn J (2003) Sharing intellectual property rights--an exploratory study of joint patenting amongst companies. Industrial & Corporate Change, 12(5):1035-1050

Hagedoorn J, Duysters G (2002) External sources of innovative capabilities: The preferences for strategic alliances or mergers and acquisitions. Journal of Management Studies, 39(2):167-188

Hallbauer S (1997) Prototypenmanagement im Entwicklungsverbund - Ein Gestaltungskonzept auf Basis des Modells lebensfähiger Systeme. Rosch-Buch GmbH, Schesslitz

Haman G (1996) Techniques and tools to generate breakthrough products. In: Rosenau MD (ed) PDMA Handbook of New Product Development. John Wiley and Sons, New York, pp 167-178

Hamel G, Doz YL, Prahalad CK (1989) Collaborate with your competitors and win. Harvard Business Review, 67(1):133-139

Handelsblatt (2006) Gründerszene Chitodent. Handelsblatt, 02.02.2006, pp 9

Harhoff D, Henkel J, von Hippel E (2003) Profiting from voluntary information spillovers: how users benefit by freely revealing their innovations. Research Policy, 32(10):1753-1769

Hatch MJ (1997) Organization theory: Modern, symbolic, and postmodern perspectives. Oxhord University Press, New York

Hattori R, Lapidus T (2004) Collaboration, trust and innovative change. Journal of Change Management, 4(2):97-104

Hayes RH, Wheelwright SC (1988) Dynamic manufacturing. Free Press, New York

Hedberg B, Dahlgren G, Hansson J, Olve N-G (1997) Virtual organizations and beyond: Discover imaginary systems. John Wiley & Sons, Chichester

Hedlund G, Nonaka I (1993) Models of knowledge management in the West and Japan. In: Lorange P, Chakrabari AK, Roos J (eds) Implementing Strategic

Processes, Change, Learning and cooperation. Blackwell Business, Oxford, pp 117-144

Helm R, Kloyer M (2004) Controlling contractual exchange risks in R&D interfirm cooperation: an empirical study. Research Policy, 33:1103-1122

Helten E (1994) Ist Risiko ein Konstrukt? Zur Qualifizierung des Risikobegriffs. Karlsruhe

Herstatt C (1991) Anwender als Quellen für die Produktinnovation. University of Zurich, Zurich

Herstatt C (1999) Theorie und Praxis der frühen Phasen des Innovationsprozesses. io new management, 68(10):72-81

Herstatt C (2002) Suchfelder für radikale Innovationen gemeinsam mit Lead Usern erschliessen. In: Albers S, Haßmann V, Somm F, Tomczak T (eds) Verkauf - Digitale Fachbibliothek auf CD-Rom. Symposion, Düsseldorf

Herstatt C, Lüthje C, Lettl C (2002) Wie fortschrittliche Kunden zu Innovationen stimulieren. Harvard Business Manager, 24(1):60-68

Herstatt C, Lüthje C, Lettl C (2003) Fortschrittliche Kunden zu Breakthroug-Innovationen stimulieren. In: Herstatt C, Verworn B (eds) Management der frühen Innovationsphasen. Gabler Verlag, Wiesbaden, pp 57-71

Herstatt C, Verworn B (2003) Management der frühen Innovationsphasen - Grundlagen - Methoden - Neue Ansätze. Gabler, Wiesbaden

Herstatt C, von Hippel E (1992) From experience: Developing new product concepts via the lead user method: A case study in a "low-tech" field. Journal of Product Innovation Management, 9(3):213-221

Higgins J, Wiese G (1996) Innovationsmanagement. Springer-Verlag, Berlin Heidelberg New York

Hillebrand B, Biemans WG (2003) The relationship between internal and external cooperation: literature review and propositions. Journal of Business Research, 56(9):735-743

Holmes M (1999) Product development in the new millenium - a CIPD vision. Product Development Management Association, Marco Island, Fl

Houghton (2006) Tracking youth trends on the web. accessed: January 27, 2006, www.freeprint.com/issues/100305.htm#features

Huber G (1991) Organizational learning: The contributing processes and the literature. Organization Science, 2:88-115

Hughes GD, Chafin DC (1996) Turning new product development into a continuous learning process. Journal of Product Innovation Management, 13(1):89-104

Hutt MD, Stafford ER (2000) Defining the social network of a strategic alliance. Sloan Management Review, 41(2):51

Hwang A-S (2004) Integrating technology, marketing and management innovation. Research Technology Management, 47(4):27-31

Ishii A (2004) Cooperative R&D between vertically related firms with spillovers. International Journal of Industrial Organization, 22(8-9):1213-1235

Jeppesen LB, Molin MJ (2003) Consumers as co-developers: Learning and innovation outside the firm. Carfax Publishing Company

Johannessen J-A, Olsen B, Olaisen J (1999) Aspects of innovation theory based on knowledge-management. International Journal of Information Management, 19(2):121-139

Johne A (1994) Listening to the voice of the market. International Marketing Review, 11(1):47

Johne FA, Snelson PA (1988) Success factors in product innovation: A selective review of the literature. Journal of Product Innovation Management, 5(2):114-128

Johnson CN (2003) QFD explained. Quality Progress, 36(3):104

Jonash RS, Sommerlatte T (2000) The innovation premium: How next-generation companies are achieving peak performance and profitability. Perseus Publishing, Cambridge, MA

Jones O, Conway S, Steward F (2000) Introduction: Social interaction and organisation change. In: Jones O, Conway S, Steward F (eds) Social interaction and organisation change: Aston perspectives on innovation networks. Imperial College Press, London, pp 1-40

Joy J, Griffiths D (2005) National minerals industry safety and health risk assessment guideline. MISHC, Brisbane

Kahaner L (1998) Competitive intelligence: How to gather, analyze and use information to move business to the top. Touchstone Books, New York

Kahn KB (2001) Market orientation, interdepartmental integration, and product development performance. Journal of Product Innovation Management, 18(5):314-323

Karle-Komes N (1997) Anwenderintegration in die Produktentwicklung : Generierung von Innovationsideen durch die Interaktion von Hersteller und Anwender innovativer industrieller Produkte. Lang, Frankfurt/Main; Bern [etc.]

Kausch P, Matschullat (eds) (2005) Rohstoffe der Zukunft - Neue Basisstoffe und neue Energien. Frank & Timme Verlag, Berlin

Keller W (1996) Absorptive capacity: On the creation and acquisition of technology in development. Journal of Development Economics, 49:199-210

Kelly GA (1955) The psychology of personal constructs. Norton, New York

Kern W, Schröder H-K (1977) Forschung und Entwicklung in der Unternehmung. Reinbek

Khurana A, Rosenthal SR (1997) Integrating the fuzzy front end of new product development. Sloan Management Review, 38(2):103-120

Khurana A, Rosenthal SR (1998) Towards holistic "front ends" in new product development. Journal of Product Innovation Management, 15(1):57-74

Kieser A (2001) Der situative Ansatz. In: Kieser A (ed) Organisationstheorien. Kohlhammer, Stuttgart, Berlin, Köln

Kim J, Wilemon D (2002a) Focusing the fuzzy front–end in new product development. R & D Management, 32(4):269-279

Kim J, Wilemon D (2002b) Strategic issues in managing innovation's fuzzy front-end. European Journal of Innovation Management, 5(Number 1):27-39

Kim L (1998) Crisis construction and organizational learning: Capability building in catching-up at Hyundai Motor. Organization Science, 9:506-521

Kirchmann EMW (1994) Innovationskooperation zwischen Herstellern und Anwendern. DUV Deutscher Universitäts-Verlag, Wiesbaden

Kirschbaum R (2005) Open innovation in practice. Research Technology Management, 48(4):24-28

Klee K (2004) Rewriting the rules in R&D. Corporate Dealmaker, (December):14-21

Knolmayer G (2002) On the economics of mass customization. In: Rautenstrauch C, Seelmann-Eggebrecht R, Turowski K (eds) Moving into mass customization. Springer, Berlin / Heidelberg, pp 3-17

Kobe C (2001) Integration der Technologiebeobachtung in die Frühphase von Innovationsprojekten. University of St. Gallen, St. Gallen

Koen P, Ajamian G, Burkart R, Clamen A, Davidson J, D'Amore R, Elkins C, Herald K, Incorvia M, Johnson A, Karol R, Seibert R, Slavejkov A, Wagner K (2001) Providing clarity and a common language to the 'fuzzy front end'. Research Technology Management, 44(2):46-55

Koen P, Ajamian GM, Boyce S, Clamen A, Fisher E, Fountoulakis S, Johnson A, Puri P, Seibert R (2002) Fuzzy front end: Effective methods, tools, and techniques. In: Belliveau P, Griffin A, Somermeyer S (eds) PDMA toolbook for new product development. John Wiley and Sons, New York, pp 5-36

Kogure M, Akao Y (1983) Quality function deployment and CWQC in Japan. Quality Progress:25-29

Kogut B, Zander U (1992) Knowledge of the firm, combinative capabilities, and the replication of technology. Organization Science, 3(3):383-397

Kogut B, Zander U (1996) What firms do? Coordination, identity, and learning. Organization Science, 7(5):502-518

Kohli AK, Jaworski BJ (1990) Market orientation: The construct, research propositions, and managerial implications. Journal of Marketing, 54(2):1-18

Kohn S, Niethammer R (2002) Aufgabengerechte Kundeneinbindung im Innovationsprozess. In: Barske A (ed) Das innovative Unternehmen - Digitale Fachbibliothek auf CD-Rom. Symposion, Düsseldorf

Kok RAW, Hillebrand B, Biemans WG (2003) What makes product development market oriented? Towards a conceptual framework. International Journal of Innovation Management, 7(2):137

Kollock P, Smith MA (1999) Communities in cyberspace. Routledge, London

Krapfel RE, Salmond D, Spekman R (1991) A strategic approach to managing buyer-seller relationships. European Journal of Marketing, 25(9):22-38

Krieger B, Cappuccio R, Katz R, Moskowitz H (2003) Next generation healthy soup: an exploration using conjoint analysis. Journal of Sensory Studies, 18(3):249-268

Kristensson P, Gustafsson A, Archer T (2004) Harnessing the creative potential among users. Journal of Product Innovation Management, 21:4-14

Kristensson P, Magnusson PR, Matthing J (2002) Users as a hidden resource for creativity: Findings from an experimental study on user involvement. Creativity & Innovation Management, 11(1):55ff.

Kromrey H (1995) Empirische Sozialforschung: Modelle und Methoden der Datenerhebung und Auswertung. Opladen

Krueger RA, Casey MA (2000) Focus groups: A practical guide for applied research. Sage Publications, Inc

Kubicek H (1977) Heuristische Bezugsrahmen und heuristisch angelegte Forschungsdesigns als Elemente einer Konstruktionsstrategie empirischer Forschung. In: Köhler R (ed) Empirische und handlungstheoretische Forschungskonzeptionen in der Betriebswirtschaftslehre. Stuttgart, pp 5 - 36

Kujala S (2003) User involvement: a review of the benefits and challenges. Behaviour & Information Technology, 22(1):1

Kujala S, Mäntylä M (eds) (2000) How effective are user studies? Springer, London

Kusonoki K, Nonaka I, Nagata A (1998) Organizational capabilities in product development of Japanese firms: A conceptual framework and empirical findings. Organization Science, 9(6):699-718

Lakhani KR, von Hippel E (2003) How open source software works: "free" user-to-user assistance. Research Policy, 32(6):923-943

Lamnek S (1993) Qualitative Sozialforschung: Bd. 2: Methoden und Techniken. Weinheim

Lane PJ, Koka B, Pathak S (2002) A thematic analysis and critical assessment of absorptive capacity research. Academy of Management Proceedings:M1-M6

Lane PJ, Lubatkin M (1998) Relative absorptive capacity and interorganizational learning. Strategic Management Journal, 19:461-477

Langford J, McDonagh D (2003) Focus groups. Supporting effective product development. Taylor & Francis Inc, New York

Larson CF (2001) Management for the new millenium - the challenge of change. Research Technology Management, 44(6):10-12

Lengnick-Hall CA (1996) Customer contributions to quality: A different view of the customer-oriented firm. Academy of Management Review, 21(3):791-810

Leonard-Barton D (1994) Empathic design and experimental modeling: Explorations into really new products. In: Adams ME, LaCugna J (eds) And now for something completely different: "Really" new products. Marketing Science Institute, Boston, MA

Leonard D (1995) Wellsprings of knowledge: Building and sustaining the sources of innovation. Harvard Business School Press, Boaton: Massachusetts

Leonard D (2002) The limitations of listening. Harvard Business Review, 80(1):93

Leonard D, Rayport JF (1997) Spark innovation through empathic design. Harvard Business Review, 75(6):102-108

Leonard D, Sensiper S (1998) The role of tacit knowledge in group innovation. California Management Review, 40(3):112-132

Lettl C (2004) Die Rolle von Anwender bei hochgradigen Innovationen. Deutscher Universitäts Verlag, Wiesbaden

Li T, Calantone RJ (1998) The impact of market knowledge competence on new product advantage: Conceptualization and empirical examination. Journal of Marketing, 62(4):13-29

Lichtenthaler E (2000) Organisation der Technology Intelligence in Abhängigkeit der Wettbewerbssituatio. ETH Zürich, Zürich

Lilien GL, Morrison PD, Searls K, Sonnack M, Von Hippel E (2002) Performance assessment of the lead user idea-generation process for new product development. Management Science, 48(8):1042-1059

Lilien GL, Rangaswamy A (1998) Marketing engineering: Computer-assisted marketing analysis and planning. Addison-Wesley-Longman, Reading, MA

Lim K (2000) The many faces of absorptive capacity: spillovers of copper interconnect technology for semiconductor chips. Mimeo, MIT, Cambridge

Linder JC, Jarvenpaa S, Davenport TH (2003) Toward an innovation sourcing strategy. Sloan Management Review, 44(4):43-49

Link P (2001) Risikomanagement in Innvoationskooperationen. ETH Zürich, Zürich

Link P, Marxt C (2004) Integration of risk- and chance management in the cooperation process. International Journal of Production Economics, 90(1):71-78

Linner S (1995) Konzept einer integrierten Produktentwicklung. Springer, Berlin

Linton JD, Walsh ST, Morabito J (2002) Analysis, ranking and selection of R&D projects in a portfolio. R & D Management, 32(2):139-148

Littler D, Leverick F, Bruce M (1995) Factors affecting the process of collaborative product development: A study of UK manufacturers of information and communications technology products. Journal of Product Innovation Management, 12(1):16-32

Lorange P (1991) Analytical steps in the formation of strategic alliances. Journal of Organizational Management, 14(1)

Lukas BA, Ferrell OC (2000) The effect of market orientation on product innovation. Journal of the Academy of Marketing Science, 28(2):239-247

Lüthje C (2000) Kundenorientierung im Innovationsprozess: Eine Untersuchung der Kunden-Hersteller-Interaktion in Konsumgütermärkten. Deutscher Universitätsverlag, Wiesbaden

Lüthje C (2003) Kundenorientierung als Erfolgsfaktor im Innovationsprozess. In: Herstatt C, Verworn B (eds) Management der frühen Innovationsphasen. Gabler Verlag, Wiesbaden, pp 36-56

Lüthje C (2004) Characteristics of innovating users in a consumer goods field: an empirical study of sport-related product consumers. Technovation, 24:683-695

Lüthje C, Herstatt C (2004) The lead user method: an outline of empirical findings and issues for future research. R & D Management, 34(5):553-568

Lynch P, O' Toole T (2003) After von Hippel: The state of user involvement research in new product development. 19th IMP-Conference, Lugano, Switzerland

Lynn GS, Morone JG, Paulson AS (1996) Marketing and discontinuous innovation: The probe and learn process. California Management Review, 38(3):8-37

Mabert VA, Muth JF, Schmenner RW (1992) Collapsing new product development times: six case studies. Journal of Product Innovation Management, 9(3):200-212

Madauss B-J (1994) Projektdefinition. In: Schnelle H, Reschke H, Schub A (eds) vol 2 Projekte erfolgreich managen. TèV-Verlag, Köln

Malhotra Y (2005) Integrating knowledge management technologies in organizational business processes: getting real time enterprises deliver real business performance. Journal of Knowledge Management, 9(1):7-28

March JG (1991) Exploration and exploitation in organizational learning. Organization Science, 2:71-87

Margerison C, McCann D (1984) Team mapping: A new approach to managerial leadership. Journal of European Industrial Training, 8(1):12-16

Markham SK, Griffin A (1998) The breakfast of champions: Associations between champions and product development environments... Journal of Product Innovation Management, 15(5):436

Mascitelli R (2000) From experience: Harnessing tacit knowledge to achieve breakthrough innovation. Journal of Product Innovation Management, 17(3):179-193

Massey AP, Montoya-Weiss MM, O'Driscoll TM (2002) Performance-centered design of knowledge-intensive processes. Journal of Management Information Systems, 18(4):37-58

McKenna E (2000) Business psychology and organisational behiour. Psychology Press, Howe

McNeill KL, Sanders TH, Civille GV (2000) Using focus groups to develop a quantitive consumer questionnaire for peanut butter. Journal of Sensory Studies, 15:163-178

McQuarrie EF, McIntyre SH (1986) Focus groups and the development of new products by technologically driven companies: Some guidelines. Journal of Product Innovation Management, 3(1):40-47

Meade LM, Presley A (2002) R&D project selection using the analytic network process. IEEE Transactions on Engineering Management, 49(1):59-66

Mehrwald H (1999) Das 'not invented here'-Syndrom in Forschung und Entwicklung. DUV, Wiesbaden

Miles MB, Huberman AM (1994) Qualitative data analysis. Sage Publications, Newbury Park, CA, London

Millson MR, Raj SP (1996) Strategic partnering for developing new products. Research Technology Management, 39(3):41

Millson MR, Raj SP, Wilemon D (1992) A survey of major approaches for accelerating new product development. Journal of Product Innovation Management, 9(1):53-69

Miotti L, Sachwald F (2003) Co-operative R&D: why and with whom? An integrated framework of analysis. Research Policy, 32(8):1481-1499

Moenart RK, De Meyer A, Souder WE, al. e (1995) R&D/Marketing communication during the fuzzy front-end. IEEE Transactions on Engineering Management, 42(3):243-258

Montoya-Weiss MM, O'Driscoll TM (2000) From experience: Applying performance support technology in the fuzzy front end. Journal of Product Innovation Management, 17(2):143-161

Morgan DL (1988) Focus groups as qualitative research. Sage Publications, New-bury Park

Morrison PD, Roberts JH, Midgley DF (2004) The nature of lead users and measurement of leading edge status. Research Policy, 33(2):351-362

Moskowitz HR (1985) New directions for product testing and sensory analysis of foods. Food and Nutrition Press, Trumbell Conn

Moskowitz HR (1994) Food concepts and products. Just-in-time development. Food and Nutrition Press, Trumbell Conn

Mowery DC, Oxley JE (1995) Inward technology transfer and competitiveness: the role of national innovation systems. Cambridge Journal of Economics, 19:67-93

Mowery DC, Oxley JE, Silverman BS (1996) Strategic alliances and interfirm knowledge transfer. Strategic Management Journal, 17:77-91

Muessig P (1997) Optimizing the selection of VV&A activities - a risk / benefit approach. Winter Simulation Conference,

Muller A, Välikangas L (2002) Extending the boundary of corporate innovation. Strategy and Leadership, 30(3):4-9

Muller J-P (2005) Stratégie d'innovation, concurrence et performance des nouveaux produits. Revue Française de Gestion, 31(155):57-76

Murphy SA, Kumar V (1996) The role of predevelopment activities and firm attributes in new product success. Technovation, 16(8):431-449

Murphy SA, Kumar V (1997) The front end of new product development: A Canadian survey. R & D Management, 27(1):5-15

Nagel R (1993) Lead User Innovationen: Entwicklungskooperationen am Beispiel elektronischer Leiterplatten. DUV Deutscher Universitätsverlag, Wiesbaden

Nahapiet J, Ghoshal S (1998) Social capital, intellectual capital, and the organizational advantage. Academy of Management Review, 23(2):242-266

Nambisan S (2002) Designing virtual customer environments for new product development: Toward a theory. Academy of Management Review, 27(3):392

Neef D (2005) Managing corporate risk through better knowledge management. The learning organization, 12(2):112-124

Nichani M (2002) Empathic instructional design. E-learningpost (http://www.elearningpost.com/features/archives/001003.asp): found Mai 20, 2004

Nielsen NA, Bech-Larsen T, Grunert KG (1998) Consumer purchase motives and product perceptions: a laddering study on vegetable oil in three countries. Food Quality and Preference, 9(6):455-466

Nihtilä J (1999) R&D-production integration in the early phases of new product development projects. Journal of Engineering and Technology Management, 16(1):55-81

Nobelius D, Trygg L (2002) Stop chasing the front end process - management of the early phases in product development projects. International Journal of Project Management, 20(5):331-340

Nonaka I (1991) The knowledge-creating company. Harvard Business Review, 69(6):96-104

Nonaka I (1994) A dynamic theory of organizational knowledge creation. Organization Science, 5(1):14-37

Nonaka I (2000) Knowledge emergence social, technical, and evolutionary dimensions of knowledge creation. University Press, Oxford

Nonaka I, Takeuchi H (1995) The knowledge creating company: How Japanese companies create the dynamics of innovation. Oxford University Press, New York / Oxford

Nonaka I, Takeuchi H, Mader F (1997) Die Organisation des Wissens: Wie japanische Unternehmen eine brachliegende Ressource nutzbar machen. Campus Verlag, Frankfurt am Main / New York

Nottrodt J (1999) Qualitätssteigerung in der Produktentwicklung durch frühzeitige Nutzung von Informationen zu vorhandenen Produkten. VDI-Verlag, Düsseldorf

O'Connor GC, Veryzer RW (2001) The nature of market visioning for technology-based radical innovation. Journal of Product Innovation Management, 18(4):231-246

OECD (2006) OECD factbook 2006 - economic, environmental and social statistics. OECD, Paris

Ofek E, Srinivasan V (2002) How much does the market value an improvement in a product attribute? Marketing Science, 21:398-411

Olson EL, Bakke G (2001) Implementing the lead user method in a high technology firm: a longitudinal study of intentions versus actions. Journal of Product Innovation Management, 18(6):388-395

Ornetzeder M, Rohracher H (2006) User-led innovations and participation processes: Lessons from sustainable energy technologies. Energy Policy, 34:138ff

Ozer M (2003) Using the internet in new product development. Research Technology Management, 46(1):10ff.

Park CW, Jun SY, MacInnis DJ (2000) Choosing what I want versus rejecting what I do not want: An application of decision framing to product option choice decisions. Journal of Marketing Research (JMR), 37(2):187

Paustian C (2001) Better products through virtual customers. Sloan Management Review, 42(3):2p

Pfeffer J, Salancik GR (1978) The external control of orgnizations: a resource dependence perspective. Harper & Row, New York

Piller F (2003) Von Open Source zu Open Innovation. Harvard Business Manager, 25(12):114

Piller F (2004) Innovation and value co-creation. Habilitationsschrift an der Fakultät für Wirtschaftswissenschaften der Technischen Universität München, München

Pitt M, Clarke K (1999) Competing on competence: A knowledge perspective on the management of strategic innovation. Technology Analysis & Strategic Management, 11(3):301-313

Pitta D, Franzak A, Katsanis F, Prevel L (1996) Redefining new product development teams: learning to actualize consumer contributions. Journal of Product & Brand Management, 5(6):48-60

Pleschak F, Sabisch H (1996) Innovationsmanagement. Schäffer-Poeschel, Stuttgart

Polanyi M (1966) The tacit dimension. Doubleday, New York

Porter ME (1980) Competitive strategy: Techniques for analyzing industries and competitors. Free Press, New York

Porter ME (1985) Competitive advantage: Creating and sustaining superior performance. Campus, New York

Powell WW, Koput KW, Smith-Doerr L (1996) Interorganizational collaboration and the locus of innovation: Networks of learning in biotechnology. Administrative Science Quarterly, 41:116-145

Prahalad CK, Hamel G (1990) The core competence of the corporation. Harvard Business Review, 68(3):79-91

Prahalad CK, Ramaswamy V (2000) Co-opting customer competence. Harvard Business Review, 78(1):79-87

Probst G, Romhardt K, Raub S (1997) Wissen managen - Wie Unternehmen ihre wertvollste Ressource optimal nutzen. Gabler, Wiesbaden

Qualls W, Olshavsky RW, Michaels RE (1981) Shortening of the product lifecycle: an empirical test. Journal of Marketing, 5(3):76-80

Rehäuser J, Krcmar H (1996) Wissensmanagement in Unternehmen. In: Schreyoegg G, Conrad P (eds) vol 6 Wissensmanagement, Managementforschung 6. Springer, Berlin, pp 1-40

Reichart SV (2002) Kundenorientierung im Innovationsprozess: die erfolgreiche Integration von Kunden in den frühen Phasen der Produktentwicklung. Deutscher Universitäts-Verlag, Wiesbaden

Reichwald R, Piller F (2003) Von Massenproduktion zu Co-Produktion: Kunden als Wertschöpfungspartner. Wirtschaftsinformatik, 45(5):515-519

Reichwald R, Piller F (2005) Open Innovation: Kunden als Partner im Innovationsprozess. In: Habenicht W, Foschiani S, Wäscher G (eds) Festschrift für Erich Zahn. Peter Lang Verlag, Frankfurt am Main

Reid SE, de Brentani U (2004) The fuzzy front end of new product development for discontinuous innovations: A theoretical model. Journal of Product Innovation Management, 21(3):170-184

Reinertsen DG (1999) Taking the fuzziness out of the fuzzy front end. Research Technology Management, 42(6):25-31

Rice M, Kelley D, Peters L, Colarelli O'Connor G (2001) Radical innovation: triggering initiation of opportunity recognition and evaluation. R & D Management, 31(4):12p

Richardson-Harman NJ, Stevens R, Walker S, Gamble J, Miller M, Wong M, McPherson A (2000) Mapping consumer perceptions of creaminess and liking for liquid dairy products. Food Quality and Preference, 11:239-246

Rigby D, Zook C (2002) Open-market innovation. Harvard Business Review, 80(10):80-89

Ring JF (2002) Risk assessment - all risk approach. University College, Cork

Rochford L (1991) Generating and screening new product ideas. Industrial Marketing Management, 20:287-296

Rosenau MD (1997) Speeding from idea to profit. Machine Design, 69(18):103-106

Rosenau MD, Griffin A, Castellion GA, Anschuetz NF (1996) The PDMA handbook of new product development John Wiley & Sons, New York

Rothwell R, Freeman C, Horlsey A, Jervis VTP, Robertson AB, Townsend J (1974) SAPPHO updated - project SAPPHO phase II. Research Policy, 3(3):258-291

Rowe WD (1977) Anatomy of risk. Wiley, New York

Saatweber J (1997) Kundenorientierung durch Quality Function Deployment. Carl Hanser Verlag, München

Salomo S, Steinhoff F, Trommsdorff V (2003) Customer orientation in innovation projects and new product development success - The moderating effect of product innovativeness. International Journal of Technology Management, 25(6/7):442ff.

Sampson P (1972) Using the repertory grid test. Journal of Marketing Research, 9:78-81

Sandmeier P (2006) Integrating customers into industrial product innovation - Lessons from extreme programming. University of St. Gallen, St. Gallen

Savioz P, Brodbeck H, Birkenmeier B, Lichtenthaler E (2001) Ansätze zur systematischen Gestaltung der Frühphase von Innovationsprozessen. In: Meyer J-A (ed) Innovationsmanagement in kleinen und mittleren Unternehmen. Vahlen Verlag, München, pp 65-74

Saynisch M (1979) Phasenweiser Projektablauf bei Entwicklungsvorhaben. In: Saynisch M, Schub A (eds) Projektmanagement: Konzepte, Verfahren, Anwendungen. Oldenbourg, München, Wien, pp 85-172

Schewe G (2005) Produktimitation als Innovationsstrategie. In: Albers S, Gassmann O (eds) Handbuch Technologie- und Innovationsmanagement. Gabler Verlag, Wiesbaden, pp 193-206

Schilling M (1998) Technological lookout: An integrative model of the economic and strategic factors driving technology success and failure. Academy of Management Review, 23:267-284

Schilling MA, Hill CWL (1998) Managing the new product development process: Strategic imperatives. Academy of Management Executive, 12(3):67

Schlaak TM (1999) Der Innovationsgrad als Schlüsselvariable: Perspektiven für das Management von Produktentwicklungen. Deutscher Universitäts Verlag, Wiesbaden

Schlicksupp H (1989) Innovation, Kreativität und Ideenfindung. Vogel Verlag, Würzburg

Schmelzer HJ (1999) Organisation und Bewertung von Produktentwicklungsprozessen. In: Tintelnot C, Meissner D, Steinmeier I (eds) Innovationsmanagement. Springer, Berlin

Schumpeter JA (1939) Konjunkturzyklen: eine theoretische, historische und statistische Analyse des kapitalistischen Prozesses. Vandenhoeck & Ruprecht, Göttingen

Schwankl L (2002) Analyse und Dokumentation in den frühen Phasen der Produktentwicklung. Dr. Hut, München

Scott R (1992) Organizations: Rational, natural, and open systems. Prentice Hall, Englewood Cliffs, NJ

Scott R (2003) Organizations: Rational, natural and open systems. Prentice Hall, Englewood Cliffs, NJ

Shapiro C, Varian H (1999) Information rules. Harvard Business School Press, Boston

Shaw B (1985) The role of the interaction between the user and the manufacturer in medical equipment innovation. R & D Management, 15(4):283-292

Simon P (1999) Risk management in engineering projects. In: Morris P (ed) Risk Management in Engineering Projects. The Institution of Electrical Engineers. London, pp 2/1-2/15

Sitkin SB, Pablo AL (1992) Reconceptualizing the determinants of risk behavior. Academy of Management Review, 17:9-39

Smith GR, Herbein WC, Morris RC (1999) Front-end innovation at AlliedSignal and Alcoa. Research Technology Management, 42(6):15-24

Smith PG, Reinertsen D (1991) Developing products in half the time. Van Nostrand Reinhold, New York

Smith PG, Reinertsen D (1992) Shortening the product development cycle. Research Technology Management, 35(3):44-49

Souder WE, Moenart RK (1992) Integrating marketing and R&D project personnel within innovation projects: an information uncertainty model. Journal of Management Studies, 29(4):485-512

Specht G, Beckmann C (1996) F&E-Management. Schäffer-Poeschel, Stuttgart

Specht G, Zörgiebel WW (1985) Technologieorientierte Wettbewerbsstrategien. Marketing, 7:161-172

Spender J-C (1996) Making knowledge the basis of a dynamic theory of the firm. Strategic Management Journal, 17(Winter Special Issue):45-62

Stalk G (2006) Hardball innovation. Research Technology Management, 49(1):20-29

Stock GN, Greis NP, Fischer WA (2001) Absorptive capacity and new product development. Journal of High Technology Management Research, 12(1):77

Stoner JA (1982) Management. Englewood Cliffs

Stuckenschneider H, Schwair T (2005) Strategisches Innovations-Management bei Siemens. In: Albers S, Gassmann O (eds) Handbuch Technologie- und Innovationsmanagement. Gabler Verlag, Wiesbaden, pp 763-780

Stupay P (2004) Making open innovation work for you. Research and Development, 46:E5

Szulanski G (1996) Exploring internal stickiness: Impediments to the transfer of best practice within the firm. Strategic Management Journal, 17:27-43

Tanner D (1992) Applying creative thinking techniques to everyday problems. Journal of Consumer Marketing, 9(4):23

Tapon F, Thong M (1999) Research collaborations by multi-national research oriented pharmaceutical firms: 1988-1997. R&D Management, 29(3):219-231

Tauber EM (1975) Discovering new product opportunities with problem inventory analysis. Journal of Marketing, 39(1):67-70

Teece DJ (1998) Capturing value from knowledge assets: The new economy, markets for know-how, and intangible assets. California Management Review, 40(3):55-79

Thom N (1980) Grundlagen des betrieblichen Innovationsmanagements. Peter Hanstein Verlag, Königstein

Thomke S, Fujimoto T (2000) The effect of "front-loading" problem-solving on product development performance. Journal of Product Innovation Management, 17(2):128-142

Thomke S, von Hippel E (2002) Customers as innovators: A new way to create value. Harvard Business Review, 80(4):74-81

Thomson DMH, McEwan JA (1988) An application of the repertory grid to investigate consumer perceptions of foods. Appetite, 10:181-193

Tidd J (1997) Complexity, networks and learning: Integrative themes for research on the management of innovation. International Journal of Product Development, 1(1):1-19

Tidd J, Bodley K (2002) The influence of project novelty on the new product development process. R&D Management, 32(2):127-138

Tollin K (2002) Customization as a business strategy - a barrier to customer integration in product development? Total Quality Management, 13:427-439

Tomczak T (1992) Forschungsmethoden in der Marketingwissenschaft: ein Plädoyer für den qualitativen Forschungsansatz. Marketing: Zeitschrift für Forschung und Praxis, 14(2):77-87

Tsoukas H (1994) Refining common sense: Types of knowledge in management studies. Journal of Management Studies, 31(6):761

Tucker LR (1960) Psychological scaling: Theory and Applications. John Wiley & Sons, New York

Ulrich H (1981) Die Betriebswirtschaftslehre als anwendungsorientierte Sozialwissenschaft. In: Geist M, Köhler R (eds) Die Führung des Betriebes. Stuttgart, pp 1 - 26

Ulrich KT, Eppinger SD (1995) Product design and development. McGraw-Hill, New York

Ulwick AW (2002) Turn customer input into innovation. Harvard Business Review, 80(1):91-98

University of British Columbia (2004) Glossary. accessed: March 21, 2004, www.agsci.ubc.ca/fuh/courses/glossary.htm

Urban GL, Hauser JR (2004) "Listening in" to find and explore new combinations of customer needs. Journal of Marketing, 68:72–87

Urban GL, Hauser JR, Qualls WJ, Weinberg BD, Bohlmann JD, Chicos RA (1997) Information acceleration: validation and lessons from the field. Journal of Marketing Research, 34:143-153

Urban GL, Hauser JR, Roberts JH (1990) Prelaunch forecasting of new automobiles. Management Science, 36(4):401-421

Urban GL, von Hippel E (1988) Lead user analyses for the development of new industrial products. Management Science, 34(5):569-582

Urban GL, Weinberg BD, Hauser JR (1996) Premarket forecasting of really new products. Journal of Marketing, 60(1):47-60

Vahs D, Burmester R (1999) Innovationsmanagement: Von der Produktidee zur erfolgreichen Vermarktung. Schäffer-Poeschel, Stuttgart

van Kleef E, van Trijp HCM, Luning P (2005) Consumer research in the early stages of new product development: a critical review of methods and techniques. Food Quality and Preference, 16(3):181-201

Verganti R (1999) Planned flexibility: linking anticipation and reaction in product development projects. Journal of Product Innovation Management, 16(4):363-376

Verworn B (2005) Die frühen Phasen der Produktentwicklung. Deutscher Universitäts-Verlag, Wiesbaden

Veryzer RW (1998a) Discontinuous innovation and the new product development process. Journal of Product Innovation Management, 15(4):304-321

Veryzer RW (1998b) Key factors affecting customer evaluation of discontinuous new products. Journal of Product Innovation Management, 15(2):136-150

Veryzer RW, Borja de Mozota B (2005) The impact of user-oriented design on new product development: An examination of fundamental relationshops. Journal of Product Innovation Management, 22:128-143

Veugelers R (1997) International R&D expenditures and external technology sourcing. Research Policy, 26:57-91

Vicari S, Trioilo G (1997) Errors and learnings in organizations. In: von Krogh G, Roos J, Kleine D (eds) Knowing Firms. Sage Publications, London, pp 201-218

von Hippel E (1978) A customer-active paradigm for industrial product idea generation. Research Policy, 7(3):240-266

von Hippel E (1979) A customer-active paradigm for industrial product idea generation. In: Baker MJ (ed) Industrial Innovation. The Macmillan Press, London, pp 82-110

von Hippel E (1986) Lead Users: A source of novel product concepts. Management Science, 32(7):791-805

von Hippel E (1988) The sources of innovation. Oxford University Press, New York

von Hippel E (2001a) Innovation by user communities: Learning from open-source software. Sloan Management Review, 42(4):82

von Hippel E (2001b) Perspective: User toolkits for innovation. Journal of Product Innovation Management, 18(4):247-257

von Hippel E, Katz R (2002) Shifting innovation to users via toolkits. Management Science, 48(7):821-833

von Hippel E, Thomke S, Sonnack M (1999) Creating breakthroughs at 3M. Harvard Business Review, 77(5):47-55

von Hippel E, Thomke S, Sonnack M (2000) Creating breakthroughs at 3M. Health Forum Journal, 43(4):20-27

von Krogh G (2003) Open-source software development. Sloan Management Review, 44(3):14

von Krogh G, Ichijo K, Nonaka I (2000) Enabling knowledge creation: How to unlock the mystery of tacit knowledge and release the power of innovation. Oxford University Press, Oxford

von Krogh G, Nonaka I, Aben M (2001) Making the most of your company's knowledge: A strategic framework. Longe Range Planning, 34:421-439

von Krogh G, von Hippel E (2003) Special issue on open source software development. Research Policy, 32(7):1149 von Rosenstiehl L (1980) Grundlagen der Organisationspsychologie. Poeschel, Stuttgart

von Zedtwitz M (1999) Managing interfaces in international R&D. University of St. Gallen, St. Gallen

Voss C, Tsikriktsis N, Frohlich M (2002) Case research in operations management. International Journal of Operations & Production Management, 22(2):195-219

Voss CA (1985) The role of users in the development of applications software. Journal of Product Innovation Management, (2):113-121

VWA (2006) Major hazard guidance material - GN14. Victorian WorkCover Authority, Melbourne

Walker BA, Olson JC (1991) Means-end chains: connecting products with self. Journal of Business Research, 22:111-118

Walls G (2002) Defuzzing the fuzzy front end. In: Walls G (ed) Creating breakthrough ideas: The collaboration of anthropologists and designers in the product development industry. Greenwood Publishers, Westport

Wheeler J, Mansfield R, Todd D (1980) Structural implications of organizational dependence up customers and owners: Similarities and differences. Organization Studies, 1(4):327-348

Wheelwright SC, Clark KB (1992) Revolutionizing product development - Quantum leaps in speed, efficiency and quality. The Free Press, New York

Whittaker E, Bower DJ (1994) A shift to external alliances for product development in the pharmaceutical industry. R&D Management, 24(3):249-260

Williamson OE (1979) Transaction-cost economics: the governance of contractual relations. Journal of Law and Economics, 22:233-261

Wilson A, Bekker M, Johnson H, Johnson P (1996) Costs and benefits of user involvement in design: Practitioners' views People and Computers XI. Proceedings of HCI'96, London, 221-240

Wilson D, Littler D, Leverick F, Bruce M (1995) Collaborative strategy in new product development--risks and rewards. Journal of Strategic Marketing, 3(3):167

Wilson R, Crouch E (2001) Risk-benefit analysis. Harvard University Press, Boston

Winiger P (1986) Opus analysiert Kundenprobleme, um bedürfnisgerechte Produkte zu schaffen. ATAG-Praxis, 4:3-7

Witt J (1996) Produktinnovation. München

WLA (2001) Senior manager's guide to risk management. W L A - Security and Risk Management Committee, October

Wolf J (2003) Organisation, Management, Unternehmensführung - Theorien und Kritik. Gabler, Wiesbaden

Wolpert JD (2002) Breaking out of the innovation box. Harvard Business Review, (August)

Wynstra F, Pierick E (2000) Managing Supplier Involvement in New Product Development: A Portfolio Approach. European Journal of Purchasing & Supply Management, 6(1):49-57

Yin RK (1994) Case study research: Design and methods. Sage Publications, Thousand Oaks

Zahn E, Komes N, Walfort R (1995) Status der Markt- und Kundenorientierung in Innovationsprozessen. Eine Analyse auf Basis einer repräsentativen Umfrage in Unternehmen des Maschinenbaus und der elektrotechnischen Industrie. Diebold Deutschland GmbH, Eschborn

Zahra SA, George G (2002) Absorptive capacity: A review, reconceptualization, and extension. Academy of Management Review, 27(2):185-203

Zaltman G (1997) Rethinking market research: Putting people back in. Journal of Marketing Research (JMR), 34(4):424-437

Zaltman G, Coulter RH (1995) Seeing the voice of the customers: Metaphor-based advertising research. Journal of Advertising Research, 35(4):35-51

Zaltman G, Duncan R, Holbeck J (1973) Innovations and organizations. John Wiley & sons, New York

Zhang D (2006) Knowledge management in organizations. Journal of Database Management, 17(1):1-8

Zhang Q, Doll WJ (2001) The fuzzy front end and success of new product development: a causal model. European Journal of Innovation Management, 4(2):95-112

Zien KA, Buckler SA (1997) Dreams to market: crafting a culture of innovation. Journal of Product Innovation Management, 14(4):274-287

Zuberbühler M (1979) Produktinnovation in der Konsumgüterindustrie: Eine vergleichende Darstellung am Beispiel der schweizerischen Nahrungsmittelindustrie. University of Zurich, Zürich